The Underserved: Our Young Gifted Children

Edited by Merle B. Karnes

A product of the ERIC Clearinghouse on Handicapped and Gifted Children

The Council for Exceptional Children

Library of Congress Cataloging in Publication Data
Main entry title:

The Underserved: our young gifted children.

"A product of the ERIC Clearinghouse on Handicapped and Gifted Children."
1. Gifted children—Education (Preschool—Addresses, essays, lectures.   I. Karnes, Merle
B., 1916–   II. ERIC Clearinghouse on Handicapped and Gifted Children.
LC3993.218.U5   1983   371.95   83-7641
ISBN 0-86586-147-1

LC
3993.218
.U5
1983

A product of the ERIC Clearinghouse on Handicapped and Gifted Children.

Published in 1983 by The Council for Exceptional Children, 1920 Association Drive, Reston,
Virginia 22091-1589

The material in this publication was prepared pursuant to contract no. 400-76-0119 with the
National Institute of Education, U.S. Department of Education. Contractors undertaking such
projects under Government sponsorship are encouraged to express freely their judgment in
professional and technical matters. Prior to publication, the manuscript was critically reviewed
for determination of professional quality. Points of view or opinions, however, do not necessarily represent the official view or opinions of either the clearinghouse's parent organization
or the National Institute of Education.

Printed in the United States of America.

Contents

THE COUNCIL FOR EXCEPTIONAL CHILDREN

Founded in 1922, The Council for Exceptional Children (CEC) is a professional association committed to advancing the education of exceptional children and youth, both gifted and handicapped.

CEC, with 50,000 members, supports every child's right to an appropriate education and seeks to influence lccal, state, and federal legislation relating to handicapped and gifted children. CEC conducts conventions and conferences and maintains an information center with computer search services and an outstanding collection of special education literature.

In addition to its membership periodicals, *Exceptional Children,* and *TEACHING Exceptional Children,* CEC has a publications list of 75 titles including monographs, texts, workshop kits, films, and filmstrips.

Council Headquarters are at 1920 Association Drive, Reston, Virginia 22091.

THE ERIC CLEARINGHOUSE ON HANDICAPPED AND GIFTED CHILDREN

The ERIC Clearinghousee on Handicapped and Gifted Children (ERIC-EC) is one of 16 clearinghouses in a national information system funded by the National Institute of Education, U.S. Department of Education. Since 1966, ERIC-EC has been housed with The Council for Exceptional Children.

ERIC-EC collects, abstracts, and indexes special education documents and journals for the central ERIC database as well as for its own computer file and publications. Other activities include computer searches, search reprints, and publications. Address inquiries to the ERIC Clearinghouse at 1920 Association Drive, Reston, Virginia 22091.

Preface

Over the years numerous books and articles have been written on how to identify and educate older children who demonstrate giftedness. There is, however, a paucity of educational literature on the young gifted/talented child. The purpose of this publication, therefore, is (a) to emphasize the need for early identification of the gifted, (b) to foster a commitment to early educational programming for gifted/talented children, and (c) to review research, expert opinion, and current practices that may enable educators to launch exemplary programs for young gifted children. In addition, this publication may provide a needed resource to teacher trainers who include programming for the gifted in their coursework.

The audience includes administrative and supervisory personnel, teachers, teacher trainers, students, parents, and others interested in the education of young gifted/talented children. The primary audience, however, is the teacher of the young gifted and talented child, the key person determining the success or failure of differentiated programs for the gifted. This publication is addressed to kindergarten, first-, second-, and third-grade public school teachers since programs for 3- and 4-year-old gifted, nonhandicapped youngsters are essentially nonexistent. Head Start teachers are also an important audience, as are teachers in day care programs and private preschool programs. Preschool gifted children who are handicapped are found in public school programs and in private and public settings such as mental health institutions or agencies, and their teachers represent another target group.

Throughout this publication an effort has been made to include both theory and practice. It is the hope of the authors that concepts are presented in sufficient depth to enable practitioners to use them to develop or improve programs for young gifted children. Above all, the authors wish to dispel the notion that waiting until the gifted child is in the middle grades is an acceptable solution to educational programming.

The authors of the various chapters have had direct experience with young gifted children, including gifted/talented handicapped children from all socioeconomic levels, and they have functioned in various roles in programs for the young gifted child—as administrators, supervisors, teachers, psychologists, and researchers. They appreciate this opportunity to share their experiences and are especially appreciative of the interactions they have had with the parents of their gifted/talented charges. Through them they have gained insight into young gifted/talented children and how instructional programs for them can be improved.

The authors would be remiss if they failed to mention the professional staffs who have worked on various projects over a span of some 15 years, sharing ideas about giftedness, challenging traditional notions, interpreting research data, and conscientiously attempting to evaluate efforts.

Special thanks is extended to the Office of Economic Opportunity and the Office of Child Development for providing funds that permitted identification of and programming for 3-, 4-, and 5-year-old potentially gifted children from low-income families. State funds from the Illinois Gifted Program funded research with low-income populations who met the criteria for potential giftedness. For 7 years the Bureau of Education for the Handicapped, now known as Special Education Programs, funded the development of a model for gifted/talented handicapped preschoolers and its nationwide dissemination. The State of Illinois, Illinois Gifted Program, has financed research relative to gifted children at the preschool level from all socioeconomic levels. The now-abolished federal Office of the Gifted provided funds to develop and demonstrate a model for preschool gifted children. Currently, parents of young gifted children are financing this program through school fees. The Research Board of the University of Illinois has provided funds to conduct research with parents of gifted children. Without these sources of funding, this book could not have been written, for its authors would not have accumulated the experience to undertake the task.

The willing support we received from the secretarial staff who typed and retyped the manuscript deserves mention, as do Audrey Hodgins and Terry Colbert, who edited the manuscript before it was submitted to The Council for Exceptional Children.

Appreciation is also extended to June B. Jordan, Editor in Chief of Publications of The Council for Exceptional Children, for her patience and encouragement during the development of the manuscript and to the National Institute of Education, which financed its development.

Merle B. Karnes

About the Authors

Merle B. Karnes directs two research and demonstration projects at the University of Illinois, one for the young bright and gifted nonhandicapped preschooler and one for the gifted/talented handicapped (RAPYHT). For seven years RAPYHT has been in the outreach stage, and the model is being replicated nationwide. The development of both of these projects was partially funded by the federal government, one by the Office of the Gifted and the other by the Bureau of Education for the Handicapped, now known as Special Education Programs (SEP). In the 1960's Dr. Karnes conducted research with elementary age children who were underachievers. For over ten years she has concentrated on the young gifted child and has written many journal articles and book chapters on the young gifted child. She has been active in the State of Illinois promoting improved educational programming for the gifted.

Kippy I. Abroms, Associate Professor in the Department of Education of Tulane University, New Orleans, is currently writing a book with Merle B. Karnes on preschool education with a heavy emphasis on the young gifted child. She began empirical research on the affective development of preschool gifted children in 1977 at the laboratory school of Tulane University, Newcomb College Nursery School, and received the Louisiana Outstanding Educational Research Award for this study. She has written a number of articles and presented many talks on the social development of gifted preschoolers.

Cynthia Denton-Ade has her own consulting firm in Fairfax, Virginia. She was formerly the coordinator of the outreach project Retrieval and Acceleration of Promising Young Handicapped and Talented (RAPYHT) at the University of Illinois.

Andrew S. Gunsberg is Assistant Professor for Early Childhood in the Department of Exceptional Education of the University of Wisconsin-Milwaukee. He has taught young nonhandicapped, handicapped, and gifted children and taught the demonstration class for 3- to 5-year old gifted/talented handicapped children at the University of Illinois. Music is an integral part of his preschool curriculum, and he has published original songs for young children.

Bernita P. (Polly) Kemp is a master teacher and supervisor of the University of Illinois Program for Young Bright and Gifted Children. For over ten years she has been a teacher of young gifted children and has participated actively in teacher training programs for students in early childhood at the University of Illinois. In 1982 she was named Preschool Teacher of the Year by the East Central Association for the Education of Young Children in the State of Illinois.

Susan A. Linnemeyer, a doctoral student at the University of Illinois, has taught in the University of Illinois Program for Young Bright and Gifted Children.

Allan M. Shwedel, an educational research consultant with the Massachusetts Board of Regents of Higher Education, has served as the program evaluator of two programs for young gifted children at the University of Illinois, the RAPYHT Project (Retrieval and Acceleration of Promising Young Handicapped and Talented) and the University of Illinois Preschool Program for the Gifted. In addition to developing various identification and assessment procedures for these two projects, he has taught courses on the young gifted child at the University of Illinois and the University of New Mexico. He has also coauthored several articles on the preschool gifted and preschool gifted and handicapped.

Robert L. Stoneburner is with the Brim School, a private school for the learning disabled at Carbondale, Illinois, which is associated with Southern Illinois University. He has been a school psychologist in the public schools, a researcher at the University of Illinois, and a teacher/trainer and researcher at Southern Illinois University.

Mark B. Williams is a San Francisco-based consultant in the field of computer-controlled interactive video instruction. He spent ten years at the University of Illinois as a teacher, curriculum writer, researcher, and lecturer.

The Underserved: Our Young Gifted Children

CHAPTER 1

The Challenge

Merle B. Karnes

As Epstein (1979) so aptly put it:

> Something about the American spirit does not love a smart kid. No one is quite
> sure why. The athletically gifted and the artistically talented are acceptable,
> but not the intellectually bright. People react with hostility to the notion of the
> "egghead." They do not rush in droves to push for special programs for gifted
> children.
>
> If gifted children are 3 to 5 percent of the school-age population, they do
> not have a large political base. Someone has to take up their banner. (p. 85)

To convince persons in power that financial resources must be invested in
gifted children, someone, or better still a number of persons, must give time,
energy, and expertise: parents, superintendents of schools, principals, directors of day care or Head Start centers, teachers, psychologists, school board
members, service club members, lay persons who have a commitment to this
segment of the population. Improved programs for the gifted are unlikely to
be established without advocates who can relate to a wide variety of groups:
legislators (who have the power to allocate funds), administrators, directors,
and board members of programs for the young. Those in positions of power
must be convinced that programming is needed for this group of young
children and that funds must be allocated.

Of all young children, the gifted and talented may well be the most neglected
in terms of educational programming. The earlier the gifts and talents of the
young are nutured, the better their chances for optimal development, but only
recently have attempts been made to meet their needs. In a national survey,
Jenkins (1979) reported only five programs for gifted/talented children below
kindergarten age. When Karnes, Shwedel, and Linnemeyer (1982) surveyed
programs for gifted children under age 5, they identified 18 such programs

nationwide, but program definition was sometimes vague and the extent of the commitment could not always be determined. Although interest in programming for gifted preschoolers seems to have increased, the number of programs fails to meet the need.

Unfortunately, the maxim "giftedness will out" is untrue, for even very young children learn to hide their talents if the significant adults in their lives do not value behavior that deviates from the norm. They soon learn to behave like the average child because they are praised for doing so. Even when adults recognize that a child deviates in positive ways, there is little assurance that the school curriculum will offer opportunities different from those provided the average child.

The growth of programs for young handicapped children, programs that emphasize differentiation of instruction, have had a beneficial effect on preschool programs in general and on programs for the gifted specifically. The passage of the Children's Early Assistance Act in 1968 encouraged states and local communities through funding by the Bureau of Education for the Handicapped (BEH) to identify young handicapped children and to initiate programs worthy of replication. These federally funded programs made clear the need for early programming, as had research documenting that the longer the child's handicap persists without intervention, the more difficult it is to compensate for or reverse its effects. The efficacy of early intervention with handicapped children has ceased to be debatable. An entire issue of the *Journal of the Division of Early Childhood* (December, 1981) was devoted to follow-up studies of handicapped children who received special preschool programming. Results clearly endorse the value of early identification and programming. While no research has been reported on the results of such programming for gifted children, it seems reasonable to assume that the arguments for early programming for the handicapped will apply to the gifted and talented as well. For the good of the young gifted child and for the good of society, every effort should be made to foster the full development of these youngsters.

WHY SO FEW PROGRAMS FOR THE GIFTED?

There are a number of reasons why programs for young gifted children have been slow to develop, and these explanations are closely related. First, specialists trained to work with the gifted are usually not trained to work with young children, and thus they focus on the age groups most compatible with their training and experience. Teachers of young children, on the other hand, are seldom trained in the education of the gifted and tend not to differentiate instruction. Second, public schools are not charged with educating children below the age of 5, with the exception of the handicapped and except in Connecticut, which allows education to be provided to gifted children as young as age 4. Were states to provide legislation for the gifted down to age 3, classes would have to be homogeneous, a practice incompatible with the current mainstreaming philosophy. Third, special programming for the gifted is rare in Head Start, day care, and private preschool programs because their philosophy does not include educational planning above and beyond that appropriate for the average child. Lack of financial and administrative backing is a fourth reason for the lack of programming for gifted youngsters. A fifth is that few courses at the university level train teachers to develop challenging programs for young gifted children. The absence of such courses is understandable because the demand for such teachers is negligible, and thus the cycle is self-perpetuating.

RATIONALE FOR EARLY IDENTIFICATION AND PROGRAMMING

The focus of this publication on gifted/talented children from 3 to 8 years of age does not mean that identification and programming need not be considered until a child reaches age 3. Commitment to early identification prompted Karnes and her associates at the University of Illinois to conduct a pilot project for parents of infants who met criteria felt to be related to above-average abilities (Karnes, Shwedel, & Linnemeyer, 1982). Fathers and mothers met weekly to discuss aspects of child development and how they could best enhance the total development of their children, especially in the affective and cognitive and language areas.

The workshops were based on a needs assessment of the parents, who then implemented infant curricula developed by Karnes (1979, 1981) as a means of teaching the infants and refining parental abilities to interact with their infants. Input from professionals who conducted the workshops indicated that parents were indeed interested in fostering optimal development of their infants and that fathers were as concerned about their role as were mothers. But such programs are rare, usually experimental in nature, and necessarily short-lived. Further, the knowledge base for infant programming is so limited that until new knowledge provides answers to critical questions about giftedness in infancy, we are unlikely to move in that direction in any widespread fashion.

A major argument for early identification of the potentially or funtionally gifted is that parents need to know their young child's potential if they are to provide the supportive and nourishing environment the child requires. Parents need access to knowledgeable professionals who can provide them with the information and skill to interact with and stimulate their gifted child. Then, too, the knowledge that a young child is potentially or functionally gifted encourages parents to make careful plans for the child's educational program both at home and at school. Selection of a school that meets a gifted child's needs is an important reponsibility of parents. As will be reiterated in Chapter 8, parents can and should be the best advocates for their gifted child throughout the school years. The sooner parents are able to begin their advocacy, the better the chances of their gifted child's having a consistently challenging program as he or she proceeds in school.

Early identification and appropriate programming can foster habits and attitudes toward learning and toward the self that may prevent the gifted child from becoming an underachiever. Pringle (1970), in an intensive London-based study, made a plea for prevention of underachievement. Recognizing the importance of early identification and programming as means of ensuring a challenging and nourishing environment, she had this to say:

> Much remains to be learned about how best to promote the development of able children. But enough is known already to justify taking action now. It needs to be on two fronts simultaneously, preventive and rehabilitative, and in each case the earlier it is attempted the higher the chances for its success. Preventive action would aim at the early identification of able children to ensure the optimum environment for the development of their potentialities. Rehabilitation would aim at an early detection of able misfits so that appropriate help can be given before the difficulties have become too intractable. (p. 127)

CHARACTERISTICS OF THE GIFTED/TALENTED PRESCHOOLER

When one speaks of programming, the first question raised is "Who *is* the gifted child?" Amidst many definitions of giftedness, there is general agreement that it involves more than a high IQ, although IQ becomes an almost inevitable criterion in gauging functional or potential giftedness. While IQ is not a prime consideration in determining musical talent, for instance, most musically talented youngsters are above average in intelligence. In 1972 the U.S. Office of Education (Marland, 1972) published this definition:

> Gifted and talented children are those identified by professionally qualified persons, who by virtue of outstanding abilities, are capable of higher performance. These are children who require differentiated educational programs in order to realize their contribution to self and society. Children capable of high performance include those with demonstrated achievement and/or potential ability in any of the following areas, singly or in combination:
>
> - General intellectual ability
> - Specific academic aptitude
> - Creative or productive thinking
> - Leadership ability
> - Visual and performing arts
> - Psychomotor ability. (p. 2)

In recent years psychomotor ability has been dropped from the definition. The U.S. Office of Education originally included it to ensure that a wider range of individuals would qualify as gifted/talented. Clark (1979) pointed out, however, as have others, that this definition has led to confusion in both identification and programming. She made it clear that the term *gifted* refers to cognitive ability and that *talent* includes other dimensions of development.

She recognized, however, the interdependence of the human system in the development of intelligence and conjectured that a gifted person can become more fully functional with a total integration of sensing, thinking, feeling, and interaction. Her position in this regard drew upon Jung's (1964) organization of human experience.

No two gifted/talented children are alike, of course, but the following six areas of giftedness and talent are found in a large number of such children. These particular characteristics, gleaned from the observations of experts in various fields of talent; from administrators, teachers, and ancillary personnel working with young children; and from other lists of characteristics delineated in the literature; were compiled over a 3-year period in a project at the University of Illinois—Retrieval and Acceleration of Promising Young Handicapped and Talented (RAPYHT). They have been found useful with non-handicapped gifted/talented children as well.

1. *Intellectual.* The child is highly alert and observant, demonstrates exceptional retention of material, is very curious about a great variety of things, is often absorbed in activity, learns easily and readily, conveys ideas exceptionally well, demonstrates advanced ability to apply knowledge to practical situations, knows about many things of which other children comparable in age are unaware, and demonstrates exceptional ability to solve problems.

2. *Academic.* Reading: The child often selects books as an activity; uses advanced vocabulary and sentence structure; has a long attention span for reading activities; demonstrates understanding and exceptional retention of what has been read to him or her; shows exceptional retention of symbols, letters, and words; shows unusual interest in printing names, letters, and words; demonstrates an ability to read. Math: The child shows strong interest in counting, measuring, weighing, or ordering objects; has a long attention span for math and math-related activities; demonstrates an advanced understanding of mathematical relationships (e.g., sets, number); demonstrates advanced understanding and retention of mathematical symbols (e.g., numerals, operation signs); performs simple operations of addition and subtraction easily; shows strong interest in or advanced understanding of concepts related to time (clocks, calendar) or money; and often applies math skills and concepts to activities and projects other than math. Science: The child examines objects carefully and observes events closely; shows strong interest or exceptional skill in classifying; has a long attention span for activities related to science or nature; often inquires about the nature or function of things; shows strong interest in science projects or experiments; demonstrates advanced understanding of cause and effect; and demonstrates advanced understanding of abstract concepts (e.g., metamorphosis, evaporation).

3. *Creative*. The child is highly inquisitive, often examining things closely and asking many questions; has a keen sense of humor; is often busily involved in work of great interest to him or her; demonstrates a high energy level through high productivity or interest in many different things; often does things in his or her own way (independent, nonconforming); is highly imaginative in art work, play, use of materials or ideas; often has many ideas for a given situation; is able to attack a problem or use materials in more than one way (flexibility); often has original ideas or makes original products; and elaborates in great detail in art work, play, or conversation.

4. *Leadership*. The child adapts readily to new situations; is frequently sought out by other children as a play and work companion; is self-confident around others; tends to direct activities in which he or she is involved; interacts easily with other children and adults; generates ideas for activities and solutions to problems; takes initiative with peers; shows an awareness of the needs of others; assumes responsibility beyond what is expected for his or her age; and is often used as a resource by other children.

5. *Visual and performing arts*. Art: The child shows a very strong interest in the visual; remembers in great detail what he or she has seen; spends a great deal of time drawing, painting, or modeling; works seriously on art projects and derives much satisfaction from them; demonstrates accelerated development of technical skill in art production; uses art media in original ways; experiments with alternative or innovative uses for art materials; deliberately plans ahead the use and placement of elements in his or her pictures; includes considerable detail and/or embellishments in his or her drawings; produces art work that is superior in composition (balance, unity, use of space), design, and color; and produces art work that is highly original and has a very distinctive style. Music: The child shows unusually high interest in music activities; responds sensitively to the mood or character of music; repeats short rhythmic patterns with ease; sings in tune or very nearly in tune; identifies two short rhythmic patterns as the same or different; identifies familiar songs from the rhythm alone; sings on the same pitch as a model (within the child's natural range); identifies the higher or lower of two tones; and identifies two short melodies as the same or different.

6. *Psychomotoric*. The child shows strong interest in fine motor activities; demonstrates advanced eye-hand efficiency; enjoys movement for its own sake (running, jumping, climbing); demonstrates a wide range of movement (e.g., slow to fast, gentle to strong); shows exceptional balance while performing motor tasks (e.g., balance beam, trampoline); shows exceptional agility in maneuvering his or her body (e.g., stopping and starting, changing direction with control); shows exceptional strength for his or her age; demonstrates advanced development of basic motor skills (walking, running, climbing, jumping, kicking, throwing, catching); shows outstanding ability to combine previously learned motor skills (e.g., combining running with jumping); and demonstrates advanced ability to adapt basic

motor skills or combinations of motor skills to goal-directed activities (e.g., games).

In summary, the intellectually gifted as a group are superior in most respects (Abraham, 1976; Clark, 1979; Gallagher, 1975; Newland, 1976). Emotionally and socially better adjusted, taller, and healthier than average children, they learn more readily and retain what they learn better. They have longer attention spans and a larger vocabulary and are better at solving problems and engaging in abstract thinking. They resist conformity and drill; have more varied interests; are more competitive and independent; have higher social values and greater integrity; are more curious; have a greater fund of information; have more ideas; are more persistent, more creative, and more perceptive of the feelings of others; have a greater sense of humor; and are more sensitive to injustices. Not only do they manifest in talent areas the abilities of children chronologically ahead of them, but the processes and products they exhibit are unique.

SPECIAL GROUPS OF GIFTED/TALENTED YOUNGSTERS

Potentially gifted children sometimes come from low-income homes, and there is reason to believe there may be as many gifted/talented among the low-income population as there are among the more economically advantaged. Head Start is a viable program with the potential for identifying young gifted/talented children, and a deliberate effort should be made to identify the potentially gifted among the Head Start population and to program more adequately for them. Fine (1967) cited a young gifted child in a Head Start class in Detroit who had never held a book in her hands, did not converse with other children, and did not know her name. After the child had been in Head Start for 2 weeks, the teacher told Dr. Fine: "Given half a chance, what a smart little girl she would be" (p. 128).

One of the major problems of potentially gifted children from low-income homes is their almost invariable low self-esteem. They anticipate failure and live up to their expectations by failing. Unfortunately, these children have more physical problems than their privileged peers, and their psychological problems are likely to be more severe. Then, too, child-rearing practices in low-income homes may be less appropriate and intellectual stimulation lacking or inadequate.

The potentially gifted Head Start child is not only predisposed to poor self-esteem but also likely to lack motivation to learn. The child's value system does not usually include pursuing intellectual tasks felt to be important by the school, and the child may tend to need immediate gratification. Among underachievers from low-income homes a high percentage are poor readers (Fine, 1967), and their weak grasp of standard English hampers the development of their abilities.

There may be fewer functionally gifted and more potentially gifted children among low-income groups because they have not had experiences comparable to those of middle- and upper-socioeconomic-group children, but until day care and Head Start programs can do a better job of programming for low-income gifted children they are likely to go unidentified and underserved.

As is true for the low-income gifted child, the gifted/talented handicapped child is likely to be overlooked or identified as potentially rather than functionally gifted/talented. The handicapping condition tends to obscure the gifts and talents. Only when the handicapping condition has been minimized or alleviated can functional giftedness emerge.

Three preschool programs for gifted and talented handicapped children have been in the literature. Two were originally funded by the Bureau of Education for the Handicapped, one in the public schools at Chapel Hill, North Carolina and the other at the University of Illinois—RAPYHT (Retrieval and Acceleration of Promising Young Handicapped Talented). The third, funded by the United States Office of Education, is Panhandle Child Development Association, Inc., Coeur D'Alene, Idaho.

Teachers of handicapped children are untrained in the education of the gifted. One advantage of their training, however, is that they have been taught to differentiate instruction and to write individualized education programs. These concepts and procedures can be applied to the instruction of gifted children.

GUIDELINES FOR THE DEVELOPMENT OF PROGRAMS FOR THE YOUNG GIFTED/TALENTED

Karnes, Shwedel, and Linnemeyer (1982) have delineated the following principles for instituting a program for young gifted/talented children:

1. Each young gifted child is unique. One child may have advanced reading skills, but his or her computation skills may be more in keeping with those of normal-developing peers. Another may have unusual talent in music but be academically on a par with his or her chronological age-mates. Another gifted child may have a high IQ but a poor self-concept. Thus each child's strengths and weaknesses must be determined, and a challenging program that meets those needs must be developed.
2. Gifted children are very self-critical and sometimes have poor self-concepts. Every effort should be made to help them develop realistic self-concepts. Feedback from significant adults is very important. A discrepancy between the child's intellectual functioning and motoric development can be very frustrating and lead to a poor perception of self. A 4-year-old, for example, may be able to develop and verbalize a story at a very advanced level but finds it arduous and trying to write the same story. When the child cannot record the story on paper, he or she may feel inadequate. Such a child needs assurance that he or she is doing fine and that it is appropriate for someone older to transcribe the story.

3. The family must play the principal role in the education of gifted children. Gains made in an educational program are best sustained and extended if school and home form a partnership where there is consistency and compatibility of programming.

4. A program for young gifted children must have a wide range of instructional materials to meet children's interests and instructional needs. Instructional materials appropriate for children of a given chronological age may not meet the needs of gifted children of similar age. Gifted children typically have many interests and advanced academic skills.

5. A program for young gifted children must be well balanced and provide opportunities for progress in all facets of development. Gifted children may have advanced cognitive skills, but programming should foster development in the motor and social/emotional areas as well.

6. The gifted child, even when mainstreamed with normally developing children, should have opportunities to interact with other gifted children of the same chronological age. This may mean transporting children from one center to another to allow for more than one gifted child in a class.

7. A program for the gifted child fares best when there is a supervisor trained in the education of young gifted children to monitor the program. Such a person should have training and experience working with young children of all socioeconomic levels who have a wide range of abilities and talents. It would also be advantageous for this person to have training and experience working with handicapped children, since there are gifted/talented children among the handicapped.

8. An exemplary program for the young gifted/talented child requires that staff participate in ongoing in-service training. Since there are only a limited number of programs that train personnel to work with young gifted children, in-service training is of paramount importance.

9. It is important that parents and professional staff work closely together to determine mutual goals for the young gifted child and delineate ways of helping the child achieve program goals. When school staff and parents work together in such a manner, the gifted child will make the progress of which he or she is capable.

10. An evaluation plan should be an integral part of the child's program. It is important to determine the extent to which children achieve goals set for them, the extent to which the parents are satisfied with the program, and areas in which the program has not been as effective as one might desire. It is only when there is an effective plan for evaluating the program that professionals and parents can judge whether the program is meeting children's needs and whether children are making the progress expected of them.

11. An exemplary program must have a well-organized, effective, ongoing identification plan that includes parents. The identification process should reflect what the program offers. For example, if the plan provides a program only for the intellectually gifted, it would seem illogical to identify children with talents in the performing arts.

12. The program must have built-in plans for helping each child make the best possible transition to the next level, so that children continue to make the progress of which they are capable. Such a transition involves the coop-

eration of administrators, teachers, ancillary personnel, and parents. (pp. 206–208)

In addition to the dozen principles already outlined, the following are also deemed important.

13. The program must promote task persistence. It is not enough to have a high IQ; sustained interest and motivation to see a task through to completion may be equally important.
14. Fostering creativity is also an important goal of an exemplary program. A differentiated curriculum for gifted children most certainly does not omit this important aspect of their development.
15. Use of community resources is essential because gifted children need talented mentors. The school and home need access to persons with expertise that neither can offer the young gifted child.

PREVENTING UNDERACHIEVEMENT

Gifted children are unusually sensitive. Hence, they are more perceptive of the attitudes of others and more apt to react keenly to mishandling or to an unstimulating environment than are their peers of lesser ability. Prevention of underachievement among young gifted children is a special challenge. Most research on underachievement among gifted children was conducted during the 1960s, and rarely did studies including children as early as first grade. Much can be gleaned, however, from studies with older gifted underachievers: causes of underachievement, implications for working with parents, and child-rearing practices.

While underachievement is baffling and complex, a number of causes are generally agreed upon (Bricklin & Bricklin, 1967; Combs, 1965; Fine, 1967; Gallagher, 1975; Karnes, McCoy, Zehrbach, Wollersheim, Clarizio, Costin, & Stanley, 1961; Pringle, 1970; Whitmore, 1980). These causes fall into four categories. The first has to do with a physical handicap such as blindness or deafness. A handicapped child, even though intellectually gifted, may not have access to a particular modality for learning and therefore may achieve at a level below his or her mental age. A child with a learning disability in language development, for example, even though gifted, is not likely to achieve at a level commensurate with his or her mental age unless remedial services are made available—ideally at an early age. Since physical problems can interfere with the development of the young gifted child, screening programs in vision and hearing are essential during the preschool years, and plans for amelioration and remediation should be implemented as early as possible. In addition, every child should have periodical physical examinations to detect physical deviations requiring medical attention. Good nutrition, of course, is essential to the well-being of the child. Good health, a high energy level, and a reasonable attitude toward learning are interrelated.

A second cause of underachievement—poor teaching and curricula that fail to challenge the gifted child—is discussed in Chapters 4 and 5. A third cause is sociological in nature: children from low-income homes are apt to place little value on education and may lack the experiential background necessary to full development. The fourth, and for the young child the most important consideration of all, is the psychological basis for underachievement, the genesis of which is often the home. It is imperative that parents be provided with the knowledge and skills that will enable them to foster the development of their gifted/talented child. (Chapter 8 addresses these issues more fully.)

While no two underachievers are alike, the following characteristics are associated frequently with underachievement (Fine, 1967; Gallagher, 1975; Pringle, 1970; Whitmore, 1980):

Negative attitudes toward school and learning
Immature relationships with parents or feelings of parental rejection
Moodiness, depression, rebellion
Male gender
Poor self-esteem, feelings of persecution
Rationalization of shortcomings, transfer of blame to others
Proneness to fantasize
Poor interpersonal relationships, distrust of others
Lack of persistence, susceptibility to distraction, procrastination
Hostility toward authority figures
Boredom
Lack of self-discipline and failure to accept responsibility for actions
Deficient leadership ability
Either a shortage of hobbies or over-commitment to them
Dislike of competition
High incidence of emotional problems
Sensitivity to criticism; tendency to criticize others
Unrealistic goals.

PROBLEMS GIFTED CHILDREN ARE PRONE TO FACE

Leta Hollingworth (1923, 1926, 1931, 1936, 1942) contributed a great deal to our understanding of the adjustment problems that highly intellectually gifted individuals face. These are problems that parents and educators must reckon with in programming for the gifted:

1. *Distaste for school.* This attitude often stems from boredom with the curriculum. Gifted children may demonstrate behavior problems simply because they are not provided a challenging curriculum.
2. *Play interests.* Gifted children enjoy complex games and are often disinterested in the games enjoyed by their average-ability peers. As a result, the gifted become isolated and withdrawn.
3. *Conformity.* Gifted children tend to resist and argue about routine requirements, especially if those requirements interfere with their interests or do not make sense to them.

4. *Problems of origin and destiny.* Gifted children tend to be more concerned about such matters as death, the hereafter, religious beliefs, and philosophical problems than are average children.
5. *Discrepancy between physical size, intellectual, and social development.* Oftentimes gifted children seek older playmates. As a result, they sometimes have difficulty becoming leaders because they are smaller.

Other researchers have added to this list. Whitmore (1980) discussed the vulnerability of the gifted and cited these problems:

1. *Perfectionism.* Gifted children have an inner drive for perfection. They are not content unless they excel. This characteristic manifests itself early.
2. *Feelings of inadequacy.* This attitude toward themselves is closely related to the desire of gifted children to reach perfection in everything they attempt. The gifted are highly critical of their work and frequently dissatisfied; as a result, they often feel inadequate and experience low self-esteem.
3. *Unrealistic goals.* The gifted tend to set unrealistic goals for themselves. When they are unable to meet those expectations, they feel inferior. On the other hand, this desire for perfection is the motivating force that results in high achievement and excellence. According to Whitmore (1980), if the gifted recognize their tendencies to demand perfection and keep these attitudes under control, this attribute has a positive influence.
4. *Supersensitivity.* Because the gifted are more sensitive to sensory stimuli and more perceptive of relationships, they seem to be more critical of others as well as of themselves. The gifted child is more vulnerable, quick to perceive verbal and nonverbal cues as rejection, and often considered hyperactive and distractable because he or she is continously reacting to stimuli.
5. *Demand for adult attention.* Because gifted children are inquisitive and eager to learn, they often usurp the attention of teachers, parents, or other adults. These demands cause problems with other children, who resent the gifted child's desire for adult attention.
6. *Intolerance.* Because gifted youngsters learn so readily and see relationships so quickly, they often become intolerant of children who are not on an intellectual par with them. They can alienate others by remarks and expressions that convey disgust or impatience.

STAFFING AND ADMINISTRATIVE ALTERNATIVES AND PROGRAM CONTINUITY

In larger public schools a staff member at the administrative or supervisory level often is in charge of the identification of young gifted/talented children (kindergarten through third grade) and the individualized programming that follows. Ancillary personnel (speech and language therapists, psychologists, social workers, motor specialists) should be available in programs for gifted children, but the key to a successful program is the teacher.

The director or supervisor of the gifted program would, of course, be in charge of inservice training. In some cases a local college can be persuaded to offer courses on the gifted and to concentrate on the young gifted child in at least one course.

Head Start programs need to be persuaded to employ coordinators for the gifted, a practice that would require reordering priorities in expenditures for staff. In some instances, the coordinator for the handicapped might also be given responsibility for the gifted. The extent to which Head Start directors are concerned about programming for gifted preschoolers is not known, but individual Head Start directors (such as the one in Champaign and Vermillion Counties in Illinois) have indicated their concern about the need for better programming for the more able Head Start enrollees.

Day care directors and directors of private schools are in key positions to provide leadership in the identification of and programming for young gifted children. While it is desirable for these programs to employ additional staff to help existing personnel modify program offerings, such a course may not be feasible. One option might be the practicum placement of graduate students from nearby colleges and universities who are in training programs in gifted education. Such on-the-job experience might prove mutually beneficial to the student and to the preschool or day care program.

All school programs need designated persons to work with parents, but it is especially important for programs for the gifted to develop close, ongoing relationships with the home. Administrators must support this point of view: parents must play an integral part in programs for gifted preschoolers.

Although research has not identified a single administrative plan that best serves the young gifted population, we do know that administrative flexibility is important. At present, mainstreaming the gifted in preschool programs with children of varying abilities, talents, and socioeconomic levels is the most acceptable plan. Differentiation of instruction is, of course, essential. Within the mainstream setting, gifted children can be encouraged to pursue independent work for a portion of the day. "Pull-out" programs, where children go to a resource room for a block of time, meet the needs of gifted children in some preschool programs. We do know that gifted children need to be with peers who are functioning at a comparable level (Karnes, 1980), and administrators may need to move children from one school to another to permit this interaction.

Halbert Robinson, when interviewed about the effects of homogeneous classes on highly gifted children, stated that he had no reason to believe there were ill effects (Epstein, 1979). It may be that children who are highly gifted, or as Clark (1979) referred to them, "severely gifted," fare best in a tutorial situation.

Parents are especially concerned about what happens to their child in moving from one program to another. A single individual must take responsibility for this transition, and it may have to be the parent. On the other hand, the school should have written data to share with the receiving school and teachers. Young gifted children who are already reading have sometimes been given reading readiness materials upon entering first grade from kindergarten; some have been assigned beginning addition activities when they are already using multiplication and division. Inappropriate programming is not conducive to child growth and development.

Most school systems have a plan whereby all kindergartners are seen in a ''kindergarten round-up,'' during which each child has a physical examination and forms are completed by parents. During this contact, school personnel can inquire into the child's preschool experiences. Since parents play an important role in determining whether or not a child is gifted, a questionnaire to solicit information from them may be useful at this time. Contact with personnel in prior programs may be indicated; whenever possible, a receiving teacher should visit a gifted child in a preschool or day care program prior to admittance to kindergarten.

Whatever plans are developed, through written reports, case conferences, or a combination of approaches, the program should be challenging, consistent with the child's stage of development, and compatible with the interests and abilities of the child.

INSERVICE TRAINING FOR TEACHERS OF GIFTED/TALENTED YOUNGSTERS

Staff training is an integral part of every high quality preschool program. Some of the requirements of an ongoing inservice training program have been listed by Karnes (1980):

1. *Inservice programs must be individualized.* Since staff differ on such variables as experiential background, formal training (especially coursework and practicum experiences with gifted children), philosophy, and interests, inservice training must be flexible to meet the needs of individuals and groups.
2. *Staff must participate actively in assessing their own needs and those of the group.* Administrators who try to determine what the inservice training program should be without input from their staff are doomed to failure. Furthermore, staff self-assessment must be ongoing in order to respond to emerging or changing needs.
3. *One person must take responsibility for developing and coordinating the inservice program.* These important activities cannot be left to chance. Plans must be thoroughly developed and executed, with long-term goals as well as short-term objectives. The coordinator must monitor inservice activities to make sure goals and objectives are met.
4. *Time must be allotted for inservice training.* If inservice is to be an im-

portant part of the program, then time for it must follow as a matter of course. Some programs provide a day a month for inservice. Day care workers are often paid for the time they invest in inservice beyond their workday. In public schools certain days are provided in the school calendar for inservice education.

5. *The budget should include funds for inservice training.* A budget item for inservice training convinces staff that such training is important. If an expert is needed to meet a group's needs and the expert the group would like to have lives some distance away, there should be money available to bring that person in. Funds are also needed to purchase the latest books on the gifted for the professional library and to enable staff to visit exemplary programs.

6. *A good inservice program uses varied approaches.* An inservice program is more than bringing in speakers. In fact, a deliberate effort should be made to use a variety of methods and techniques to ensure that the inservice program is creative and exciting. In some programs each staff member develops an IEP (inservice education plan) with goals, objectives, and activities designed to suit that individual.

7. *Ongoing evaluation of individual and group inservice training is essential.* An administrator or supervisor should assist individual staff members in evaluating the extent to which their inservice education plans are successful. Evaluation of the total inservice program is equally important. If the staff is particularly interested in fostering creative and productive thinking among its young charges, then an evaluative plan may be to gather pretest and posttest data on children and determine whether or not improved teacher skills are reflected in the behavior of the children.

Kaplan (1980) added a noteworthy dimension to the guidelines noted here when she said there should be an analysis of the current status and the desired status of a program as well as of the individuals in the program. Analyzing the desired status of a program entails defining the need for inservice; the procedures Kaplan has suggested to determine desired status are test data, product review, and inventories, whereas current status can be arrived at by observation, needs assessment, and questionnaires.

Providing appropriate educational programs for gifted/talented youngsters is indeed a challenge, but the rewards are commensurate with the magnitude of the problem. The research data base is scant and existing program models few, yet enough is known to warrant action now. Gifted youngsters with their exciting academic and creative potentials are highly rewarding students, and if the number of specifically trained teachers is small, the potential of inservice training is great. With innovative staffing patterns and administrative flexibility, the challenge of educating young gifted children may yet be met in this decade.

REFERENCES

Abraham, W. Counseling the gifted. *Focus on guidance*, 1976, *9*, 1–11.

Bricklin, B., & Bricklin, P. *Bright child—poor grades: The psychology of underachievement*. New York: Delacorte Press, 1967.

Clark, B. *Growing up gifted*. Columbus OH: Charles E. Merrill, 1979.

Combs, A. *The professional education of teachers: A perceptual view of teacher preparation*.Boston: Allyn & Bacon, 1965.

Epstein, C. *The gifted and talented: Programs that work*. Arlington VA: National School Publishing Association, 1979.

Fine, B. *Underachievers: How can they be helped?* New York: E. P. Dutton, 1967.

Gallagher, J. *Teaching the gifted child*. Boston: Allyn & Bacon, 1975.

Hollingworth, L. *Special talents and defects: Their significance for education*. New York: Macmillan, 1923.

Hollingworth, L. *Gifted children: their nature and nurture*. New York: Macmillan, 1926.

Hollingworth, L. The child of very superior intelligence as a special problem in social adjustment. *Mental Hygiene*, 1931, *15*, 3–16.

Hollingworth, L. *The development of personality in highly intelligent children* (Fifteenth yearbook of the Department of Elementary School Principals). Washington DC: National Education Association, 1936.

Hollingworth, L. *Children above 180 IQ*. Yonkers-on-Hudson NY: World Book, 1942.

Jenkins, R. *A resource guide to preschools and primary programs of the gifted and talented*. Mansfield CT: Creative Learning Press, 1979.

Jung, C. (Ed.). *Man and his symbols*. New York: Dell, 1964.

Karnes, M. Elements of an exemplary preschool/primary program for gifted and talented. In S. M. Kaplan (Ed.), *Educating the preschool primary gifted and talented*. Los Angeles: National/State Leadership Training Insitute on the Gifted and Talented, 1980.

Karnes, M. *Small wonder: Level I*. Circle Pines MN: American Guidance Service, 1979.

Karnes, M. *Small wonder: Level II*. Circle Pines MN: American Guidance Service, 1981.

Karnes, M., McCoy, G., Zehrbach, R., Wollersheim, J., Clarizio, H., Costin, L., & Stanley, L. Factors associated with underachievement and overachievement of intellectually gifted children. *Exceptional Children*, 1961, *28*, 167–175.

Karnes, M., Shwedel, A., & Linnemeyer, S. The young gifted/talented child: Progress at the University of Illinois. *The Elementary School Journal*, 1982, *82*, 195–213.

Marland, S. *Education of the gifted and talented* (Report to the Congress of the United States, Commissioner of Education). Washington DC: U.S. Government Printing Office, 1972.

Newland, T. *The gifted in socio-educational perspective*. Englewood Cliffs NJ: Prentice-Hall, 1976.

Pringle, M. *Able misfits*. London: Langman Group, 1970.

Whitmore, J. *Giftedness, conflict, and underachievement*. Boston: Allyn & Bacon, 1980.

CHAPTER 2

Identification

Allan M. Shwedel
Robert Stoneburner

From an educational perspective, the goal of an identification plan is to achieve an effective match between a group of children and a specific educational program. In terms of special programs for gifted and talented preschoolers, the goal of an identification plan is to select those gifted and talented children who would benefit most from the special programming to be offered. Issues concerning the development and implementation of a plan to select gifted and talented preschoolers will be discussed in this chapter. Topics to be covered include: definitions of giftedness, identification models, assessment techniques, identifying the young child from a special population, eligibility consideration, and a description of an actual identification plan.

DEFINITIONS OF GIFTEDNESS

Before we can describe specific approaches to the identification of gifted preschoolers, it is necessary to discuss definitions of giftedness and the relationships among definitions, identification, procedures, and special programming.

At present the definition of giftedness is in flux. Historically, identification procedures have been developed by psychometrists who were interested in individual differences and personality. Much of the work was based on the assumption that individuals possessed certain underlying abilities or traits. Since the traits were assumed to exist, the psychometrist's goal was to develop reliable and valid instruments to measure the degree to which these traits were present in individuals (Riegle, 1979). The monumental study by Terman (Terman & Oden, 1959), which demonstrated both the long-term stability of intelligence as measured by the Stanford-Binet and the apparent validity of the measurement instrument itself, led to a reliance on intelligence as an indicator of giftedness. Gallagher (1966) has pointed out that for many years superior intelligence as measured by standardized intelligence tests actually became the working definition of "giftedness."

For the past few years the statement proposed by the United States Office of Education (USOE) has served as a working definition of giftedness and talent (Marland, 1972). This statement recognizes that an individual may have demonstrated or potential prowess in any of a number of domains: intellectual, academic, creative, artistic, leadership, or psychomotoric. This broad definition has proved to be useful as a basis for developing procedures to identify gifted and talented handicapped preschoolers (Karnes & Associates, 1978). Recently, however, the USOE definition has been criticized by Renzulli (1978). He had pointed out that the statement lumps together processes— i.e., intellectual, creative, and leadership functioning—with performance, such as artistic and academic accomplishment. Renzulli has also pointed out that an important characteristic—motivation—has been left out of the USOE definition.

Renzulli's Definition

An alternative definition, based upon characteristics observed among gifted adults, has been offered by Renzulli. According to this definition, giftedness results from an interaction among three characteristics: above average intellectual ability, creativity, and task commitment. For preschoolers, the relationship among these interacting characteristics and future success has not been investigated. Thus, while Renzulli's definition of giftedness in adults is conceptually eloquent and perhaps valid, its utility as a model for establishing identification criteria among preschoolers remains to be demonstrated.

Another important issue concerning Renzulli's definition centers on the modifiability of the three underlying characteristics or the interaction among them. If either the characteristics or their interactions are modifiable, then it is likely that early educational experience can have some impact on the emergence of giftedness during adulthood. But conversely, if the characteristics or interactions are not modifiable, then the importance of early educational experience would probably be minimal. The assumption that guides this chapter is that giftedness in adulthood *is* related to early childhood experiences, although the precise nature of the relationship is still unclear.

Linking Universal and Unique Levels of Development

As the work of Feldman (1980) suggested, the importance of preschool programs for the gifted, and particularly the important role played by the teacher of the young gifted child, lies in the fact that intellectual and social development do not follow universally determined paths throughout an individual's lifespan. The issue is not simply heredity versus environment but rather that development, i.e., sequential change, occurs on a number of levels that according to Feldman (1980) range from universal to unique.

For example, universal aspects of cognitive development include the acquisition of time regularities, object permanence, and communication skills. Cultural aspects of cognitive development include those skills acquired by individuals within a particular culture such as rules of cleanliness and religious practices. Feldman identified another important area of development, "discipline-based" development such as learning to play chess or becoming an airplane pilot. Here the levels of mastery and criteria for attainment are stated, and an individual can select a domain to master. These discipline-based domains cut across cultural boundaries, but not all individuals are able to master a given discipline. Feldman pointed out that much of the development that leads to positive changes in society spring from development that occurs within a discipline-based domain such as painting or molecular biology. It is the discipline-based domain that gives a framework in which change can occur.

The educational system can provide the linkage from the universal and cultural aspects of development to the disciplined-based and unique aspects of development. A gifted preschooler will become a gifted adult only if he or she masters the requirements of a discipline and is able to persevere in the task, which is often a lonely one, of going beyond the confines of the discipline to create either a useful innovation within the discipline or an innovation that bridges a number of disciplines (e.g., Darwin's theory of evolution and its impact on both biology and political/social philosophy in the late nineteenth century).

If it is recognized that early education is important for fostering giftedness, but it is also recognized that a clear yet valid definition of giftedness— especially at the preschool level—is lacking, how can a defensible identification plan be established?

If one keeps in mind that the goal of the identification plan is to match students with programs, a defensible approach is for administrators to look at both the characteristics of the special program and characteristics of preschoolers in order to select children who would not only succeed but would flourish within the special program. For example, if it is assumed that giftedness is primarily due to superior intellectual ability, then academic acceleration or enrichment would be logical choices as the focus of the special preschool program. In this case, identification should be geared to the selection of preschoolers who show evidence of potential for high academic achievement. On the other hand, if it is assumed that creativity is the major factor in giftedness and if the special program is designed to encourage creativity, then the identification process should be geared to the selection of children who show evidence of high creative potential. However, if a program emphasizes creativity, using only tests of academic aptitude for identification would probably lead to the selection of an inappropriate group of children (Wallach, 1976; Wallach & Wing, 1969).

Alternatives to Identification

An alternative defensible approach to identification is to use a variety of procedures for the tentative selection of children for entry into the program in combination with ongoing monitoring of their success once they enter. If children are not making gains in terms of both successful achievement and positive motivation, then they can easily be placed in a more appropriate class, that is, one better suited to their needs and capabilities. Or, if the special programming occurs within a mainstreamed classroom, the teacher can simply discontinue the special activities for those particular children. Thus, with this approach the establishment of an effective identification process becomes an empirical issue to be determined on an ongoing basis for each program.

A variant of this ongoing monitoring approach is the revolving door model proposed by Renzulli, Reis, and Smith (1981). With this approach a large pool of candidates is identified as eligible for the special program. Children enter and leave the program at various times throughout the year depending on their interests and accomplishments while both in and out of the program.

No matter which approach is used, program planners should be able to justify both the identification procedures and the special curriculum on the basis of their working definition of giftedness.

IDENTIFICATION MODELS

There are two basic approaches to the identification process. One involves a single means of entry and the other involves multiple means of entry. The traditional system, in which a child had to score above 135 on the Stanford-Binet, is an example of the single means of entry. Another example is the sequential process whereby a child is given a more formal assessment only after performing well on a screening instrument. In this case, a child is admitted into the program only if he or she is successful on the follow-up assessment. This process of screening plus follow-up assessment can be a cost-effective procedure, but so long as the final decision is based on a total score from a single test or even a cluster of tests, this is still a single-point-of-entry approach. See, for example, the *Baldwin Identification Matrix* (Baldwin, 1979).

Multiple-Entry Identification

In recent years some programs for the gifted have used a multiple-entry-point identification process. An example of this approach is Gowan's "reservoir model" (Gowan, 1975). Gowan's model is designed so that a pool of potential candidates can be assembled on the basis of multiple assessment procedures including scores on group aptitude tests, classroom teacher nomination, and staff nomination. With this information, children have three separate ways to enter the special program: (a) by scoring at the top on any three of the four measure assessment procedures; (b) by being placed at the top on any two lists and scoring above the minimal cut-off on a follow-up assessment with the Stanford-Binet; and (c) by being admitted with special consideration by the selection committee. Gowan's model is geared to somewhat older children, but it could easily be adapted to the needs of a preschool age population.

The RAPYHT Project, at the University of Illinois, a federally funded program for gifted and talented handicapped preschoolers, uses a variant of the multiple-entry identification process (Karnes, Shwedel, & Lewis, submitted for publication). The RAPYHT project identification process is based on a set of talent checklists that are filled out by the teacher for each child in the class and by each child's parent. There are checklists for each of the following ability areas: creative, intellectual, scientific, mathematical, reading, musical, leadership, artistic, and psychomotoric. If either the teacher or a parent rates a child above a predetermined cut-off on any one of the checklists, the child will be considered for entry into the RAPYHT program. Thus, two very different sources of information—teachers and parents—are used to select handicapped preschoolers who are functionally or potentially gifted or talented. As a verification of the results from the checklists, these provisionally identified children participate in especially designed small group activities within their talent area. If the children perform adequately on at least one of two activities, they are enrolled in the supplemental program. For some children with severe handicaps, additional standardized tests data are taken into consideration to determine whether or not they could benefit from RAPYHT programming.

A major advantage of the multiple-entry process is that since it can be set up both to assess a wide range of abilities and to make use of different sources of information regarding the young child's behavior, the approach will increase the probability of including children from various ethnic, racial, and socioeconomic groups into the special program. The issue of special populations will be discussed in a later section of this chapter. Both the Seattle Preschool Project at the University of Washington (Robinson, Jackson, & Roedell, 1978) and the University of Illinois Preschool Program for the Gifted (Karnes, Shwedel, & Linnemeyer, 1982) use multiple-entry procedures to maximize opportunities for children to demonstrate their abilities and thus maximize the chances that a child will qualify for the program.

While the use of a multiple-entry procedure is being advocated, it is important to realize that the target characteristics, the instruments, and the entry criteria should all be geared to achieve an effective match between the services that the special program will provide and the young children to be chosen as participants.

ASSESSMENT TECHNIQUES

With the conceptual and practical expansion of the descriptor *gifted* and the subsequent recognition of the presence of gifted and talented children among and within varying segments of the population, the instrumentation and techniques traditionally used to identify gifted and talented children are being modified to reflect this expansion. Traditional employment of intelligence tests, achievement measures, and creativity tests can and should be augmented through the use of teacher rating scales, parent information, observation techniques, and criterion-referenced tests. Combinations of identification measurements and techniques should be coupled with the realization that identification of gifted and talented children is an ongoing, dynamic process that cannot effectively be carried out through a "one-shot" measurement procedure.

In this section the following types of identification procedures will be discussed: (a) standardized tests; (b) rating scales; (c) systematic observational data; (d) criterion-referenced tasks; (e) anecdotal records; (f) case studies; and (g) community nominations.

Standardized Measures of Intelligence

Standardized measures of intelligence are the most widely used and accepted means of identifying gifted populations. Both verbal and performance tests are available, with greater credence usually given to instruments that tap the cognitive/language development of the child. The cut-off scores indicated here separate the top 7% of the preschoolers from the rest of their peers.

Stanford-Binet Intelligence Scale, Form L-M (Terman & Merrill, 1973)

The Stanford-Binet Intelligence Scale is an individually administered intelligence test designed to measure intellectual functioning in children and adults (age range: 2 through adult). In general, items on the Stanford-Binet place great emphasis on verbal skills and responses, although many items at the early age levels require fine motor responses. Two scores are yielded by this instrument, a mental age (MA) and a deviation IQ ($\overline{X} = 100$, SD $= 16$). Scoring criteria indicate that a child must obtain an intelligence quotient score of 124 or greater to place within the intellectually gifted range as measured by this test. Procedures are also available for analyzing the child's response on the Stanford-Binet in terms of Guilford's Structure of the Intellect Model (Landig & Naumann, 1978; Tucker, 1972).

The Wechsler Preschool and Primary Scale of Intelligence (WPPSI) (Wechsler, 1967)

The Wechsler Preschool and Primary Scale of Intelligence (WPPSI) is an individually administered intelligence test designed to measure general intellectual functioning. The scale is presented in two parts: a verbal scale comprised of five subtests and a performance scale comprised of four subtests. Subtests on the verbal scale include information, comprehension, arithmetic, similarities, and vocabulary. Picture completion, block design, mazes, and coding/animal house represent the subtest areas of the performance scale.

Raw scores obtained on each of the subtests are transformed to scaled scores with a mean of 10 and a standard deviation of 3. The scaled scores of all subtests are combined to yield verbal, performance, and full scale intelligence quotients. Deviation intelligence quotients are reported with a mean of 100 and standard deviation of 15. Scoring criteria reveal that a child must obtain an IQ score of 123 or above to be considered as functioning in the gifted range as measured by this instrument.

The Slosson Intelligence Test for Children and Adults (SIT) (Slosson, 1981)

The Slosson Intelligence Test is designed as an individually administered measure of verbal intelligence usable with children and adults. All items are administered verbally and, with few exceptions, require a verbal response. Some items at younger age levels require a gestural or fine motor (paper and pencil) response. The SIT yields a mental age score and a ratio intelligence quotient score. Scoring criteria indicate that a child must obtain an intelligence quotient score of 120 or above to be included in the gifted range of intellectual functioning as measured by this test.

The Columbia Mental Maturity Scale (CMMS), Third Edition (Burgemeister, Blum, & Lorge, 1972)

The Columbia Mental Maturity Scale is designed for individual evaluation of children who demonstrate sensory or motor defects or who demonstrate difficulty in verbalization. Administration involves presenting of 92 pictorial cards to the child and requesting the child to respond by pointing to the picture on each card that is different from the others. The test is designed to measure general reasoning ability through demonstration of skill in the area of perceptual discrimination of color, shape, size, use, numbers, naming parts, and symbolic material. It includes perceptual classification tasks as well as tasks requesting abstract manipulation of symbolic concepts. The CMMS yields an age deviation score with a mean of 100 and standard deviaiton of 16. Scoring criteria indicate that a child must obtain an age deviation score of 124 or above to be included in the gifted range of intellectual functioning as measured by this test.

The Pictorial Test of Intelligence (French, 1964)

The Pictorial Test of Intelligence is designed as a measure of general intelligence of nonhandicapped and handicapped children between the ages of 3 and 8 years. Six subtests are employed to measure picture vocabulary, form information and comprehension, similarities, size and number, and immediate recall. Items are arranged in multiple-choice format, requiring a gestural (pointing) response from the child. The test yields a raw score that is converted to mental age units, which are subsequently converted to a deviation score. The General Cognitive Index score is noted as the indicator of overall intellectual development. Four types of scores are yielded by this instrument: general cognitive index (mean = 100, SD = 16), scale indexes (mean = 50, SD = 10), percentile ranks, and mental age score. Scoring criteria indicate that a child must obtain a general cognitive index score of 124 or above to be considered within the gifted range of intellectual functioning as measured by this test.

Standardized Achievement/Readiness Tests for Preschool Children

Standardized readiness and achievement tests may be used to identify children with unique skills in the basic academic areas of reading, math, and science. Even though measure of academic attainment are not typically associated with preschool populations, the intellectually gifted and/or academically talented child may demonstrate levels of readiness skills or academic attainment well above chronological age expectations.

The Metropolitan Readiness Test, Level I (Nurss & McGauvran, 1976)

The Metropolitan Readiness Test is designed as a norm-referenced, multiple-skill battery, developed to assess a kindergarten-age child's readiness for school-related tasks. It is comprised of seven subtests: Auditory Memory, Rhyming, Letter Recognition, Visual Matching, School Language and Listening, Qualitative Language, and Copying. The test yields percentile and stanine scores for visual and language skills and presents a composite pre-reading score. Percentiles are given within stanines with a resulting mean score of the fiftieth percentile of the fifth stanine and a cut-off identification score of the eightieth percentile of the eighth stanine.

Stanford Early School Achievement Test, Level I (Madden & Gardner, 1969)

The Stanford Early School Achievement Test is a measure of cognitive-academic skill development designed for use with kindergarten and first grade populations. The test measures the areas of mathematics, environment, letters and sounds, and aural comprehension. Scoring patterns yield percentile and stanine scores for each of the subparts of the test and a composite test score. The test mean is the fiftieth percentile of the fifth stanine with a cut-off score for advanced development being identified as the ninetieth percentile of the ninth stanine.

Test of Basic Experiences, Level K (Moss, 1971)

The Test of Basic Experiences is a readiness measure that taps the child's mastery of concepts related to early academic achievement. The test is comprised of five subtest assessing mathematics, language, science, social science, and general concepts. Each subtest yields a score that is interpreted through stanines and percentiles. The mean score is the fiftieth percentile of the fifth stanine, with cut-off levels established for advanced development at the ninetieth percentile of the eighth stanine.

Standardized Tests of Perceptual-Motor Development

Standardized tests of perceptual-motor development may be used with preschoolers to help identify unique development in children's ability to accomplish fine motor, paper and pencil tasks; to work through problem situations on a performance level; and to accomplish gross motor tasks.

Basic Motor Ability Test (Arnheim & Sinclair, 1974)

The Basic Motor Ability Test is designed for use with children 4 through 12 years of age. The test measures responses requiring small and large motor control, eye-hand coordination, and static and dynamic balance. Test scores are reported in percentiles, with a mean score at the fiftieth percentile and a cut-off score for advanced development established at the ninetieth percentile. The test is normed by sex and age levels.

Developmental Test of Visual-Motor Integration (Berry, 1967)

The Developmental Test of Visual-Motor Integration is a paper and pencil test of fine motor coordination and visual perception. The test is comprised of 24 geometric drawings, arranged in order of increasing difficulty, that are reproduced by the child. The test yields a VMI age equivalence score with a cut-off score for advanced development of +1 year for younger children and +2 or more years for older subjects.

Purdue Perceptual-Motor Survey (Roach & Kephart, 1966)

The Purdue Perceptual Motor Survey includes 11 subtests that assess three major areas of motor development: laterality, directionality, and perceptual-motor matching. Test scoring yields a 1 to 4 rating on a category scale and a total score. A summary profile may be developed, and test norms permit interpretation by grade level and the total score by socioeconomic status level.

Wechsler Preschool and Primary Scale of Intelligence (Wechsler, 1967)

The performance scale of the Wechsler Preschool and Primary Scale of Intelligence presents five subtests that measure visual discrimination, fine motor coordination, and nonverbal problem solving. Subtests include animal house, picture completion, mazes, geometric designs, and block design. The test yields a performance IQ with a mean of 100 and a standard deviation of 15. The cut-off score for advanced development is a performance IQ of 123.

Standardized Test of Social Development

Measures of social competencies and maturity are useful with preschool-age populations in helping to determine the child's level of personal, social, and interpersonal skill development. Social competencies are critical to the child's adjustment in the school setting, and advanced social development is often associated with leadership qualities.

California Preschool Competency Scale (Levine, Elzey, & Lewis, 1969)

The California Preschool Competency Scale is designed to be used with children 2 through 6 years of age using an informant format (i.e., teacher or parent support). It is a rating scale measure that assesses the child's development in terms of interpersonal skills and assumption of personal responsibility. The test scores are reported in percentiles that reflect considerations for age, sex, and socioeconomic level. The mean score for the test is at the fiftieth percentile with a cut-off score of the ninetieth percentile being used to identify advanced development.

Vineland Social Maturity Scale (Doll, 1965)

The Vineland Social Maturity Scale assesses a child's personal/social development across eight areas: general self-help, self-help in eating, self-help in dressing, self-direction, occupation, communication, locomotion, and socialization. It is an informant-type scale, which involves reporting on the child by an informed adult (i.e., parent or teacher). The test yields a social age score and a social quotient score. The mean social quotient is 100 with a cut-off score for advanced development established as 124.

Measures of Creativity

Measures of creativity are important elements in the identification and assessment of gifted and talented children. However, the complexities involved in establishing definitions and standards of creativity that have broad acceptance in the field have greatly limited test development in this area. The characteristic most generally used in defining creativity have been drawn from Guilford (1967). These include fluency, flexibility, originality, elaboration, and imagination. The most frequently used measures of creativity are those developed by Torrance (1966).

Torrance Tests of Creative Thinking: Figural Test, Forms A and B (Torrance, 1966)

Torrance's figural test of creative thinking is a nonverbal test that taps the areas of fluency, elaboration, imagination, and originality. It is normed for populations 5 years of age and older. It contains three areas of primary activity: picture construction, picture completion, and parallel lines or circles. The test yields a *t*-score for fluency, flexibility, elaboration, and originality. Each subarea has a mean of 50, and a standard deviation of 15, and a *t*-score of 65 is used for the cut-off level.

Torrance Tests of Creative Thinking: Verbal Test, Forms A and B (Torrance, 1966)

Torrance's verbal test of creative thinking uses seven subareas to assess verbal creativity, including: asking, guessing causes, guessing consequences, product improvement, unusual uses, unusual questions, and just suppose. The test is also designed to be used with ages 5 through adult and yields *T*-scores for the areas of fluency, flexibility, and originality. The test has a mean of 50 with a standard deviation of 15, and *T*-scores of 65 are used as cut-off scores.

Thinking Creativity in Action and Movement (Research Edition) (Torrance, 1980)

This recent addition to Torrance's collection of creativity tests is geared to the preschool-age child. Items on the test give the child the opportunity to demonstrate his or her creative ability by moving around the room in various ways. Like the other Torrance tests, this one assesses the child's fluency, flexibility, elaboration, and originality. Preliminary norms are provided for ages 3 to 7, but sample sizes are relatively small. Given the absence of adequate norms, communities could select a cut-off score of 1.5 standard deviations above the mean based on the distribution of scores for their local population of preschoolers.

Ratings and Observational Checklists

Observational checklists and rating scales constitute another important source of information for identifying gifted and talented youngsters. Since the use of test scores alone in the identification process is often discouraged, direct observational data may often be used as corroborative or supportive evidence of the child's level of functioning. While informal observations and rankings have been used frequently, research has generally demonstrated that these methods are less than satisfactory (Barbe, 1964, Pegnato & Birch, 1959). Observation or rating scales from established lists of characteristics of the gifted appear to hold more promise. Recent evidence shows that if teachers are trained in administration of the scales their ratings are an accurate source of information for selecting gifted students (Borland, 1979; Gear, 1978). Similarly, there is evidence that parent ratings correlate highly with intelligence test scores even among preschoolers (Ciha, Harris, & Hoffman, 1974). The Seattle Project has also found parent checklists to be a useful indicator of intellectual ability (Robinson, Jackson, & Roedell, 1979). It appears that observations or rankings are best conducted by an adult who has ongoing contact with the child and who has been provided with some level of inservice training on the use of the scale and the nature and types of responses that best characterize the gifted/talented.

Basically, then, observational data, whether in the form of checklists or rating scales, permit the evaluation of a child's behaviors and performance that are generally not assessable through the use of standardized measures. These scales need not be restricted to the requirements of formal measures of performance, and they thereby provide the observer with greater latitude in noting the more intangible characteristics of the child's behavior. Additionally, the observations of the child can be conducted in the more naturalistic environments of the classroom, playground, or home without the constraints of the structured test setting. The effectiveness of observational data appears to be increased by a prudent selection of accepted characteristics of gifted/talented children, provision of structure in the observational or ranking process, and training of the observers on the relevant behaviors to be noted.

Scale for Rating Characteristics of Superior Students

Renzulli and Hartman (1971) have developed a set of 10 checklists that can be filled out by teachers or parents. In order to make the checklists appropriate for the parents of preschool children some items would need to be modified or deleted, but nonetheless the checklists are a promising tool either for initial screening or as one among a number of assessment instruments. In general, the role of the parent in the identification process has been minimized, partly because of the existence of parents who, at any cost, want their child to be labeled as ''gifted.'' The data from the study by Ciha, Harris, and Hoffman (1974) suggest that parental bias is not a major constraint on the overall accuracy of parent responses to the items on a behavioral checklist. In the future, parent rating scales will surely play an increasingly important role in the identification of gifted preschoolers.

RAPYHT Talent Checklist (Karnes & Associates, 1978)

A set of talent identification rating scales specifically designed for use by teachers of preschool handicapped children has been developed by Karnes and Associates (1978). These rating scales encourage the teacher to look for evidence of talent or talent potential among preschoolers. Entrance eligibility cut-off scores for handicapped preschoolers have been established on all seven checklists. Following are some examples of some items for a dramatic ability rating scale that is currently being developed by the RAPYHT staff.

1. Shows exceptional memory especially for mannerisms and dialogue.
2. Often uses fantasy to guide own activities.
3. Shows high degree of ''body involvement'' when telling stories or talking to friends and adults.
4. Demonstrates advanced level of verbal expressiveness.

A modified version of this checklist has also been developed for parents.

Seattle Project Parent Questionnaire (Robinson, Jackson, & Roedell, 1979)

This questionnaire contains both general open-ended items and items about specific skills such as whether or not the child can read street signs. While normative data are not available, this questionnaire is a good source of information about the intellectual skills of young gifted children.

Criterion-Referenced Measures

In recent years criterion-referenced measures have become increasingly popular in preschool assessment. Unlike formal test materials, criterion-referenced measures do not attempt to describe the child in terms of some relative group standard, but focus more on the individual's mastery of special skills. The measures do not as a rule yield composite scores or quotients, but usually report findings in terms of developmental age levels across some combination of the critical developmental areas of cognitive skills, language skills, self-care skills, social skills, and gross motor and fine motor skills. At the preschool level test items are generally arranged in an ascending order of difficulty designed to meet the skill requisites of each age along the developmental continuum. Performances are reported in terms of age scores that reflect the child's level of skill mastery in each of the developmental areas.

Test items on criterion-referenced measures tend to be skill-specific and are most often presented in the form of performance objectives. Thus, an item from a traditional test might ask: "Can the child name five colors?" while the comparable criterion task might be stated: "The child can name five colors upon request 90% of the time." A child's response on the formal test item is interpreted in terms of the youngster's standing with relation to others, while the criterion-referenced item is directed toward an understanding of the specific skills of the child being evaluated. There are major advantages to the classroom teacher in using criterion-referenced measures in that they not only provide an ongoing assessment of the child's developmental progress, but they also serve as a valuable resource in individualizing instruction for a particular child. Teachers of the gifted should exercise some caution in the use of criterion-referenced material since no set of established guidelines, commercially produced or teacher-made, can encompass all of the unique behaviors of gifted and talented children. Attempts to restrict the child's educational program to only those tasks that are characteristic of particular skills or age levels results in the same problems as placing the child in a regular class bound by grade level curricula. Additionally, most commercially produced programs of criterion-referenced materials for young children tend to reach their upper limits at the 5- or 6-year level. This factor may result in an artificial limit being placed on the child with more advanced levels of development. The teacher must ensure that there are other measures going beyond the developmental guidelines that allow the child a full range of opportunities to demonstrate these advanced skills.

Anecdotal Records

Anecdotal records can provide a wealth of information on the gifted child, particularly with relation to the screening and identification processes. Reports from parents, teachers, and other significant adults in the child's life bring to the child-find process a broad spectrum of data pertaining to the child's background of experiences, developmental history, modes of problem-solving, special talents or skills, language development, interpersonal skills with adults and peers, unique interests, and ability to cope with a range of situations. Whether in screening or formal testing, the examiner has very limited time to observe the child, which often results in too much reliance being placed on the youngster's performance on the prescribed assessment procedures. Anecdotal information can carry the examiner beyond the limitations of the tests and testing situation and permit at least a brief account of how the child functions in the home, school, or community at large. Anecdotal data can also help point out discrete skill areas that might otherwise be overlooked in the identification process. Additionally, when observations of the child are accomplished in a systematic fashion over a period of time, such as might be done in a preschool setting, they can provide a chronology of growth that cannot be duplicated in any test setting.

The dangers associated with the use of anecdotal data are fairly obvious. Adults' perceptions of a child with whom they have frequent contact may be distorted by emotional factors, unfamiliarity with normal child development patterns, or misinformation obtained from friends or even professionals. While there is no quick, absolute means of validating the anecdotal information given, the examiner should weigh the reports against any existing "hard data" (i.e., test scores, child products, verified professional reports, etc.) that are available and against his or her own observations and clinical intuitions with regard to the child. If major discrepancies occur that cannot be resolved through further discussion, the child might be scheduled for re-evaluation, or visitations might be planned to permit the youngster to be observed in the home, preschool setting, or wherever the purported behaviors occur.

Case Studies

Throughout this chapter there has been a consistent emphasis on flexibility and openness in the identification process. It is clear that no one test or one set of observational strategies is sufficiently robust to be used exclusively in the identification process. The greater the body of information developed on the child, the greater the probability that the child will be appropriately identified. Background data and tangible evidence of the child's past products or experiences all play a role in the identification process. When all of these data are collected, one has the basic ingredients for what constitutes the best current process for identification, the case study. The case study format has served the education community well in helping to effectively identify and program for handicapped populations. If applied with the same degree of rigor, it can be an equally valuable tool in the identification of gifted/talented children (Foster, 1980).

Brief mention should also be made of personality and experiential self-report inventories. Data from these two sources can add useful information to case study reports. Unfortunately, little work regarding preschoolers has been done in the area. The interested reader is referred to the work of Davis and Rimm (1979), Grant (1974), Rekdal (1977), and Taylor and Ellison (1968).

Community Nominations

There are a significant number of other professionals in the community who can and should play a role in child-find programs. The family physician or child's pediatrician most often comes to know the child long before other professionals have access to the child or the family. Properly guided, physicians are in an ideal position to make the earliest referrals on children whom they perceive as "fast developers." Personnel in the community social service agencies have contact with many families and may be in the homes on a regular basis with the opportunity to observe children and their interactions within their families and neighborhoods. Here again, inservice training to raise the level of awareness pertaining to early identification of gifted children could result in many new referral resources. In many of the helping professions, personnel such as psychologists and social workers become involved in family counseling and are in a good position to help identify children who evidence advanced development or special skills. Community librarians, juvenile workers, recreation workers, day care staff, scout leaders, and a multitude of other persons in contact with children can all make a contribution to a truly community-wide identification network that will help promote the best interests of the community's exceptional children.

PROBLEMS IDENTIFYING YOUNG CHILDREN FROM SPECIAL POPULATIONS

So far in this chapter various aspects of the identification process have been described. The basic assumption that has guided this discussion is that there are very few preschoolers who are unequivocally gifted, that is, children who everyone is certain will grow up to make a meaningful, unique contribution to society. The identification problem is due not so much to limitations in the psychometric properties of the assessment instruments, but rather to the fact that giftedness is not an attribute like eye color or bone size. Giftedness is best understood as a characteristic that emerges, oftentimes gradually, from the "person-environment" interaction. The research literature describing underachievers attests to the fact that for giftedness to emerge there has to be some sort of "click" between the individual and his or her social milieu. Unfortunately, the nature of the "click" is still unclear.

Since giftedness is best viewed as a fragile, emerging characteristic rather than an all-or-none attribute, it is obvious that early identification is going to be somewhat inaccurate. If the selection criteria are too narrow, some or many potentially gifted individuals will miss the opportunity to nurture their talents. On the other hand, if the selection criteria are too broad, limited resources will be diluted among a relatively large group of preschoolers, many of whom will not grow up to be gifted. To dilute resources does not mean that they are being wasted, but each school must decide whether it will cast a wide or narrow net. The choice has to be made on the basis of each community's values and goals.

There is another important consequence of this conception of giftedness as a gradually emerging characteristic. Since giftedness depends on the person-environment interaction, the frequency and quality of these interactions will also determine the form of giftedness and the ease with which observers will be able to label a child as gifted. In particular, the quality of person-environment interactions varies considerably among different groups within the United States. While almost everyone can agree on what it means to be a gifted adult, it becomes much more difficult to agree upon which traits or behaviors among different groups of preschoolers are signs of potential for giftedness. The readily observable behaviors of handicapped preschoolers or preschoolers from non-middle-class groups differ considerably from the behaviors of middle-class preschoolers who are labeled as gifted. Does this mean that preschoolers who have speech delays or come from poor rural communities cannot grow up to be gifted adults? Obviously not, but the question remains: How can preschoolers from atypical populations be identified?

One way to deal with this issue is to view the task not as one to *identify* gifted preschoolers but as one to *select* preschoolers who show evidence of potential for a special program. The questions to be answered by assessment are: "What can these kids do?" and "How well can they do it?" Thus, the search becomes a search for strengths, these strengths being both signs of exceptional ability and stepping stones for further educational development. If a child can do any one thing very well or stands out from the group, no matter how, this may be interpreted as a sign that there is some potential lurking within that child. Of course, the preschool program may fail in its attempt to make the "click" between the child's potential and society, but that problem is beyond the scope of this chapter.

Gay (1978) listed some correspondences between descriptions of giftedness and their manifestations among gifted Black children. For example, research literature has suggested that gifted children are keen observers and, according to Gay, this characteristic may be observed in the Black child who "picks up more quickly on racist attitudes and practices; [and] may feel alienated by school at an early age" (p. 354). Gay recommended that teachers use these behavioral characteristics as a supplemental strategy to locate promising Black children who would be missed by traditional identification procedures. Another strategy proposed by Gay is to consider "any students who are doing adequate, grade level work but demonstrate evidences of poor attendance (75% or less), transiency, pronounced language difficulty, welfare or low socioeconomic status, or apparent neglect" (p. 356). These strategies were not designed specifically for the preschool-age Black child, but they demonstrate that preschools can develop flexible selection systems to accommodate the unique backgrounds to the children they serve. Any child who functions adequately in the face of adversity can be considered to be a promising candidate for special programming at the preschool level. Of course, the adverse conditions could stem from physical or mental handicaps as well as from social or economic hardships.

The identification procedures developed for the RAPYHT preschool program at the University of Illinois, which serves gifted handicapped children, were designed to bypass the traditional identification procedures by encouraging teachers to look for strengths in each of nine talent areas for *all* children in their classes. This process has enabled teachers to identify potentially gifted preschoolers, some of whom have mild to severe handicaps such as hearing impairments, speech delays, or cerebral palsy. It is too soon to tell whether or not these children will be labeled as "gifted" in later years, but the RAPYHT identification process has helped teachers to see their handicapped preschoolers from a new perspective so they can encourage the development of talents among these children. Some additional ideas for alternative assessment procedures can be found in Bernal (1978), Meeker (1978), Mercer and Lewis (1978), Stallings (1979), Talada (1979), and Torrance (1977).

ELIGIBILITY CONSIDERATIONS

Once assessment instruments have been selected, decisions will have to be made concerning entry criteria. Commonly used cut-off scores were indicated for some tests in an earlier section of this chapter. Nevertheless, these cut-off scores were neither theoretically nor empirically derived. Instead, the cut-off scores are the result of arbitrary decisions made by previous test users. There is nothing inherently wrong with these arbitrary decisions, but program planners should not feel bound solely by the weight of convention when establishing entry criteria for their own programs (Gowan, 1975).

While the stated goal of the identification process is to find the optimal match between preschoolers and special programs, various political, economic, and ethical considerations should and do play a role in the selection of children for entry into a program. Often, the major political consideration is to ensure that the identification process is not biased either for or against one or more subgroups within the total population. It is beyond the scope of this chapter to describe the many procedures that have been proposed to ensure that children from various racial, ethnic, and socioeconomic groups are adequately represented in programs for the gifted. Discussions of these identification plans can be found in Baldwin, Gear, and Lucito (1978), Storlie, Bellis, Powills, and Propuolenis (1978), and Torrance (1977).

Funding also has to be taken into account when selection criteria are established. Typically, the selection of the top 3% to 5% of the population in any given community as being gifted is based on cut-off scores commonly used with the Stanford-Binet. In fact, the number of "gifted" individuals will vary depending on the definition used for giftedness and, in a pragmatic sense, on the cut-off scores used by each program. Thus, some communities may find that 15% of their preschoolers are eligible for the special program. In this case, what happens if there are only funds for 5% of the preschoolers? One obvious solution is to adjust the cut-off levels. Another possibility would be to have a version of the "revolving door" program (Renzulli, Reis, & Smith, 1981). Under this plan children would participate in the special program on a periodic basis. Their length of stay in the special setting would vary depending on the type of project the individual child was working on. While Renzulli's "revolving door" plan may not be applicable to preschoolers, it does show that budgetary considerations can be handled in flexible ways without necessarily violating the assumptions underlying a program's identification plan. The cost of the identification process itself should also be considered. Renzulli and Smith (1977) have collected some cost data that suggest that costs for a case study approach were less than the costs for the more traditional group testing with follow-up individual intelligence testing.

SAMPLE IDENTIFICATION PLAN

Each program will have a unique identification plan. Following is a description of an identification plan used at the University of Illinois. This description is presented *not* as a model to follow but rather as an example of some of the issues that must be addressed in the development of a viable identification plan.

The University of Illinois Preschool Program for the Gifted is based on an open-classroom approach that encourages independence, task persistence, higher level thinking skills, and creativity (Karnes & Shwedel, submitted for publication). A multiple-entry approach to identification was designed so that a group of 22 3- to 5-year-old children who are functioning considerably above their age-mates in intellectual, creative, or cognitive fine-motor functioning could be selected for the program. The identification process involves three distinct phases: child-find, assessment, and selection.

Child-Find Phase

The first phase, child-find, involves an awareness campaign to inform parents throughout the community about opportunities for potentially gifted/talented young children to participate in a special program. Information about the program is disseminated in various ways: small signs posted in stores, bulletin boards, and outdoor kiosks; newspaper advertisements and flyers sent to Head

Start and local day care programs; and public service announcements on radio and television. This child-find process begins approximately 1 month before the individual assessments are conducted. Due to funding limitations, there is no active screening of all preschool-age children from the community. Nonetheless, last year there were approximately 200 inquiries regarding the program resulting from these relatively passive child-find procedures. Each inquiry is followed up by a telephone call from a member of the staff who describes the program in detail and in many cases invites the parent to view the classroom in operation. If the parent is still interested in the program and if the child is within the 3- to 5-year-old age range, arrangements are made for the assessment process.

Assessment Phase

The assessment phase was designed so that information about each child's intellectual, creative, and cognitive fine-motor functioning can be obtained from two independent sources: parents and the child's own performance in an individual testing situation. Parents are asked to fill out questionnaires about their child's abilities and interests. These questionnaires are modified versions of a questionnaire developed by the Seattle Project (Robinson, Jackson, & Roedell, 1979) and a questionnaire developed by the RAPYHT Project (Karnes & Associates, 1978). While the parent is completing the questionnaires, the child is being tested by a school psychologist on the Stanford-Binet (Terman & Merrill, 1973), the Draw-A-Person Test (Harris, 1963), and Thinking Creatively in Action and Movement (Torrance, 1980). These particular tests were chosen because they have been used extensively with young children. Assessment activities are carried out at the preschool, and they take approximately 1 hour per child. Occasionally the individual testing is not completed in one session, and consequently a short second session is needed. Detailed test information is not provided to parents except in rare instances. Parents are informed prior to assessment that the test information is not designed to provide a detailed picture of their child's functioning but rather the information is viewed by the project staff as a relatively efficient means of identifying young children who can benefit from the preschool program.

Selection Phase

The final phase of the identification process is selection. The goal of the selection process is twofold: to ensure that the children who enter the program are likely to benefit from the experience and to ensure that the program enrolls children from various racial, ethnic, and socioeconomic groups as well as maintaining a balance of ages and sexes. A pool of eligible candidates is established on the basis of the assessment results. Criteria for the eligibility pool are as follows: (a) scoring 2 standard deviations or more above the mean on any *one* of the identification instruments; (b) scoring 1½ standard deviations or more above the mean on any *two* of the identification instruments; and (c) for those children from low-income families, scoring at least 1 standard deviation above the mean on any *two* identification instruments. Once the eligibility pool has been established, the program staff meet to select the final candidates for entry into the program. At this point demographic information is used to make the final entry decision. There are no quotas, but the goal is to create a heterogeneous classroom. Eligible children who are not selected are placed on a waiting list in case some children do not enroll in the program or if openings occur early in the school year.

To date the information from the parent questionnaires has not played a major role in the selection process since meaningful norms to interpret parents' responses are still in the development process. Once norms are developed, it may even be possible to use the questionnaires to expand the child-find process. Instead of screening children individually, a large-scale mailing could be used to distribute the questionnaires to most of the parents of preschool-age children within the community. Those children who were rated high by their parents relative to their same-age and socioeconomic-level peers could be invited in for follow-up assessment.

In total the identification process takes 2 to 3 months since all the activities are carried out on a part-time basis. The end result is a preschool classroom filled with young gifted children who are likely to benefit from the basic orientation of the program.

SUMMARY

From an administrator's perspective, it would be much simpler if gifted children were born with a "G" etched on their foreheads, but luckily for both the individual and society, this is not the case. Admittedly, "giftedness" is a "fuzzy" construct. The act of establishing an identification plan requires each community to decide how it wants to balance needs and resources. At present there is no single solution, but there are numerous viable alternatives, many of which have been described in this chapter. Figure 2-1 represents a five-step sequential process that can serve as a guide for the development of a viable and defensible identification plan. The key to this guide is that decisions made at each step are dependent on the outcome of previous steps.

The identification of gifted preschoolers for entry into special programs is a relatively new concern to educators. It is hoped that within 5 years the content of this chapter will be subsumed by more sophisticated and precise approaches. In the meantime, teachers and program developers should be willing to experiment with the identification procedures described here in order to establish a plan that meets the unique needs of their preschool program.

FIGURE 2-1
Guidelines for the Establishment of an Effective Identification Plan

---

1. Develop a community-based operational definition of giftedness (Storlie, et al., 1978).
2. Develop a plan for the preschool gifted program.
3. Develop assessment procedures:
   (a) Performance areas to be assessed.
   (b) Type(s) of information to be collected.
4. Specify selection criteria.
5. Monitor effectiveness of the identification process.

REFERENCES

Arnheim, D., & Sinclair, W. *Basic Motor Ability Tests (BMAT)*. Long Beach CA: Institute of Sensory Motor Development, California State University, 1974.

Baldwin, A. Another perspective on identification using the Baldwin Identification Matrix. *CONN-CEPT I: Practical suggestions for gifted and talented program development*. Hartford CT: Connecticut State Department of Education, 1979.

Baldwin, A., Gear, G., & Lucito, L. *Educational planning for the gifted: Overcoming cultural, geographic, and socioeconomic barriers*. Reston VA: The Council for Exceptional Children, 1978.

Barbe, W. *One in a thousand—A comparative study of moderately and highly gifted elementary school children*. Columbus: Ohio State Department of Education, 1964.

Bernal, E. The identification of gifted Chicano children. In A. Baldwin, G. Gear, & L. Lucito (Eds.), *Educational planning for the gifted: Overcoming cultural, geographic, and socioeconomic barriers*. Reston VA: The Council for Exceptional Children, 1978.

Berry, K. *Developmental Test of Visual-Motor Integration (VMI)*. Chicago: Follett, 1967.

Borland, J. Teacher identification of the gifted: A new look. *Journal for the Education of the Gifted*, 1979, *2*, 20–33.

Burgemeister, B., Blum, L., & Lorge, I. *Columbia Mental Maturity Scale (3rd Ed.)*. New York: Harcourt Brace Jovanovich, 1972.

Ciha, T., Harris, R., Hoffman, C., & Potter, M. Parents as identifiers of giftedness: Ignored but accurate. *The Gifted Child Quarterly*, 1974, *18*, 191–199.

Davis, G., & Rimm, S. Characteristics of creatively gifted children. *The Gifted Child Quarterly*, 1977, *21*, 546, 551.

Doll, E. *Vineland Social Maturity Scale*. Circle Pines MN: American Guidance Service, 1965.

Feldman, D. *Beyond universals in cognitive development*. Norwood NJ: Ablex Publishers, 1980.

Foster, W. *Clinical approaches to research on the gifted*. Paper presented at the American Educational Research Association Annual Convention, Boston, 1980.

French, J. *Pictoral Test of Intelligence*. Boston: Houghton Mifflin, 1964.

Gallagher, J. *Research summary on gifted child education.* Springfield IL: Office of the Superintendent of Public Instruction, 1966.

Gay, J. A proposed plan for identifying black gifted children. *The Gifted Child Quarterly*, 1978, *22*, 353–360.

Gear, G. Effects of training on teacher judged giftedness. *The Gifted Child Quarterly*, 1978, *22*, 90–97.

Gowan, J. How to identify students for a gifted child program. *The Gifted Child Quarterly*, 1975, *19*, 260–263.

Grant, T. *Relevant aspects of potential.* Marlborough CT: RAP Researchers, 1974.

Guilford, J. *The nature of human intelligence.* New York: McGraw-Hill, 1967.

Harris, D. *Children's drawings as measures of intellectual ability: A revision and extension of the Goodenough Draw-A-Man test.* New York: Harcourt Brace Jovanovich, 1963.

Karnes, M., & Associates. *Preschool talent checklists manual.* Urbana IL: Publications Office, Institute for Child Behavior and Development, 1978.

Karnes, M., & Shwedel, A. Maximizing the potential of the young gifted child. Submitted for publication, 1982.

Karnes, M., Shwedel, A., & Lewis G. Serving the underserved: The young gifted/talented handicapped. Submitted for publication, 1982.

Karnes, M., Shwedel, A., & Linnemeyer, S. The young gifted/talented child: Programs at the University of Illinois. *The Elementary School Journal*, 1982, *83*, 195–214.

Landig, H., & Naumann, T. Aspects of intelligence in gifted preschoolers. *The Gifted Child Quarterly*, 1978, *22,* 85–89.

Levine, S., Elzey, F., & Lewis, M. *California preschool social competency scale.* Palo Alto CA: Consulting Psychologists Press, 1969.

Madden, R., & Gardner, E. *Stanford Early School Achievement Test (SESAT).* New York: Harcourt Brace Jovanovich, 1969.

Marland, S. *Education of the gifted and talented, I: Report to the Congress of the United States by the Commissioner of Education.* Washington DC: U.S. Office of Education, 1972.

Meeker, M. Nondiscriminatory testing procedures to assess giftedness in Black, Chicano, Navajo, and Anglo children. In A. Baldwin, G. Gear, & L. Lucito (Eds.), *Educational planning for the gifted: Overcoming cultural, geographic, and socioeconomic barriers.* Reston VA: The Council for Exceptional Children, 1978.

Mercer, J., & Lewis, J. Using the system of multicultural assessment (SOMPA) to identify the gifted minority child. In A. Baldwin, G. Gear, & L. Lucito (Eds.), *Educational planning for the gifted: Overcoming cultural, geographic, and socioeconomic barriers.* Reston VA: The Council for Exceptional Children, 1978.

Moss, M. *Tests of Basic Experiences (TOBE).* Monterey CA: CTB/McGraw-Hill, 1971.

Nurss, J., & McGauvran, M. *Metropolitan Readiness Tests.* New York: Harcourt Brace Jovanovich, 1976.

Pegnato, C., & Birch, J. Locating gifted children in junior high school: A comparison of methods. *Exceptional Children*, 1959, 25, 300–304.

Rekdal, C. In search of wild duck: Personality inventories as tests of creative potential and their use as measurements in programs for the gifted. *The Gifted Child Quarterly*, 1977, *21*, 501–516.

Renzulli, J. What makes giftedness? Reexamining a definition. *Phi Delta Kappan*, 1978, *60*, 180–184, 261.

Renzulli, J., & Hartman, R. Scale for rating behavioral characteristics of superior students. *Exceptional Children*, 1971, *38*, 243–248.

Renzulli, J., Reiss, S., & Smith, L. The revolving-door model: A new way of identifying the gifted. *Phi Delta Kappan*, 1981, *62*, 648–649.

Renzulli, J., & Smith, L. Two approaches to identification of gifted students. *Exceptional Children*, 1977, *43*, 512–518.

Riegle, K. *Foundations of dialectical psychology*. New York: Academic Press, 1979.

Roach, E., & Kephart, N. *Purdue Perceptual-Motor Survey*. Columbus OH: Charles E. Merrill, 1966.

Robinson, H., Jackson, N., & Roedell, W. *Annual report to the Spencer Foundation: Identification and nurturance of extraordinarily precocious young children*. Seattle: University of Washington Child Development Research Group, 1978. (ERIC Document Reproduction Service No. ED 162 756.)

Robinson, H., Jackson, W., & Roedell, W. *Seattle Project Parent Questionnaire* (1979 version). Seattle: University of Washington Child Development Research Group, 1979.

Slosson, R. *Slossen Intelligence Tests for Children and Adults*. East Aurora NY: Slosson Educational Publications, 1981.

Stallings, C. *California program model: Learning through methods of inquiry, an individualized approach*. San Diego CA: San Diego City Schools, 1979.

Storlie, T., Bellis, D., Powills, J., & Propuolenis, P. *The development of a culturally fair model for the early identification and selection of gifted children*. August 1978. (ERIC Document Reproduction Service No. ED 159 229.)

Talada, E. Project search: Identification of creative talent potential among the gifted. *CONN-CEPT I: Practical suggestion for gifted and talented program development*. Hartford: Connecticut State Department of Education, 1979.

Taylor, C., & Ellison, R. *Manual for Alpha Biographical Inventory (Rev. Ed.)*. Salt Lake City: Institute for Behavioral Research in Creativity, 1968.

Terman, L., & Merrill, M. *Stanford-Binet Intelligence Scale* (Form L-M, 1972 norms ed.) Boston: Houghton Mifflin, 1973.

Terman, L., & Oden, M. *Genetic studies of genius, V: The gifted child grows up*. Stanford CA: Stanford University Press, 1959.

Torrance, E. *Torrance Tests of Creative Thinking*. Bensenville IL: Scholastic Testing Service, 1966.

Torrance, E. *Discovery and nurturance of giftedness in the culturally different*. Reston VA: The Council for Exceptional Children, 1977.

Torrance, E. *Thinking creatively in action and movement* (Research ed.). Bensenville IL: Scholastic Testing Service, 1980.

Tucker, J. *Structure of intellect analysis for the Stanford-Binet Form L-M*. Austin TX: Author, 1972.

Wallach, M. Tests tell us little about talent. *American Scientist*, 1976, *64*, 57.

Wallach, M., & Wing, C. *The talent student: A validation of the creativity intelligence distinction*. New York: Holt, Rinehart, & Winston, 1969.

Wechsler, D. *Wechsler Preschool and Primary Scale of Intelligence*. New York: Psychological Corporation, 1967.

CHAPTER 3

Conceptual Models

Merle B. Karnes
Polly Kemp
Mark Williams

Four conceptual models have been used in developing instructional programs for young gifted/talented children, nonhandicapped and handicapped: the Open Classroom, Guilford's Structure of the Intellect (SOI), Renzulli's Enrichment Triad Model, and Bloom's Taxonomy. This chapter focuses largely on these four models. While Williams' Cognitive-Affective Model has not been used with preschool children, it is a potentially useful model and is, therefore, discussed briefly. Use of multimodels is also addressed because many preschool programs are eclectic in nature.

Models are used because they provide a framework to guide instruction. They help the program planner to develop individualized programs for gifted/talented children. Programs that adopt a model are apt to be more consistent and better organized than programs that do not (Karnes, 1980). Another important reason for using a conceptual model is that it helps to interpret the program to other professionals, parents, and the lay public. Interpreting how a program for the gifted child differs from a program for the average child is a persistent problem. Merely stating that the "higher level thought processes" are reached by "enriching the curriculum" does not differentiate between a program for gifted and talented children and other programs. Finally, the use of a model tends to make the program staff better observers of each gifted/talented child. A model defines the parameters within which the program focuses and therefore dictates what is to be observed and evaluated.

In the last 12 years, developmental milestones have been used to assess young children's development, especially for children with handicapping conditions. These milestones have been derived from standardized tests, expert opinion on child development, and the experience of practitioners working with normal children. Teachers rely on these guidelines for ongoing assessment and in planning individualized instruction programs that match the child's level in critical areas such as cognition/language, gross and fine motor development, and social/emotional growth. Guidelines that have been used to program for handicapped children have also proved helpful for assessing gifted children, and many programs for the gifted rely on developmental guidelines along with a conceptual model. Developmental guidelines help the teacher to be more observant of a child and more realistic about the child's total development.

No research evidence to date verifies that one conceptual model is superior to another in promoting the gifts and talents of the young child. Nevertheless, it is important that there be a theoretical framework of some kind, that the goals of the program be congruent with this framework, and that the procedures for evaluating the program be compatible with the theoretical framework and instructional program.

Two models used at the University of Illinois for over 10 years with culturally different preschoolers, preschoolers from all socioeconomic levels and races, and handicapped children who are also gifted and talented will be discussed first and in considerable detail. These are the Open Classroom and the SOI models.

THE OPEN CLASSROOM MODEL

The open classroom seems particularly suitable for teaching gifted preschool children. Its child-oriented philosophy together with its unique use of time, space, curriculum, and staff offers many opportunities for gifted children to develop their potential. Gallagher (1975) pointed out that:

> The potential of this approach for gifted students seems manifest. It makes the design of independent student research a more practical possibility and can allow the gifted student to move more at his or her own pace. (p. 278)

Individual and discovery learning are stressed in the open classroom. Children move at their own pace, in their own time, pursuing their own interests. The teacher in the open classroom encourages, in fact expects, a child to take the initiative, to be independent, resourceful, and creative—all characteristics of a gifted child.

No two open classrooms are alike. Each reflects the interests, backgrounds, values, and personalities of the children and teacher. Even though the classrooms are different, sometimes strikingly so, open classroom teachers share a common philosophy; that each child, with help, can make decisions determining the scope, the means, and the pace of his or her education. This philosophical concept dramatically changes the traditional method of teaching. The classroom is no longer *only* teacher-directed, rather it is teacher/child-directed. Children make decisions about their own learning activities, and the teacher's role is to help each child, when he or she is ready, to acquire basic skills that explain, describe, and organize experience.

The philosophy and principles of the open classroom seem highly compatible with the needs of gifted children. The informal approach offers gifted children the opportunity to select their learning experiences on the basis of curiosity, interest, and ability. The children are not fettered by age or grade. In addition to a shared philosophy, teachers in the open classroom use time, space, curriculum, and staff in unconventional ways. These four dimensions provide a framework for the organization and operation of the classroom.

Time

The daily schedule of an open classroom is an extended block of time within which children work on activities they have chosen. The teacher moves about the room, observing and listening and talking to children. At opportune moments she assists them by giving information, suggesting a resource, raising a question, teaching a skill, or directing an activity into more constructive channels. Children usually group and regroup themselves voluntarily on the basis of interests. A child may choose to work alone, with another child, with a teacher, or with a group of children. Self-directed learning occurs naturally because children have time to investigate and experiment. A child can pursue one learning activity for a whole day, for several days, even for weeks. A child can explore an interest in depth and the teacher has time to assist this exploration. Sustained work over a period of time is encouraged. Children are rarely interrupted or cut off from finishing what they have begun. In fact, they are expected to begin and complete a task to the best of their abilities and within their own time frames.

Without the time restraints inherent in a formal classroom, where the teacher selects the activities and moves the children from one structure to another every 15 or 20 minutes, children and teachers in the open classroom manipulate time to suit individual needs and desires. The teacher has time to become well acquainted with each child. Free to observe and work with children informally, the teacher gains a broad understanding and appreciation of the unique characteristics and abilities of each child. This in turn leads to highly individualized and realistic educational goals for the intellectual, social, and emotional development of every student in the classroom.

Children have time to learn from each other in the classroom as well as on the playground. Throughout the day they share experiences and ideas, feelings and fantasies, knowledge and skills, materials and space. The teacher expects children to use their time productively and to value work and learning. This would appear to be a most suitable environment for gifted children, who are task-committed and who need flexible periods of time to pursue their interests. Time is never a factor in determining what can and cannot be done in the open classroom.

Space

Space is adapted to accommodate the interests, ideas, and needs of the children and teachers. Activities revolve around a number of learning centers such as woodworking, housekeeping, dramatic play, reading, math, art, science, music, blocks, and water play. Although each center contains the materials related to it, each is part of a larger organizational scheme, and materials and equipment can be and often are used in other parts of the room. The centers and other work areas vary in size and are separated by bookshelves, dividers, chalkboards, display cases, and screens. Materials and equipment are available at all times and are placed so children can reach them easily. Each child has his or her own mailbox for personal books and treasures. There are always one or two private nooks where a child or teacher can be alone to think, read, or work. An open classroom is rarely a tidy environment, yet excessive tidiness may inhibit children and discourage "learning in what David Hawkins has called the concrete mode—messing around with stuff" (Featherstone, 1971, p. 4).

Materials, equipment, and furniture are often rearranged. The teacher and children decide when and how to transform several smaller spaces into a larger one if room is needed for a growing city, a miniature solar system, or a papier-mâché dinosaur. Hallways and corridors frequently become art galleries, science museums, or dance studios. Every inch of space is used. Children and teachers work on the floor, at tables, in the hall, and in the library as well as outside. Art work, stories, and experiments are artistically displayed in many parts of the room, creating a rich and interesting milieu.

Children and teachers move freely about the room observing and talking to each other. Their movements and activities are influenced by the spatial arrangements of the room. A large open space beckons a child to use it—to run, jump, slide, yell—while a number of smaller spaces cue a child to slow down, stop, explore. This in itself often sparks the creative impulse.

The flexible use of space in the open classroom increases the diversity as well as the number of learning experiences for children. More materials can be added to several small areas than to one larger space. Then, too, children working in close proximity spontaneously look at and discuss each other's work, a practice that stimulates other ideas or projects. The freedom to manipulate space encourages the children to act on the environment, be involved in decision making, spontaneously participate in dialogue, and integrate their learning experiences.

Curriculum

No prescribed curriculum is taught in the open classroom. Rather, parts of many different curricula are used as well as an enormous range and variety of materials and equipment. Books of every description fill shelves placed in many parts of the room. Children frequently dictate, illustrate, and bind their own books, which are used in the library as reference books and sometimes as part of a reading program. Manipulative materials are supplied in great diversity and range, with little duplication. Some of the materials are commercial and are found in many preschool classrooms and kindergartens; some are common household items; some are junk collected by the children and teachers; and some are developed by the children and teachers. This profuse and eclectic mass of curriculum materials stimulates the natural curiosity of children and prompts them to initiate many of their own learning activities.

The range of learning experiences in the open classroom is large and variable, and many different kinds of activities go on simultaneously. For example, on a typical day one might see three children playing a game of alphabet concentration while another reads books in the quiet room; others are creating a complex structure from blocks while another small group conducts a simple science experiment, the results of which they will later dictate to the teacher.

The open classroom approach to learning is interdisciplinary. Neither children nor teachers are expected to confine themselves to a single subject area while learning. The content areas of reading, math, science, art, and, sometimes, music and movement are integrated into an activity whenever possible.

Children's learning experiences in the open classroom are pursuits, extensions, and elaborations of their own spontaneous interests, rather than activities selected by the teacher. Children, especially gifted children, usually know what they want to learn and when they are ready to learn it. The joy and enthusiasm with which a child applies himself to a task he wants to do is evident to anyone who has observed children. The teacher avoids whole-class assignments. Instead, he or she directs and shapes the activities children have chosen through dialogue, introducing related materials, integrating content areas, or direct instruction.

Staff

The teacher in the open classroom is not locked into teaching specific content areas at a predetermined time each day. Rather, he or she is free to spend time observing, talking, and listening to children and learns to know each of them very well. As the teacher works with the children, the focus is on the cognitive processes the children are using as well as on their social and emotional levels of development. These informal observations, along with formal assessments and information from parents, help the teacher determine when adult intervention is appropriate, what resources to make available to extend a child's learning, and what kinds of suggestions, questions, and elaborations of an activity will best stimulate the thinking of a particular child.

Teaching in the open classroom is closely related to child development theories. Children, even gifted children, differ greatly in experiences, abilities, and backgrounds. Some need more time to complete a task than others; some work well independently with only occasional assistance while others need more help and direction; some read while others are just beginning to discover the relationship between letter and sound. In the open classroom each child starts where he or she is and moves forward in a unique way, time, and pace. For example, the basics—"reading, writing, and arithmetic"—are all taught in the open classroom, although not in the way they are taught in a traditional classroom. The major difference between the two approaches is *how* and *when* the basics are taught. In the traditional classroom, groups of children are usually taught a specific content area, using similar materials, when the teacher decides it is time to teach it. In the open classroom, basics are most often taught to one child, using a variety of materials based on that child's interests and when that child is ready.

The teacher is a facilitator who encourages discovery learning, independent thinking, risk-taking, problem-solving, and open examination and expression of ideas and feelings. The teacher's language is used intelligently, geared to a child's interests, work, and level of functioning. Good communication skills are modeled by the teacher as he or she listens, responds, paraphrases, clarifies, questions, and engages others in dialogue. The teacher also models and stimulates critical thinking by asking questions such as "Why do you think that's happening?" or "What else could you use or do?" Children learn a great deal from modeling and soon incorporate many of these learning behaviors into their own learning style.

Teacher and children share the responsibility of running the classroom. Each day children make decisions. They select and plan many of their own learning experiences, group and regroup themselves, and decide which pieces of their work they want to display and where to display them. Each child keeps a major portion of his or her work in a notebook or in labeled folders that assist the child and teacher in planning that child's program and evaluating that child's progress. The teacher also keeps an extensive file on each child: daily anecdotal records, informal inventories, formal assessments, and notes from parent-teacher conferences. This information is reviewed and updated regularly.

The teacher in the open classroom must be enthusiastic and committed to this philosophical approach to teaching children. Each child is recognized as an individual who has unique knowledge and experiences, values and opinions, abilities and needs. The teacher must believe that each child, with help, can determine the scope, the means, and the pace of his or her education and the teacher must *act* on this belief day after day. The teacher must be a perceptive and thoughtful observer, knowledgeable about child development theories and practices, skillful in diagnostic techniques, experienced in teaching all of the content areas, and willing to change the focus or direction of instruction if the child's interest or response dictates a change.

Excellent organizational skills are imperative for the teacher in the open classroom as well as a willingness to spend hours in planning, gathering materials, and developing a classroom environment that is both appealing and challenging to children. The teacher should have, or quickly develop, total classroom awareness. Many children are involved in diverse activities simultaneously, and the teacher must be aware of what is happening with each child or group of children at any time. Finally, the open classroom teacher must genuinely respect and enjoy children and be sensitive and eager to talk with; listen to; and share experiences, ideas, problems, feelings, and fantasies with all of the children.

RAPYD II Open Classroom

An exemplary open classroom was developed for 20 gifted children at the University of Illinois in 1972–1973 as one component of the RAPYD II project (Retrieval and Acceleration of Potentially Young Disadvantaged), a project financed by the gifted program, State of Illinois. One purpose of the project as stated in the proposal was "to evaluate the effect of open education in the development of potentially gifted-disadvantaged children and middle- or upper-class gifted children." Research data at the end of the project indicated that the open classroom was, indeed, a viable approach for developing the potential of gifted preschool children. However, another feature was added to the curriculum: The RAPYD II proposal stated that the teacher in the classroom would "identify and implement twenty-five original ideas initiated by the children." Thus, children's projects became an important element in the development of this particular open classroom. Used as a focal point, the children's projects helped the teacher implement the philosophy and principles of the open classroom. The vacuum that occurred the first few days of school was quickly and easily filled by the children, who began to initiate their own activities. A child/teacher-directed classroom evolved rather than a teacher-directed one.

A project was defined as a series of related activities or lessons, initiated by a child's interest, identified by the teacher, and developed by the child and teacher over an extended period of time. A project could be developed by one child and the teacher or by a group of children and the teacher. Some of the projects were long (the Solar System, Dinosaur, Plant, City, and Hospital projects extended over several months); others (the Fashion Show, Band Concert, Parade, Beauty Shop, and Restaurant projects) were short, running only 10 days to 2 weeks. A project was terminated on completion or when members lost interest. Each child who initiated an idea decided whether or not he or she wanted that interest developed into a project. Each child decided whether or not to join a particular project and was free to leave when interest waned. All of the project members were committed to attending frequent meetings for planning and discussion as well as to spending some time each week working on the project. Although the projects were an important feature of the RAPYD II open classroom, they were only a small part of the hundreds of other learning experiences initiated and pursued by the children.

Summary of Open Classroom Model

The philosophy, principles, and practices of the open classroom approach seem to match the needs and abilities of many gifted preschool children. The literature and experience tell us that gifted children need ample time, enough space, a wide-ranging curriculum, and individual attention from the teacher to develop their talents. Each of these four dimensions is an integral part of the open approach. The time framework of this approach encourages discovery learning. The focus is on *how* to learn rather than on *what* to learn. The gifted child is more likely to perceive relationships and apply them if he or she is not hurried from one assignment to the next. The children and the teacher have time to investigate, hypothesize, experiment, and reflect. Ideas, concepts, and problems can be explored in depth over extended periods of time, providing the gifted child with the opportunity to exercise inquisitiveness and use analytical and critical skills.

Not confined to traditional practices, the teacher in the open classroom is free to challenge and direct the curiosity, inquisitiveness, inventiveness, originality, independence, and intellectual and creative abilities of the gifted child. The philosophy, principles, and practices of the open approach offer gifted preschool children a variety of opportunities to develop their potential.

GUILFORD'S STRUCTURE OF THE INTELLECT (SOI) MODEL

J. P. Guilford's (1967) Structure of the Intellect is a conceptual model of intellectual functioning that educators of elementary and high school gifted children have found extremely useful as a framework on which to base instructional programs and activities. The comprehensive nature of this model provides many and varied avenues for intellectual pursuits, and teachers can readily use it to encourage gifted children to employ thinking processes beyond those required in the regular school curriculum. The Structure of the Intellect (SOI) model postulates 120 different thinking abilities. Whether or not all these ways of thinking are in fact distinct from one another, the rich and varied possibilities that this model presents have provided teachers, especially those concerned with the gifted, with a wealth of ideas for stimulating lessons, activities, and projects. Examination of Guilford's model quickly explains its widespread popularity among educators of school-age gifted children. In fact, a book about the education of gifted children can hardly be found that does not contain a discussion of the SOI model and its usefulness. However, the authors have found little evidence of the use of this model at the preschool level, save in Karnes's own programs for preschool gifted and talented children. A discussion of the use of the model in these programs follows the description of the model given here.

The Structure of the Intellect model is an organized system that presents all the different ways in which people think. In this model, 120 different intellectual processes or abilities result from the combinations of five kinds of thinking *operations* applied to four types of materials, or *contents*, which result in six types of *products*. A thorough knowledge of the model is gained not through the memorization of the 120 abilities, but rather by becoming familiar with the 15 descriptors of the model's three dimensions and by understanding how these descriptors are combined to comprise intellectual abilities. The most useful approach to learning the model is to master one of the three dimensions at a time.

Operations

The operations dimension of the model describes ways of thinking or of procesing information. This dimension is the most important of the three and should be learned thoroughly before the others are introduced. The five operations are Cognition, Memory, Divergent Productive Thinking, Convergent Productive Thinking, and Evaluation.

Cognition is the process of becoming aware of, perceiving, recognizing, or understanding information. Cognition includes discovery through all five senses as well as the comprehension of ideas, concepts, or principles. It is the way in which we acquire new information, and is thus the source for the information that we store and use in various ways (i.e., the *other* four operations). This is a very important process for preschoolers to exercise, but unfortunately most preschool programs concentrate on this intellectual process to the exclusion of all others. The SOI model helps teachers to become aware of the fact that cognition is only one of five ways of dealing with information and therefore should not receive undue emphasis in the classroom.

The second operation, *Memory*, is the storage and retrieval of information, both on a long-term and a short-term basis. The information retrieved is basically the same as what was learned, and it is recalled in connection with the same cues with which it was learned. This is also a very useful intellectual operation, but again is one that receives too much emphasis in the classroom at the expense of the productive and evaluative thinking operations described below.

Divergent Productive Thinking is imaginative, original, self-expressive thinking. The child is asked either to generate new information or to recall stored information in relation to new cues. There is no one correct answer to a question that calls for divergent thinking, nor can all the possible answers be predicted. Divergent thinking plays a large role in what we know about creative activity, and the practice of this thinking operation is very important in developing independent, imaginative, original minds. Preschool-age children quickly learn to be successful at this type of thinking and often greatly enjoy doing it. A program for gifted children of preschool age should provide a healthy diet of divergent thinking activities on a regular basis.

Convergent Productive Thinking is the process of organizing information to deduce the one correct answer. As in divergent thinking, new information is generated, but convergent tasks are highly structured and restrictive, and the answer can be deduced from the information given. Convergent thinking requires "zeroing in" on the answer as opposed to "expanding out" to all possibilities in divergent thought. Although the range of convergent activities appropriate for preschool-age children is limited, this is an important process that should not be ignored. (A riddle is an example of a convergent activity that can be used at the preschool level; certain sorting and classifying tasks are also convergent.)

Evaluative Thinking makes comparisons with standards or criteria and includes judgments concerning identity, suitability, desirability, and morality. Evaluation differs from convergent thinking because no new information is produced; one makes a judgment about material present, remembered, or previously produced. Certain theorists have argued that higher level processes such as critical thinking are not yet developed in children of preschool age, but the authors have found that 4- and 5-year-old gifted children can, in fact, make choices based upon their own reasoning in activities that are carefully structured by the teacher. Independent thought and judgment are important intellectual habits for children to develop as soon as they are ready to do so.

Contents

The contents dimension of the SOI model describes four types of material that one can think about. That is, any of the five *operations* described above can be performed upon any of the following types of "substance" or information: figural, symbolic, semantic, or behavioral. *Figural* content is concrete information and is perceived, recalled, and manipulated in the form of images. It concerns the physical aspects of an object—its shape, color, or texture—and has no meaning beyond pure sensation. *Symbolic* information refers to signs that stand for things, such as letters, numerals, codes, road signs, and musical notation. *Semantic* content concerns verbal ideas and concepts; the focus is upon the *meaning* conveyed in words or pictures. Finally, *behavioral* content is about the feelings, thoughts, moods, desires, and interactions of people.

Products

The third dimension of the Structure of the Intellect model describes how the end products of thinking can be organized. One can process, in any of five ways (operations), information of any of four kinds (contents). The *form* in which this information is dealt with can be any of the following six *products*: units, classes, relations, systems, transformations, or implications. *Units* are single items of information, each having its unique character. *Classes* refer to aggregates of information grouped according to a common element or property, such as red circles or four-legged animals. *Relations* deal with the explicit connections between things; "greater than" and "opposite" describe different relations. *Systems* are patterns of information comprised of a number of interrelated and interdependent parts. A system is a whole network that forms a single concept yet is made up of many organized parts. Examples of systems include complex designs, equations, sentences, and stories. *Transformations* are shifts, modifications, transitions, or redefinitions of information. They involve seeing something in a new and different way and are characteristic of creative people. Finally, *implications* are possible consequences, or circumstantial connections between items of information. They are not as clear-cut as relations, but rather are just "things that go together."

Summary of SOI Model

In summary, each of the 120 different intellectual abilities described by the Structure of the Intellect model is a unique combination of one descriptor from each of the three dimensions. The thinker performs one of the operations on some kind of material (content), which is organized in a particular form (product). Each ability can then be labeled with an abbreviation, called a *trigram*, which names the particular operation, content, and product, in that order. Each ability, or "cell," in the Structure of the Intellect cube has its own unique classification and trigram. (Abbreviations consist of the first letter of the descriptor, with two exceptions. Because two operations, cognition and convergent productive thinking, begin with the same letter, C refers to cognition and N refers to convergent thinking. Likewise, semantic content is abbreviated with the letter M to avoid confusion with symbolic content.) To illustrate, the trigram CMC refers to the cell representing Cognition of Semantic Classes; NSR stands for Convergent Production of Symbolic Relations.

Classroom Use

The Structure of the Intellect model has been used in classrooms for 4- and 5-year-old gifted and talented children at the University of Illinois (Karnes & Bertschi, 1978; Karnes & Zehrbach, 1973). The teachers in these classrooms make use of the model to stimulate the children's creative and productive thinking throughout the day. Each day, a teacher-directed lesson is taught to all children in groups of five to eight children per teacher. Lessons are scheduled to tap a variety of thinking abilities each week. The lessons are written in game format to make them highly appealing to the children and to encourage maximum participation. Often the teachers themselves write these lesson plans, based upon their knowledge of the model, or they adapt lessons written by others to their particular group.

In addition to teaching SOI-based lesson plans, teachers in these classrooms set up activities during free play, music, and other less directed periods of the school day that stimulate the children to think productively and creatively. For example, in arts and crafts activities, teachers attempt to have each child make something different from what other children make out of available materials. Creative movements and original words to songs are encouraged during music activities. Knowledge of the SOI model gained during ongoing inservice training also helps the teachers of these young gifted children to ask questions throughout the school day, which stimulate the children to move beyond the basic levels of thought. Teachers are often heard to ask: "How else could that be done?" "What are all the different ways to do this you can think of?'' ''Why do *you* think this is best?'' Teachers trained in the use of the model were also found to be effective in encouraging divergent and evaluative thinking when teaching in more informal classroom situations (Karnes & Zehrbach, 1973).

The usefulness of the Structure of the Intellect model in programs for gifted children of school age has been acknowledged for many years. The model has also been shown to be effective when used with gifted and talented preschoolers and will probably be in more general use at the preschool level in the coming years.

COMPARISON OF THE OPEN CLASS AND SOI MODELS

Karnes and Bertschi (1978) have compared the open classroom and the SOI models as they are interpreted and implemented at the University of Illinois. The differences between the two approaches are best understood by examining the performance of each in determining the following: theoretical base, curriculum, instructional methods and materials, child assessment, teacher role, teacher-child interactions, use of time, and use of space.

Theoretical Base

The Structure of Intellect approach assumes that children learn best when teachers provide sequenced activities based on individualized instructional objectives. The SOI model helps teachers stimulate a variety of intellectual abilities, including convergent, divergent, and evaluative thinking. The SOI model aids in programming for talent development as well as in the remediation of handicaps.

The open classroom assumes that children, with teacher help, are capable of determining the direction, scope, means, and pace of their education. The teacher helps children to acquire basic skills, the learning tools that will enable them to explore, observe, describe, and organize experience. It provides an environment that encourages and nurtures talent in children and also meets their special needs.

Curriculum

SOI teachers rely on prepared curriculum and materials to plan lessons. They also use a game format to present math, language, and prereading lessons. Art and music activities are included in the daily plan. Children learn songs; use musical instruments; and participate in yoga, dance, and creative movement exercises. Teachers also plan lessons using talk sheets, puppets, and role plays that help children explore their feelings and learn appropriate social behavior.

In the open classroom children initiate their own learning activities. Instead of planning structured lessons, teachers attempt to extend or channel the children's activities in ways that integrate the learning of specific skills. Thus, teachers base instruction on their knowledge of each child and use the child's interests as a springboard to facilitate skill development. For example, if Billy is playing with his favorite animal, a gray rubber hippopotamus, his teacher may ask what the hippopotamus eats. Billy, some of the other children, and the teacher may decide to find out by looking up the answer in an animal book. The group may spend a half hour learning about the eating habits of the hippopotamus and other wild animals.

Instructional Methods and Materials

SOI lesson plans are matched to individual needs. Sometimes children with similar needs are grouped together for an activity, and sometimes teachers place materials and instructions for an activity in a separate envelope for each child. The children call these tasks "workjobs" and perform them independently, usually sitting together in small groups with a teacher nearby to provide help when needed.

During directed play time, children in the SOI classroom have access to a variety of materials. This is a time for child-initiated projects, play, and individual tutoring. Teachers encourage social interaction among children interested in using the same materials and take advantage of every opportunity to teach children directly.

A variety of materials is available at all times in the open classroom. They are placed so that children can reach them easily. Teachers listen carefully in order to engage children in dialogue and activities that lead to an exploration of subjects in which they have expressed interest. Content areas such as math, reading readiness, and fine motor coordination are integrated into a child's activity whenever possible. Teachers and children also discuss problems that come up and make decisions together.

Child Assessment

Both the SOI and the open classroom approaches use the same sequenced set of skills in six developmental areas as a guideline for child assessment and as an aid in determining individual priorities. In the SOI classroom, skills are observed in gamelike activities that provide an opportunity for the child to demonstrate specific skills. In the open classroom procedure, teachers observe and record each child's performance of specific skills during spontaneous classroom activity. For skills unlikely to be demonstrated spontaneously, the teacher gives each child a simple task in which the desired skill can be observed. Such tasks are generally incorporated into the child's normal activities.

Teacher Role

SOI teachers plan precisely the daily experiences for all children in the classroom. They meet together daily to discuss their plans, to record child progress, and to set new objectives. Although teachers provide materials and direct children in using them, they take care to involve them actively in the learning situation and encourage them to act as freely as possible within the context of planned activities.

In the open classroom, teachers help children to understand their environment and their feelings. Teachers give encouragement, feedback, guidance, information, and clarification to children throughout the day. Teachers create a purposeful atmosphere by expecting and helping children to use time productively and to value work and learning. Teachers in the open classroom meet for at least 1 hour each day to discuss their observations and to devise new strategies for extending learning experiences.

Teacher-Child Interactions

Most interactions between teacher and children in the SOI classroom are initiated by the teacher. Teachers make a conscious effort to ask questions that require divergent, convergent, and evaluative thinking when working with groups of children as well as when working with individuals.

In the open classroom interactions are spontaneous and informal and usually are initiated by the child. Teachers are more likely to work with individuals than with a group.

Use of Time

A specific daily schedule is followed in the SOI classroom. During the first period of the day, children are allowed to choose their own activities. Later, 15-minute lessons for small groups of children are alternated with periods of less structured activity and with activities such as music, when the whole group is together. Snacks are served in a family atmosphere, and self-help, social, and expressive language skills are encouraged. Children spend about 20 minutes each day on the playground.

The daily schedule in the open classroom consists of flexible blocks of time. Many learning activities take place simultaneously. A child may work alone, with a friend, or in a group. Snacks are available on a small table throughout the day. When children are hungry, they may help themselves to the portions illustrated on a menu card. Group meeting is the only time of the day when all children and teachers meet together. During each day's meeting teachers record topics or activities in which individual children wish to participate. The children involved in planning usually share responsibility for leadership during the meeting. Each child cleans up his or her own work space and everyone helps put the room in order at the end of the day. In the open classroom, as in the SOI classroom, children spend about 20 minutes each day on the playground.

Use of Space

The use of space varies in the SOI classroom. During directed play, children and teachers are scattered in various parts of the room. During structured lessons, there may be two or three small clusters, each including one teacher and three to five children. During music and snack, teachers and children are together in one part of the room.

The use of space in the open classroom changes to meet the interests and needs of the children. Children move freely about the room throughout the day. The classroom is divided into areas with consideration for the type of work likely to occur, the supplies needed, and the proximity to other areas. The art area, for example, has a large table with bins underneath it that contain ingredients and tools for making playdough. On the wall is an illustrated recipe for making playdough, and next to that table is a toaster oven where playdough creations can be baked. Other art supplies—paper, crayons, tape, glue, paint, scissors, boxes, and "junk"—are at the child's level in the same work area. A corner for reading is set off from noisy activity areas and contains a carpet, pillows, and a wide variety of children's books, attractively displayed.

RENZULLI'S ENRICHMENT TRIAD MODEL

The third model to be discussed is the Enrichment Triad Model. This model is similar to, and compatible with, the open classroom previously discussed, and Type II processes seem to be similar to the SOI and Bloom's Taxonomy processes. The Enrichment Triad Model has been widely used since it was published in 1977, and even prior to that time Renzulli conducted workshops introducing the model to educators of the gifted. Renzulli (1977) noted that there are many who criticize gifted programs, charging that

> Many of the practices that typify gifted programs are little more than a random collection of kits, games, puzzles, and artsy-craftsy activities and that what we call differential education is basically a cosmetic reshuffling of many time-honored curricular practices that are essentially good for all students. (Preface)

For this reason, Renzulli has designed a framework into which "many innovative practices can be placed" (Preface).

> Just as buildings that are constructed without architectural plans are likely to result in wasted space and duplicated facilities, so can educational programs without appropriate models result in wasted time, indefensible practices, and a great deal of "ammunition" for persons who question both the value and the quality of special services for gifted youngsters. (Preface)

Renzulli's model should dispel the idea that the needs of gifted children can be met by giving them "more of the same" or letting them cover the material at a faster rate than is expected of their average peers. In discussing such practices, Renzulli (1977) has commented, "Individualization of rate or pace without additional differentiation in areas such as content, learning style, and teaching strategies fails to respect the total set of characteristics that bring gifted and talented youngsters to our attention" (p. 2).

A program that makes use of the Enrichment Triad Model must be committed to the following two major program objectives, according to Renzulli (1977).

Program Objective No. 1

For the majority of the time spent in the gifted programs, students will have an opportunity to pursue their own interests to whatever depth and extent they so desire; and they will be allowed to pursue these interests in a manner that is consistent with their own preferred styles of learning. (p. 5)

Program Objective No. 2

The primary role of each teacher in the program for gifted and talented students will be to provide each student with assistance in (1) identifying and structuring realistic solvable problems that are consistent with the student's interest, (2) acquiring the necessary methodological resources and investigative skills that are necessary for solving these particular problems, and (3) finding appropriate outlets for student products. (p. 10)

Renzulli's Enrichment Triad Model reflects his concern that educators of the gifted are often preoccupied with process and forget that "process is the path rather than the goal of learning" (p. 8).

The Enrichment Triad Model offers three types of enrichment. The first two types of activities are suitable for all learners, according to Renzulli, but are important for gifted children for two reasons:

First, they deal with strategies for expanding student interests and developing the thinking and feeling processes. . . . Second, and perhaps more importantly, these two types of enrichment represent logical input and support systems for Type III Enrichment which is considered to be the only type that is appropriate mainly for gifted students. (p. 13)

Type III Enrichment is concerned with individuals and/or small groups investigating problems that are real to them. Renzulli's recommendation is that approximately half of the time a gifted child spends in enrichment activities should be devoted to Type III activities.

Renzulli (1977) has defined enrichment experiences or activities as those "above and beyond the so-called 'regular curriculum'" (pp. 13, 14). Following is an explanation of the three types of enrichment discussed by Renzulli (1977).

Type I Enrichment: General Exploratory Activities

These experiences or activities involve very little structure but expose the learners to a variety of areas of study that may be of potential interest to them. Through such exploration, gifted children can determine which areas they wish to study in more depth. From the very beginning of their explorations, they must be cognizant of the fact that they must choose an area of study. The teacher's role is to assist them in this exploration, which may entail encouraging them to broaden their interests and explore areas not previously experienced. The teacher can generate interests by setting up interest centers stocked with a variety of appropriate materials. Another strategy is to invite carefully selected people to make presentations to gifted children. Carefully conducted field trips are still another strategy to use in Type I enrichment experiences. Type I enrichment is an ongoing process, and even though students are involved in projects they must continuously be encouraged to broaden their interests.

Type II Enrichment: Group Training Activities

These experiences or activities have to do with methods, materials, and instructional techniques. These activities are concerned with the child's development of effective thinking and feeling processes. This part of the model focuses on training activities. During participation in these enrichment activities the learners acquire the higher-level thought processes that will enable them to deal more effectively with content. Some of these processes are brainstorming, observing, evaluating, comparing, synthesizing, hypothesizing, elaborating, and classifying. This portion of the model is similar to the processes included in Bloom's Taxonomy and Guilford's Structure of the Intellect Model.

Type II Enrichment Activities can often lead to Type III activities, because learners master skills necessary to solve problems in a wide range of areas. In fact, the skills they learn are valuable tools for more advanced types of inquiry. It is important for teachers to recognize that Type II activities are not a program just for gifted children; instead, these activities lead to the acquisition of tools essential in Type III enrichment activities.

Type III Enrichment: Individual and Small Group Investigations of Real Problems

In this type of activity, the type specifically appropriate for the gifted, children become the investigators of real problems. They must, of course, use appropriate methods of inquiry. In essence, Type III Enrichment activities are vastly different from Type II:

> First, the child takes an active part in formulating both the problem and the methods by which the problem will be attacked. Second, there is no routine method of solution or recognized correct answer although there may be appropriate investigative techniques on which to draw and criteria by which a product can be judged. Third, the area of investigation is a sincere interest to an individual (or small group) rather than a teacher-determined topic or activity. And

consumer attitude, and in so doing, takes the necessary steps to communicate his or her results in a professionally appropriate manner. (pp. 29, 30)

In Type III Enrichment the teacher is a manager and a resource person. The teacher uses a variety of methods to get at the child's interests, including centers of interest and exposure to a wide variety of experiences. The teacher's role is not to put pressure on a child to engage in an activity, but rather to encourage and support the child. Renzulli has stressed the importance of exposure to creative/producer individuals—even for children as young as 3 and 4 years of age.

It might seem that finding appropriate outlets for the products of a child might not be appropriate for the preschool child. This is not the case. At Colonel Wolfe School, at the University of Illinois, one teacher who promotes creativity in art has an annual exhibit. Artwork is sold to students, staff, the public, and parents. This artwork is attractively displayed in a meeting room, and a price is on each piece of art. The children play a major role in planning the art show and in deciding what to do with the money. Each year a drawing is selected by the children to use as the design on a T-shirt that also contains the words, "Colonel Wolfe School."

Experience stories dictated by gifted students can be made into a book with accompanying illustrations. These books can be produced inexpensively and sold to retrieve the initial investment. The same holds true for artwork of clay or papier-mâché. If a written product shows unusual promise, a children's magazine might prove to be a source for publication.

According to Renzulli, teachers of gifted children are responsible for providing methodological assistance. A gifted child as young as age 5 might need to be trained in the use of a library. Children who are talented in music and/or movement may need specific training by a specialist.

Renzulli has made a real contribution to the field in conceptualizing the Enrichment Triad Model and in suggesting specific ways teachers of the gifted can provide programs for these children above and beyond what is provided for children with average abilities.

BLOOM'S TAXONOMY OF EDUCATIONAL OBJECTIVES MODEL

Bloom's Taxonomy, which concentrates on the cognitive domain, has also proved to be a useful model in programs for gifted children. A good definition of taxonomy has been provided by Plowman (1968): "a system of classifying objects, principles, and facts in a manner consistent with their natural or logical relationships" (p. 2).

Bloom, Engelhart, Furst, Hill, and Krathwohl (1956) pointed out some of the ways their taxonomy of educational objectives can help teachers. They specifically stated that teachers building a curriculum should find a wide range of possible goals or outcomes in the cognitive area. By comparing the goals of their curriculum with this range of possible outcomes, they should be able to determine the kinds of objectives and additional goals they wish to include in their own curriculum, in this case for their gifted children.

Bloom and his associates stated that the taxonomy should help teachers specify objectives to facilitate the planning of learning experiences and to prepare evaluation plans and procedures. "In short, teachers and curriculum makers should find this a relatively concise model for the analysis of educational outcomes in the cognitive area of remembering, thinking, and problem solving" (Bloom, et al., 1956, p. 2). In fact, "Properly used, a taxonomy should provide a very suggestive source of ideas and materials for each worker and should result in many economies in effort" (p. 1).

Bloom's *Taxonomy of Educational Objectives* (1956) is divided into six major classes: knowledge, comprehension, application, analysis, synthesis, and evaluation. The authors perceived that these classes represent a hierarchical order of the different classes of objectives. The handbook, which delineates the classification scheme, is useful to teachers of the gifted if they study its contents carefully. The authors have suggested first reading the introduction and a condensed version of the taxonomy in the appendix to get a concise overview of the publication. Then, to obtain a more thorough understanding of the taxonomy and its uses, the chapter on educational objectives and curriculum development should be thoroughly studied, followed by the chapter on the classification of educational objectives and the test exercises. The remainder of the handbook should be referred to when the teacher finds sections relevant to specific teaching, curriculum, or testing.

Before attempting to use the model, as is true for all models, teachers need inservice training. If the model is to be used to develop a curriculum for gifted children, the inservice training should involve a group of teachers who have gifted children in their classes.

WILLIAMS' COGNITIVE AFFECTIVE MODEL

Williams' model (1970) has attempted to combine the cognitive and affective domains. To date this model has been implemented only with elementary-age gifted children, but it has potential for preschool children. The model has three dimensions. Dimension 1 deals with subject matter—music, art, science, arithmetic, social studies, and language. Dimension 2 focuses on teacher behavior (strategies of teaching) including attributes, analogies, discrepancies, paradoxes, provocative questions, examples of habit, examples of change, organized random search, skills of search, tolerance for ambiguity, adjustment to developments, intuitive expression, study of creative people and processes, evaluation of situations, creative listening skills, reading skills, creative writing skills, and visualization skills. Dimension 3 centers on pupil behaviors (cognitive/intellective)—fluent thinking, flexible thinking, original thinking, elaborative thinking—and affective/feeling—curiosity, risk-taking, complexity, and imagination.

Williams (1970) asserted that affective development is closely akin to cognitive development. Children who feel good about themselves pursue cognitive activities to a greater degree; conversely, children who do well cognitively tend to value themselves more.

What Williams has attempted to do in his model is to link the cognitive traits included in Bloom's Taxonomy (1956)—knowledge, comprehension, application, analysis, synthesis, and evaluation—with the affective traits in Krathwohl's Taxonomy (Krathwohl, Bloom, & Mosia, 1964)—receiving, responding, valuing, conceptualizing, and internalizing.

Combining the cognitive domain with the affective domain in developing curriculum has also been addressed by Michaelis (1967). A reader who is interested in placing more emphasis on affective development within the framework of fostering cognitive development may wish to read what this author has to say.

USE OF MULTIMODELS

Almost all programs for young gifted children to date use more than one conceptual model. For example, in the University of Illinois programs for gifted/talented handicapped and nonhandicapped children, two models are demonstrated—one classroom uses the SOI model and the other the open classroom model. In addition, both use a developmental model to assess the child's development in important areas. A program for gifted/talented handicapped youngsters at Coeur D'Alene, Idaho, uses Bloom's Taxonomy and Type I Enrichment of the Enrichment Triad Model. They also use a developmental model. In a new program that is being developed for gifted/talented nonhandicapped children at the University of Illinois, the open classroom and SOI models are being combined and implemented in the same classroom. A developmental model is also being used.

SUMMARY

The four conceptual models most frequently used with preschool-age gifted/talented children are the open classroom, Guilford's Structure of the Intellect (SOI), Renzulli's Enrichment Triad Model, and Bloom's Taxonomy. There are other models that program planners may wish to investigate and that may have merit for use with preschool-age children. No conceptual model has proved to be more effective than any other model. The selection of a model, however, is contingent upon the major goals of the program and upon the philosophy of the personnel developing the program.

Developmental guidelines have proved particularly useful in programming for handicapped children, and these can be used with gifted children to determine the level of development of a child in critical areas. These developmental milestones can be used with any conceptual model.

Regardless of which conceptual model is selected, it will provide a framework for carefully planning an individualized program. It enables personnel to become better observers of children and helps delineate aspects of the program that should be evaluated. In addition, a model facilitates the interpretation of the program so that there is a better understanding of how the program for the gifted child differs from that for the average child. There seems little doubt that programs that adopt a model are apt to be more consistent and better organized than programs that do not.

REFERENCES

Bloom, B., Engelhart, M., Furst, E., Hill, W., & Krathwohl, D. (Eds.) *Taxonomy of educational objectives, Handbook I: Cognitive domain.* New York: David McKay, 1956.

Featherstone, J. *Schools where children learn.* New York: Liveright, 1971.

Gallagher, J. *Teaching the gifted child.* Boston: Allyn & Bacon, 1975.

Guilford, J. *The nature of human intelligence.* New York: McGraw-Hill, 1967.

Karnes, M. *Elements of an exemplary preschool/primary program for gifted and talented* (S. Kaplan, Ed.). National/State Leadership Training Institute of the Gifted and the Talented. Ventura CA: Ventura County Superintendent of Schools, 1980, pp. 103–140.

Karnes, M., & Bertschi, J. Identifying and educating gifted/talented nonhandicapped and handicapped preschoolers. *TEACHING Exceptional Children,* 1978, *10*(4), 114–119.

Karnes, M., & Zehrbach, R. *A comparison of different approaches for educating young gifted children (RAPYD II).* RAPYD II (Retrieval and Acceleration of Promising Young Disadvantaged) Project Final Report, Illinois Office of Superintendent of Public Instruction (OSPI), Gifted Children's Section (Project #E-508). Urbana IL: Institute for Research on Exceptional Children, College of Education, University of Illinois, 1973.

Krathwohl, D., Bloom, B., & Mosia, B. *Taxonomy of educational objectives, Handbook II: Affective domain.* New York: David McKay, 1964.

Michealis, J., Grossman, R., & Scott, L. *New designs for the elementary school curricula.* New York: McGraw-Hill, 1967.

Plowman, R. *An interpretation of the taxonomy of educational objectives.* Sacramento: Author, 1968.

Renzulli, J. *The enrichment triad model: A guide for developing programs for the gifted and talented.* Wethersfield CT: Creative Learning Press, 1977.

Williams, F. *Classroom ideas for encouraging thinking and feeling.* Buffalo NY: DOK Publishers, 1970.

CHAPTER 4

Teachers

Merle B. Karnes

Much has been noted about the characteristics of teachers who work with gifted/talented children. When listing these desirable characteristics, one is prone to add: "That's right, but every child deserves a teacher with those characteristics." It seems almost discriminatory to hold out for a better teacher for gifted children than for nongifted children. Indeed, some contend that gifted children will get along well under any circumstances, but anyone who has worked with a mediocre or poor teacher knows well that such teachers are likely to be more intolerant of and intolerable to gifted children than to the so-called "average" child.

Not everyone loves a gifted child. For a long time we have suspected that many teachers would rather have the gifted child in someone else's classroom. While we do not have data on teacher attitudes toward gifted preschool children, it may well be that what Rothney and Sanborn (1968) and Wiener (1978) found to be true of teachers of older children is also true of teachers at the preschool level. Essentially, these researchers found that many teachers of older children feel hostility toward those who are gifted. This finding is not surprising if one recognizes that among teachers, as among professionals in general, there are some who are mediocre and some who are, unfortunately, incompetent. Because of the difficulty schools have in firing incompetent teachers, gifted children in mainstream settings must sometimes endure teachers who are ill equipped to teach the average child, much less the gifted youngster.

Gallagher (1975) asked the question, "Who is afraid of the gifted child?" and gave the answer, "Just about everybody" (p. 313). It is not surprising that some teachers are threatened even by young gifted children. We do have some evidence that a significant proportion of underachievement may be attributed to poor teaching, negative teacher-pupil attitudes, and curricula that do not meet the needs of gifted children (Shaw & Alves, 1963; Thiel & Thiel, 1977; Watson, 1960). Granted the weight of these negative factors, what are the positive attributes to consider in selecting teachers for talented youngsters?

CHARACTERISTICS OF TEACHERS OF YOUNG GIFTED CHILDREN

Criteria Used in the Astor Program

A review of the few programs that have been developed for young gifted children suggests that the Astor Program for intellectually gifted children from prekindergarten (age 4) through grade 3 has determined rather specifically the salient characteristics of teachers of gifted children (Eurlich, 1978). These characteristics are generally in accord with the profiles of teachers of the gifted reported in the literature (Bishop, 1968; Freehill, 1961; Newland, 1962; Spaulding, 1963; Ward, 1961). The following characteristics were sought in teachers of the gifted employed in the Astor Program during the period in which it was funded by the Astor Foundation:

1. A sympathetic understanding and feeling for gifted children
2. An understanding of the needs and psychology of gifted children
3. Experience with early childhood classes, nursery schools, very young children (their own, especially)
4. Intellectual superiority
5. A broad range of interests and skills
6. Educational background reflecting a variety of interests and at least one field of specialization other than education *per se*
7. A willingness to undertake the many allied assignments required of this particular effort
8. A dynamic and alert personality
9. A sense of humor (not sarcasm)
10. Flexibility. Readiness to learn, revise, change
11. A creative, perhaps unconventional, personal philosophy
12. Good health and vitality
13. Graduate course work in education of the gifted and a readiness to continue such education (Ehrlich, 1978, p. 60)

In addition to this list, the director of the Astor Program asked teachers of the gifted in the program what characteristics they considered especially important for teachers of gifted children. The responses of the teachers generally agreed with the selection criteria. Characteristics delineated by the teachers included commitment to children, warmth, empathy, sensitivity, sense of humor, enthusiasm, open-mindedness, personal security, energy, and intellectual superiority (p. 61).

Other Teacher Selection Criteria

The criteria used for teacher selection in the Astor Program seem valid; however, the definition of giftedness used in that program was restricted to intellectual giftedness. When a broader definition of giftedness and/or talent is used, other selection criteria may be desirable.

Good Self-Concept

A good self-concept may be one of the most important characteristics of a teacher of young gifted children. The importance of self-concept to the gifted child is rarely overlooked, but the recognition of its importance to the teacher of the gifted is frequently by-passed. A number of researchers and psychologists have reminded us that the more positive the teacher feels about himself or herself, the more positive he or she will feel toward the children (Combs, 1965; Coopersmith, 1967; Jerslid, 1965). Obversely, the teacher who has a weak self-concept can easily be threatened by a bright child, even a 4-year-old.

Dorothy Sisk (1976), in discussing the importance of self-concept, had this to say: "More and more educators are beginning to realize the ever increasing importance of the self-concept. . . . One's self-picture can open vistas, or it can keep an ever tight door between the individual and new opportunities" (p. 13). While Sisk was focusing on the gifted child, what she had to say is applicable to teachers and to parents of these children.

Task Commitment

If one accepts Renzulli's (1977) point that giftedness cannot be identified by a single criterion such as intelligence but is a cluster of interlocking behaviors, then the definition of giftedness should be reflected in the criteria for selecting a gifted teacher. The cluster in identifying the gifted, according to Renzulli, includes (a) above-average but not necessarily superior intelligence, (b) task commitment, and (c) creativity. Thus, it would seem reasonable to insist that the teacher of young gifted children demonstrate task commitment. The teacher who flits from school system to school sytem and from one teaching approach to another without really giving each approach a fair try does not seem a likely candidate. Another facet of task commitment as it applies here is the sustained commitment to identifying and meeting the unique needs of gifted children. Bishop (1975) found that effective teachers of the gifted had a strong need to achieve. This characteristic seems to be closely akin to task commitment.

Maturity

Maturity is not synonymous with age, and the dictionary definition seems to apply here: "Full development, brought by time, treatment, etc., to the condition of full excellence." While the Astor Program did not specifically list experience as a criterion, initially they had hoped to employ teachers from within the New York school system. Although experience may not assure maturity, an inexperienced teacher is not as a general rule ready to launch a program for young gifted children.

Mature teachers convey to others that they know what they are doing and why they are doing it. Mature teachers inspire confidence among their charges and are recognized by peers as outstanding teachers. They are not threatened by gifted children but, in fact, enjoy the challenge they present. Mature teachers understand learning styles and strategies and can match each child's needs with an appropriate strategy.

Emotional Stability

This characteristic is closely associated with a positive self-concept, flexibility, and good physical health. A teacher with unresolved personal problems is usually a poor teacher for any child, but such a teacher may be even more ineffective with the gifted, since understanding the complex nature of the gifted child and his or her special needs can tax the emotions of even stable teachers. Gifted children need good models; therefore, teachers of young gifted children need to be composed, and in control of their emotions. They need to model appropriate ways of handling feelings.

Sensitivity

Another important characteristic is sensitivity to the feelings and needs of others, especially of the gifted children in the teacher's classroom. Gifted children are sensitive; they sometimes set unrealistically high standards for themselves and feel very bad when they do not achieve as much as they think they should. They are sensitive about their interactions with others and are sometimes resented by adults and children. The teacher of the gifted needs to perceive what troubles gifted children and to help them work through their feelings. This kind of support enables gifted children to develop their abilities and to cope more effectively with the attitudes of others and with problems that are related to being gifted.

Ability to Individualize Instruction

The teacher of the gifted must be sensitive to individual differences in abilities and able to individualize instruction. Even when the teacher is assigned to a homogenous class of intellectually gifted children, the unique abilities and needs of each child will require an individualized curriculum. In most cases, however, gifted children are found in mainstream classrooms, and thus, the range of individual differences is even greater.

Commitment to Parent Involvement

Involvement of the parents and family is critical in working with the young gifted/talented child, and the teacher must not only be committed to the notion of parent involvement but must also have the skills to work effectively with parents.

COMPETENCIES OF TEACHERS OF YOUNG GIFTED CHILDREN

Formal coursework in the area of education of the gifted is essential, but supervised practicum experience is also necessary to ensure that a teacher is competent to teach gifted children. The heart of a training program should be a carefully monitored internship in classes where young gifted children are enrolled in the mainstream. These classes may even include handicapped children, especially the gifted handicapped. Above all, these classes should be taught by teachers who have demonstrated the qualities that are thought to be critical for teachers of the gifted. Internship experiences are considered important by a number of persons in the field of gifted education (Feldhausen, 1977; Frasier, 1977; Jenkins & Stewart, 1979; Maker, 1975; Nix, 1976).

A number of competencies have been identified by researchers and teacher trainers, and these should be considered in developing a competency-based training program for teachers of the gifted. Seeley (1979) sent a questionnaire to every college and university training program listed with the National/State Leadership Institute on the gifted and to all teachers and principals in the state of Colorado to determine the competencies that should be basic to certification for teachers of the gifted. The five competencies ranked in order of importance were:

1. Diagnostic-prescriptive teaching skills.
2. Curriculum modification strategies.
3. Higher cognitive teaching and questioning.
4. Special curriculum development.
5. Student counseling strategies.

Since preschool for gifted children down to age 3 is not a part of the public schools and since Colorado programs for the gifted do not extend to the preschool level, teachers, principals, and teacher trainers did not consider the competencies specifically needed for teachers of the preschool gifted. Nevertheless, the only competency not appropriate for preschoolers is "student counseling." It would seem that "parent counseling strategies," which received a lower rating, would be one of the primary competencies needed by teachers of young gifted/talented children.

It is to be hoped that teacher training programs that develop in the future will carefully screen candidates for the personal qualifications and professional background that will ensure outstanding teachers of the gifted when they have completed the program.

Admittedly, there is at present no full-blown program for training teachers of young gifted/talented children, but some of the knowledge and skills needed to be effective in working with these children and their parents have been identified.

Familiarity with Gifted Characteristics, Child Development, Research, and Programs

Teachers of gifted children must recognize the characteristics of giftedness in the areas of intellectual functioning, academic achievement, creativity, visual and performing arts, social development (leadership), and psychomotor abilities. In addition, they should be able to assess task commitment. Although psychomotor abilities is no longer considered an area of talent by the U.S. Office of the Gifted, teachers need to be aware of such talents and to program for them appropriately.

Fundamental to an understanding of gifted children and the ability to program for them is knowledge of normal child development. Only when the teacher understands the normally developing child can he or she program for the gifted child. Developmental information is essential if the teacher is to match the child's stage of development in a given area with the curricular offerings.

Admittedly, little research has been conducted on the very young gifted child, but research with older gifted children often has relevance, and teachers of the gifted must be familiar with this material. Research having to do with adult-child interactions, self-concept, and ways of effectively mainstreaming children represent some areas in which teachers of young gifted children must be knowledgeable. Teachers who work at the juncture of research and practice must be capable of interpreting research findings and determining their implications for practice.

While programs for young gifted children are few in number, teachers of the young gifted should know about them and be able to apply information derived from those programs to a program in which they are involved.

Competence in Identification and Measurement

A teacher of young gifted/talented children should be aware that there are gifted/talented children among the handicapped. To have the expertise to identify these children and to program appropriately for them is a skill.

In order to appropriately program for young children, the teacher of the gifted/talented should be competent in the interpretation of the results of standardized tests and in the use of observation procedures to be able to obtain accurate and meaningful information about young children.

Skill in Child Management

Frequently, a gifted child in a day care, Head Start, or kindergarten program is singled out as a troublemaker. A careful study of the situation often reveals that this child is simply bored with an unchallenging learning environment.

If the teacher is not perceptive, he or she may treat the symptom and not discover the cause. It is true that a gifted child can be demanding, asking many more questions than his or her average peers. Skill in child management methods that will enable the young gifted child to be busily engaged in activities that are meaningful and challenging is a requisite of the teacher of gifted youngsters.

Knowledge of Effective Instructional Methods

Newland (1976) listed instructional methods particularly useful in teaching the intellectually gifted child:

> Teaching methods employed with the gifted 1) should focus upon helping them to learn, 2) should be appropriate a) to the level of the intellectual and social development of the child, and b) to the varying kinds of demands and opportunities inherent in the different kinds of learning situations encountered by the child, 3) should reflect a dominant and consistent, though not sole, nurturance of the relatively high capacity of the gifted in the cognitive area, and 4) should reflect persistently a sensitivity to the importance of the progression from the perceptual or low conceptual level to the higher conceptual kinds of cognitive operation. (pp. 153–154)

There is no one best method for teaching gifted children, but some techniques are more appropriate than others. Gifted children, as is true of all children, need feedback from significant adults, and since gifted children tend to be self-critical, it is important that teachers let gifted children know how they are doing so that they will gain confidence in themselves and their ability to learn. While teachers want children to experience intrinsic motivation from completing a task and doing it well, they recognize that a few words of praise often spur children to put forth greater effort. Gifted children, unlike their less gifted peers, however, do not always need immediate gratification. They are often able to work on a project for days or even weeks without becoming impatient.

Newland (1976) concluded that:

> No teaching method is of value uniquely in regard to the gifted. Many methods, adapted appropriately to differing situations, have potential merits in facilitating the learning of all children. Some, however, have a greater potential yield, at times, with the gifted because of the different kinds of learning behaviors they involve. None of these, though, can be generalized as the method always to be used with the gifted. (p. 155)

Barbe and Frierson (1975) have pointed out that teachers of the gifted have traditionally been more concerned about the product of learning than the process. They have emphasized the importance of introducing material at the exploratory level, a practice in keeping with Renzulli's (1977) Enrichment Triad Model Type I. Teachers of young gifted children need to foster the acquisition of effective processes of learning, and at the same time they must be certain that there are no gaps in the young child's learning.

The open classroom lends itself to a process-oriented approach, for there the teacher is a learner-participant, an integral part of the learning process itself. Since a process-oriented approach is more flexible than a product-oriented approach, creativity is more likely to flourish. This does not mean, however, that product is not important also. The role of teachers is to provide an environment where children will learn how to learn and at the same time achieve something in the way of a product.

Methods and techniques are admittedly important, but Nelson and Cleland (1975) have added this caution:

> The way the teacher proceeds is more important than the materials or the specific methods utilized. It is the teacher who sets the environment which inspires or destroys self-confidence, encourages or suppresses interests, develops or neglects abilities, fosters or banishes creativity, stimulates or discourages critical thinking, and facilitates or frustrates achievement. (p. 439)

Torrance (1975) listed those factors mentioned most frequently by his students in *Creative Ways of Teaching:*

Recognizing some heretofore unrecognized and unused potential
Respecting a child's need to work alone
Inhibiting the censorship role long enough for a creative response to occur
Allowing or encouraging a child to go ahead and achieve success in an area and in a way possible for him
Permitting the curriculum to be different for different pupils
Giving concrete embodiment to the creative ideas of children
Giving a chance to make a contribution to the welfare of the group
Encouraging or permitting self-initiated projects
Reducing pressure, providing a relatively non-punitive environment
Providing approval in one area to provide courage to try in others
Voicing the beauty of individual differences
Respecting the potential of low achievers
Demonstrating enthusiasm
Giving support of the teacher against peer pressures to conformity
Placing an unproductive child in contact with a productive, creative child
Using fantasy ability to establish contacts with reality
Capitalizing upon hobby and special interests and enthusiasms
Tolerating complexity and disorder, at least for a period
Achieving a high level of involvement
Being uninhibited in bodily contact with children
Communicating that the teacher is "for" rather than "against" the child (p. 468)

If promoting creativity in gifted children is as important as it is generally thought to be, then these techniques must be taken into account in the selection and training of teachers of the gifted.

Knowledge of Conceptual Models

Familiarity with the conceptual models that have been used to develop curricula for young gifted children sensitizes the teacher to the complexities of the learning process. For example, when the teacher learns the Guilford Structure of the Intellect Model, he or she becomes more aware of the kinds of thinking that can be encouraged among the children in the classroom, especially among those gifted young children who are capable of utilizing symbols and constructs in acquiring concepts and moving from concrete to more abstract learning.

Skill in Working With Parents

It is no secret that teachers in general are not comfortable working with parents, and working with parents of gifted children, who may be as talented as their children, represents an even greater threat. Thus, teachers of the gifted must possess skills in working with parents of the gifted. They must recognize alternative ways of involving parents, be capable of developing a needs assessment instrument, and be able to assist parents in assessing their own needs. They need to know how to train parents to become better observers of their children, to assess child development, and to promote the development of their children. Parents of gifted children may need training in behavior management techniques. Teachers of the gifted need to be competent reporters of child progress to parents and able to assist parents in assessing the progress of their own children. Finally, they should be able to train the parents to be the advocates for their children so that gifted youngsters will receive services that meet their special needs. Parents also need to learn how to make use of community resources that have something to offer their gifted children.

Familiarity With Other Disciplines and Instructional Materials

Identification and programming for the gifted entails *a team approach*. Teachers of gifted children need to know what other disciplines have to offer; they need to know what information they should gather and share with ancillary personnel to enable them to contribute more fully to educational planning for gifted children. Regardless of the strengths gifted children may have, they too need special services. Teachers of gifted children should be alert to the weaknesses of their gifted students, especially those that stand in the way of the full development of talent.

Teachers of young gifted children need to be aware of instructional materials that meet a wide range of abilities, especially when the gifted are mainstreamed with average, below average, and handicapped youngsters.

Teacher Talent

It is particularly advantageous if the teacher of gifted children demonstrates talent in one of the talent areas in addition to being superior in intelligence and academic achievement. For example, the teacher might be talented in music, art, drama, or dance. At the minimum, the teacher of the gifted should have some training in at least one of these talent areas.

Skill in Assessment

To ensure child progress the teacher must know how to assess the ongoing progress of each gifted child in his or her program as well as the effectiveness of family involvement. The teacher must have this information to make decisions regarding future programming.

Advocacy Skills

The teacher must have the knowledge and skills to be *an advocate* for the program. He or she must be able to interpret the program in order to win the support of the administration, other teachers, parents, and the public in general. The teacher must also achieve continuity in the programming for young gifted children as they move on through school. Only when continuity is ensured can an early intervention program be judged successful.

Self-Knowledge

Finally, the teacher of gifted children needs a good understanding of his or her own feelings, strengths, weaknesses, and motivations. As Nelson and Cleland (1975) pointed out, "It would be foolish to assume that a person can understand the needs, feelings, and behaviors of others if he does not understand himself" (p. 440).

OTHER FACTORS IN SELECTING TEACHERS

While there is some redundancy or overlap between the following three factors and the teacher competencies/characteristics discussed earlier, these factors are so important that a separate section has been set aside for their discussion.

Teacher Intelligence

Newland (1976) has devoted considerable attention to teacher intelligence. He noted:

> The intellectual capability of teachers of the gifted should be appropriated to the educational level of their pupils. This is crucial for three principal and somewhat overlapping reasons. First, it is important that no intellectually based communication gap exist between the gifted child and his teacher. The teacher must be capable of understanding the vocabulary and concepts employed by the child in his learning, and the teacher should not typically communicate with the child by means of a vocabulary or in terms of concepts which are either disconcertingly, frustratingly higher or unnaturally lower than the level of the child's capability. Second, the teacher must be intellectually capable of understanding relatively fully the concepts essential to the learning of the gifted child. Third, the teacher of the gifted must be sufficiently psychologically

insightful and intellectually competent to understand and work with such children in their necessary progress from behavior that is essentially perceptual to behavior that involves higher level conceptualization. (p. 148)

Newland went on to say that "the teacher or worker at the elementary level should be in at least the top 10 percent of the adult population, with the criterion of the top 5 percent being applied with respect to those working in substantive areas at the junior-senior high school level" (p. 149). Using this frame of reference, it is suggested that teachers should fall within the top 15 percent of the adult population in intelligence if they are to work effectively with preschool gifted children.

Program Goals

Goals of the program are another consideration in selecting teachers. If a major goal of the preschool program is to promote the talent of youngsters in the visual and performing arts, then a major selection criterion for teachers would be talent in music, art, or dance, as well as experience and formal training in the visual arts. Other characteristics included in this chapter would, of course, need to be taken into consideration.

Cultural Background of Students

The culture of the young gifted child to be served in the program is another consideration. For example, if young Black children or low-income Italian children in the ghetto areas of a large city were the population to be served, a selection criterion might be that the teacher represent the culture of the children being served in order to ensure that the children would be understood in terms of significant cultural factors. If the youngsters to be served were handicapped, then the teacher should have special training in early education of the handicapped as well as the gifted.

ONGOING INSERVICE TRAINING

It is unlikely that a newly initiated program for young gifted children would be able to select teachers with all of the personal attributes and professional training delineated in this chapter. Thus, administrators will employ teachers who meet as many of these requirements as possible and through inservice training assist staff members to become more competent.

GUIDELINES IN SELECTING TEACHERS FOR YOUNG GIFTED/ TALENTED CHILDREN

The following guidelines highlight the major points covered in this chapter:

1. The teacher is the single most influential factor in the school setting relative to the development of gifted children.

2. Teachers of the gifted should possess a high level of those characteristics deemed to be important for all teachers.

3. Not all teachers are committed to teaching young gifted children; therefore, it is important for administrators to identify those teachers who are not effective or do not wish to work with gifted children and avoid placing gifted children in their classrooms.

4. A good self-concept may be one of the most important characteristics of a teacher of the gifted. A teacher who has a weak self-concept can be threatened by a young gifted child. Such teachers are likely not to have the respect for gifted children that they should. Other characteristics that should be emphasized are maturity, successful experience teaching young children, emotional stability, task commitment, and creativity.

5. Competencies of teachers of young gifted children should be acquired through formal coursework closely tied with practicum experiences whenever possible.

6. Coursework and practicum experiences should include work with non-handicapped children, handicapped, gifted/talented handicapped, and gifted/talented nonhandicapped children. Since gifted/talented children will likely be educated in the mainstream, teachers must have the knowledge and skills to work with children having a wide range of abilities and handicaps.

7. Teachers of young gifted children should be aware of programs for the gifted at the preschool level and should learn from the experience of others in improving their own programs.

8. Teachers must be familiar with appropriate conceptual models for educating the young gifted child and be able to select and implement a model(s) compatible with their philosophy.

9. In programming, teachers of the gifted need to understand and make use of other disciplines. They also need to be aware of community resources for young gifted children and to assess such resources.

10. Selection of appropriate instructional materials is another competency teachers of young gifted children must possess.

11. Still another is the competency to evaluate the young gifted child's progress.

12. Since it is often difficult to persuade other professionals and the lay public to support special programs for the gifted, the teacher should have the skills to advocate for gifted children and to train others to be advocates.

13. Another consideration in selecting teachers of the young gifted/talented is the cultural background of the children to be served. It seems advantageous whenever possible for the teacher to represent the culture of the children he or she teaches.

REFERENCES

Barbe, W., & Frierson, E. Teaching the gifted—A new frame of reference. In W. Barbe & J. Renzulli (Eds.), *Psychology and education of the gifted*. New York: Irvington Publishers, 1975.

Bishop, W. Successful teachers of the gifted. *Exceptional Children*, 1968, *34*, 317–325.

Bishop, W. Characteristics of teachers judged successful by intellectually gifted, high achieving high school students. In W. Barbe & J. Renzulli (Eds.), *Psychology and education of the gifted*. New York: Irvington Publishers, 1975.

Combs, A. The professional education of teachers: A perceptual view of teacher preparation. Boston: Allyn & Bacon, 1965.

Coopersmith, S. *The antecedents of self-esteem*. San Francisco: W. H. Freeman, 1967.

Enrlich, V. *The Astor program for gifted children: Pre-kindergarten through grade three*. New York: Teacher's College, Columbia University, 1978.

Feldhausen, J. Meeting the needs of gifted children and teachers in a university course. *The Gifted Child Quarterly*, 1977, *21*, 195–199.

Frasier, M. A national survey: The third dimension. *The Gifted Child Quarterly*, 1977, *21*, 207–212.

Freehill, M. *Gifted children: Their psychology and education*. New York: Macmillan, 1961.

Gallagher, J. *Teaching the gifted child*. Boston: Allyn & Bacon, 1975.

Jenkins, R., & Stewart, E. . . . And into the fire: A guide to G/C/T internship experiences for pre-professionals. *Journal for the Education of the Gifted*, 1979, *3*(1), 1–6.

Jerslid, A. Voice of the self. *NEA Journal*, 1965, *54*, 23–25.

Maker, C. *Training teachers for the gifted and talented: A comparison of models*. Reston VA: The ERIC Clearinghouse on the Gifted and Talented, The Council for Exceptional Children, 1975.

Nelson, J., & Cleland, D. The role of the teachers of the gifted and creative children. In W. Barbe & J. Renzulli (Eds.), *Psychology and education of the gifted*. New York: Irvington Publishers, 1975.

Newland, T. *The gifted in socioeducational perspective*. Englewood Cliffs NJ: Prentice-Hall, 1976.

Newland, T. Some observations on essential qualifications of teachers of the mentally superior. *Exceptional Children*, 1962, *29*, 111–114.

Nix, J., Teague, W., & Busher, C. *Guidelines for inservice education: Gifted and talented*. Georgia Department of Education in cooperation with Title V, Section 505 Project, Interstate Cooperative Effort for the Gifted and Talented, 1976.

Renzulli, J. *The Enrichment Triad Model: A guide for developing programs for the gifted and talented*. Wethersfield CT: Creative Learning Press, 1977.

Rothney, J., & Sanborn, M. *Promising practices in the education of superior students: A demonstration program*. Madison WI: University of Wisconsin, 1968.

Seeley, K. Competencies for teachers of gifted and talented children. *Journal for the Education of the Gifted*, 1979, *3*(1), 7–13.

Shaw, M., & Alves, G. The self-concept of bright academic underachievers. *Personnel and Guidance Journal*, 1963, *42*, 401–403.

Sisk, D. Helping children know themselves. In B. Cherry (Ed.), *A handbook of bright ideas facilitating giftedness*. Manatee FL: Manatee Gifted Program, Manatee Junior College, 1976. (ERIC OBC. 093, ED 135 174)

Spaulding, R. What teacher attributes bring out the best in gifted children? Affective dimensions of creative processes. In J. Gallagher (Ed.), *Teaching gifted students*. Boston: Allyn & Bacon, 1965.

Thiel, R., & Thiel, A. A structural analysis of family interaction patterns, and the underachieving gifted child. *The Gifted Child Quarterly*, 1977, *21*, 267–275.

Torrance, E. Creative teaching makes a difference. In W. Barbe & J. Renzulli (Eds.), *Psychology and education of the gifted*. New York: Irvington Publishers, 1975.

Ward, V. *Educating the gifted*. Columbus OH: Charles E. Merrill, 1961.

Watson, G. Emotional problems of gifted students. *Personnel and Guidance Journal*, 1960, *39*, 98–105.

Wiener, J. Attitudes of psychologists and psychometrists toward gifted children and programs for the gifted. *Exceptional Children*, 1978, *44*, 531–534.

CHAPTER 5

Differentiating the Curriculum

Merle B. Karnes
Susan A. Linnemeyer
Cynthia N. Denton-Ade

Experts agree that an appropriate curriculum for young gifted children is qualitatively different from that provided average children. It does not merely provide more of the same kind of experience or pace experiences more rapidly. Gifted children are a unique population and therefore require a differentiated curriculum.

THE CASE FOR DIFFERENTIATION

How to differentiate instruction for gifted children has long been a concern of educators. Over a quarter of a century ago in the 49th yearbook of the National Society for the Study of Education, Part II, Sumption, Norris, and Terman (1950) addressed this issue, noting that there is "greater emphasis placed on creative effort, intellectual initiation, critical thinking, social adjustment, social responsibility, and the development of unselfish qualities of leadership" (p. 278). Thus, it seemed clear even then that differentiating instruction for the gifted involved more than enrichment of the regular curriculum or inclusion of experiences and skills customarily reserved for older children.

More recently, Renzulli (1977), in discussing enrichment and qualitative curriculum differences, stated that experiences in a curriculum for the gifted must (a) be above and beyond the regular curriculum, (b) take into account the specific content interests of students, (c) accommodate their preferred styles of learning, and (d) give them opportunities to pursue topic areas to unlimited levels of inquiry. These criteria are appropriate to preschool as well as elementary and secondary curricula. Renzulli (1977) further suggested that "an important part of all programs for the gifted should be the systematic development of the cognitive and affective processes which brought these youngsters to our attention in the first place" (p. 22).

According to Kaplan (1980), "a differentiated curriculum for young gifted learners reflects the differences that distinguish them from their non-gifted peers" (p. 62). She went on to observe: "The literature discussing the appropriate learning experiences for the gifted/talented outlines the development of creative thinking and problem-solving processes and the acquisition of advanced content as necessary objectives for these children" (p. 63). Kaplan's (1974) procedures for presenting learning opportunities to the young gifted child include the following:

Exposure: Students are exposed to experiences, materials, and information which is outside the bounds of the regular curriculum, does not match age-grade expectations, and introduces something new or unusual.

Extension: Students are afforded opportunities to elaborate on the regular curriculum through additional allocation of working time, materials, and experiences, and/or further self-initiated or related study.

Development: Students are provided with instruction which focuses on thorough or new exploration of a concept or skill which is part of a general learning activity within the regular curriculum. (p. 123)

Maker (1982) has discussed how expectations for gifted children differ from those for children in general, observing that the input for the gifted is

(a) Accelerated or advanced, (b) more complex, (c) beyond the regular curriculum, (d) selected by the students according to their interests, and (e) concerned with the more abstract concepts in each content area. The level and type of resources used or available to these individuals are different from those available to all students. (p. 6)

Maker went on to cite six ways in which expectations for gifted learners are different:

These young learners may be able (a) to benefit from longer time periods for learning; (b) to create new information, ideas, and products; (c) to achieve greater depth of thought or investigation; (d) to show personal growth or sophistication in affective areas; (e) to develop new generalizations; (f) to develop higher levels of thinking; and (g) to design and implement their own study. (p.6)

Gallagher (1975) proposed three ways to differentiate instruction for the gifted:

1. The content of material presented to gifted children must be changed to emphasize greater complexity and higher levels of abstraction.
2. The method of presentation must also be different. [Mere presentation of information is not enough, warns Gallagher, for gifted children must develop a learning style that will serve them well later on.]
3. The learning environment must be modified. This might be accomplished, for example, by moving the child to a different instructional setting so that he or she can be with others of similar abilities, by acceleration to a higher grade, through the use of a different conceptual model, through an administrative device such as a resource room, a special class, or an after-school group. (p. 72)

In a recent article, Renzulli, Smith, and Reis (1982) developed a strategy for working with the gifted that they called "curriculum compacting." They began by reminding us of what is likely to happen to gifted children: they are often taught what they already know, and even when differentiated instruction is provided, gaps frequently occur in their learning. Renzulli and his colleagues, therefore, suggested a systematic plan for compacting and streamlining the regular curriculum that prevents the gifted from becoming bored by unchallenging work, especially in the basic skills, and at the same time ensures that they have mastered the skills essential for subsequent achievement. According to these authors, two requirements for successful compacting are careful diagnosis and a thorough knowledge of the content and objectives of an instructional unit. Instruments appropriate for use with preschoolers are available to diagnose such basic skills as mathematics, reading readiness or reading, and language. Careful diagnosis enables teachers to compact the curriculum so that gifted children use time more efficiently and economically and at the same time have opportunities to pursue special interests. Enrichment and acceleration, therefore, occur simultaneously. Renzulli, Smith, and Reis have cautioned, however, that we cannot conclude that a child is interested in a certain subject merely because he or she happens to do well in that subject. Gifted youngsters must have opportunities to explore a wide variety of interests.

Ward (1980), on the other hand, noted the important role regular education plays in the full development of gifted children: "General education—the education of the whole person—also involves the development of non-intellective dimensions of personality" (p. 39). Difficulties in human relations, for example, may hinder the development of the gifted child's particular abilities. "Therefore," Ward concluded, "in an indirect manner, through the education of the person with talent as distinct from the development of the talents per se, the general education curriculum does contribute to the nurture of great human abilities" (p. 39). His remarks were not meant to imply, however, that the school does not have the responsibility for identifying talents and encouraging their development, although training and experience in a marked talent area may have to be provided outside the school, possibly by a mentor who manifests unusual talent in that area.

In 1971 the Marland report clearly stated that gifted and talented children "require differentiated educational programs and/or services beyond those normally provided by the regular school program" (p. ix). Differentiating instruction for any child, however, is a complex task, and differentiating instruction for the gifted/talented is particularly difficult. As Passow (1982) noted:

> Though gifted/talented education overlaps with education for all children— since "all children" includes the gifted and talented—planners for the gifted must formulate a clear response to the perennial question, "Why isn't this good for all children?" Only when we can clearly indicate the unusual and unique aspects of the curriculum and instruction which we seek can we defend differentiated curriculum for gifted/talented children. . . . Developing a differentiated curriculum involves fashioning an environmental setting, providing human and material resources, and arranging teaching and facilitating strategies so that "gifted responses" will occur more readily. An appropriately differentiated curriculum will increase the likelihood of high quality learning interactions— the "stuff" of curriculum and instruction—as shown by resulting products and performances. (pp. 6–7)

Passow went on to delineate seven principles of curriculum differentiation that are appropriate for younger as well as older gifted/talented children. He noted that these principles are endorsed by the National/State Leadership Training Institute on the Gifted and Talented Curriculum Council and will likely be refined by that group.

1. The content of the curriculum for the gifted/talented should focus on and be organized to include more elaborate, complex, and in-depth study of major ideas, problems, and themes that integrate knowledge with and across systems of thought.
2. Curriculum for the gifted/talented should allow for the development and application of productive thinking skills to enable students to reconceptualize existing knowledge and/or generate new knowledge.
3. Curriculum for the gifted/talented should enable them to explore constantly changing knowledge and information and develop the attitude that knowledge is worth pursuing in an open world.
4. Curriculum for the gifted/talented should encourage exposure to, selection, and use of appropriate specialized resources.
5. Curriculum for the gifted/talented should promote self-initiated and self-directed learning and growth.
6. Curriculum for the gifted/talented should provide for the development of self-understanding and the understanding of one's relationship to personal, societal institutions, nature, and culture.

7. Evaluation of curriculum for the gifted/talented should be conducted in accordance with prior stated principles, stressing higher-level thinking skills, creativity and excellence in performance and products. (pp. 7–10)

These principles are intended to help those responsible for the education of the gifted/talented child to make decisions that will maximize learning. To the persistent question, "Wouldn't this learning activity be appropriate for all children?" Passow (1982) has raised three more: "Would all children want to be involved in such learning experiences? Could all children participate in such learning experiences? Should all children be expected to succeed in such learning experiences?" (p. 12). If the answer to these three is affirmative, then the activity isn't really providing differentiated instruction for the gifted.

Passow (1982) has suggested three strategies for differentiating instruction. The first has to do with acceleration; gifted learners cover material more rapidly or earlier than do youngsters with average ability. There are dangers in acceleration, however, and Passow has cautioned that gifted children may not have time to "reflect, savor, play around with ideas and create" (p. 15) if they are pushed too rapidly through the curriculum. In addition, acceleration may not give them sufficient opportunity to make selections for themselves. With the second strategy, gifted children are encouraged to pursue subjects in greater depth and breadth than are average learners. The third strategy focuses on instruction that differs in nature; thus, the content or process emphasized would not normally be included in the curriculum, and what is offered gifted children is neither enrichment nor extension of the regular curriculum.

In explaining how the University of Illinois Preschool Gifted Program differentiates the curriculum for young gifted children, Karnes, Shwedel, and Williams (1983) stated that the curriculum for these children provides:

- Offerings not usually a part of the standard curriculum for young children.
- Encouragement to pursue a chosen interest in depth.
- Learning based on needs rather than on predetermined order or sequence of instruction.
- Activities more complex and requiring more abstract and higher-level thinking processes.
- Greater flexibility in the use of materials, time, and resources.
- Higher expectations for independence and task persistence.
- Provision of more opportunities to acquire and demonstrate leadership abilities.
- Greater encouragement of creative and productive thinking, including higher-level thinking processes.
- More emphasis on interpreting the behavior and feelings of self and others.
- More opportunities to broaden the base of knowledge and enhance language abilities. (pp. 129–130)

VARIABLES AFFECTING CURRICULUM

There is considerable similarity among experts on what constitutes a differentiated curriculum for gifted children. There is also a consensus that each gifted child is unique and that many variables will, therefore, influence the curriculum for an individual child. Some of the variables follow.

Characteristics, Needs, and Interests of the Child

Each child has characteristics that make him or her a unique individual. Although many gifted children may be above average in all facets of development, particular children who show gifts in some areas may not be developing on a par in all respects. They may have unusually outstanding strengths in the cognitive area, have poor self-esteem and poor interpersonal skills, but be very creative in music. Or they may have the potential to become outstanding in a given area, but due to limited stimulation may not develop that potential fully. A child may have a handicapping condition that requires special attention before he or she can function at a level indicative of giftedness.

The gifted child may also vary in interests under the influence of home and of experiences prior to school attendance. If a differentiated curriculum does encourage the in-depth pursuit of interests, the teacher can expect to discover a broad spectrum of interests among young gifted children.

Expectations Based on What Is Known About Gifted Children

Research and experience give us information about the skills gifted children are capable of mastering. A curriculum for young gifted children is naturally influenced by such information. Following are some of the skills felt to be important for young gifted children to develop.

Cognitive Skills

To acquire and recall a large bank of information.

To acquire and use an extensive vocabulary.

To use words innovatively.

To transfer learnings.

To generalize.

To see cause-and-effect relationships.

To see relationships other than the obvious.

To make inferences.

To integrate and synthesize information.

To engage in high level problem-solving.

To organize information.

To comprehend complex ideas.

To perceive subtle differences.

To detect discrepancies in procedures, rules, expectations.

To use alternative ways of seeking information.

To analyze situations.

To evaluate processes/products.

To see implications.

To use a high level of reasoning.

To formulate hypotheses.
To make applications.
To make transformations.

To manifest a high level of critical thinking.
To display unusual curiosity.

Creativity Skills

To take risks.
To think divergently.
To think and act flexibly.
To think and act fluently.
To create original and/or inventive ideas, processes, products.
To elaborate on concepts.

To demonstrate imagination.
To tolerate ambiguity.
To demonstrate high aesthetic values.
To manifest a high level of intuitive thinking.

Affective Skills

To have a realistic self-concept.
To demonstrate respect for others.
To be empathetic toward others.
To be tolerant of individual differences.
To engage in self-evaluation.
To tolerate criticism.
To share belongings and ideas.
To persist at task.
To be independent in thinking and behavior.
To tolerate delayed gratification.

To tolerate lack of closure or delayed closure.
To be willing to compete.
To display a sense of humor.
To be sensitive to injustices.
To display standards of excellence.
To engage in moral reasoning.
To clarify thoughts, feelings, and values.
To display confidence in one's ability.
To be intrinsically motivated.

Teachers aware of the importance of these skills are more likely to provide gifted children with opportunities to acquire and practice them.

Goals and Involvement of Parents

Goals of the parents and the extent of their involvement in the child's educational program may influence the goals set for the child. Parents have every right to share their goals for their children with school personnel and to expect support in helping achieve the goals. If parents want their child to pursue a talent in music, the home and school may have to identify a mentor for the child. Other parents may hope to encourage a child in leadership, while still others will encourage interest in the field of science. Parents do have a marked influence on the child's values and interests, and the school whenever possible should support the parents' goals for the child. The compatibility of the goals of home and school is contingent on the extent to which they work together for the best interests of the child.

Teacher Attributes, Competencies, Attitudes, and Values

The key to the success of a school program rests largely with the teacher, who determines to a large extent the appropriateness of the curriculum for the gifted child.

Physical Make-Up of the Classroom

Space and equipment must be compatible with the kind of program the teacher wishes to implement. Important considerations, for instance, aside from room size, may include the ease with which furniture can be rearranged and the accessibility of running water.

Pupil-Teacher Ratio

Gifted children depend on adults to assist them in obtaining the knowledge and skills to pursue their interests. Since they can be especially demanding of adult time, the adult/child ratio should be relatively high.

Availability of Ancillary Services

If the child has a handicapping condition, curricular offerings will entail special services to help overcome or compensate for it. Speech and language therapy, occupational or physical therapy, or social work may be required depending on the nature of the problem. If supportive services are viewed broadly, they may include the work of a mentor who helps develop the child's artistic ability.

Community Resources and Attitudes

Some communities have a wealth of resources the family and the school can use to promote the development of the gifted child. After-school, Saturday, and summer programs are sometimes available. In other communities, singling out the gifted and providing special programs, whether in special classes or in a mainstream setting, is frowned upon as undemocratic. In such instances, community attitude has to change markedly before gifted children can be provided with a differentiated curriculum.

Financial Allocations

A truly differentiated curriculum for young gifted children will require greater financial support in terms of providing instructional materials, financing field trips, and maintaining an adequate teacher/child ratio. The parent involvement program may also be more costly than for parents of average children.

Supervisory and Administrative Support

Knowledgeable and interested supervisors and administrators are needed to make sure that the needs of the gifted are being met through a differentiated curriculum. In that light, advocates are also needed to sell the program, to interpret to the community its value and the purpose it serves.

ROLE OF INDIVIDUALIZED EDUCATION PROGRAMS

In recent years, individualized education programs (IEP's) for gifted children have followed plans similar to those for handicapped children as delineated in Public Law 94-142. Such plans involve parents, in itself a worthwhile goal that additionally tends to make school personnel more thoughtful and accountable. Procedures for developing IEP's vary among local districts, but according to Renzulli and Smith (1979), all specify the child's level of performance, including data regarding the child's characteristics and abilities; delineate long-term goals and short-term objectives; describe an instructional plan to achieve these goals and objectives; determine the time the child will spend in the regular program and in the special program; involve parents; set the starting date and duration of services; and specify how the child's needs and progress will be evaluated.

Treffinger (1979) offered further guidelines in the preparation of IEP's:

- There must be adequate time for thoughtful planning and training in instructional design so that the planning will not be busywork.
- Effective planning requires accurate assessment data that will be relevant to the instructional decisions to be made.
- An individualized program does not mean the student learns only in isolation.
- An effective IEP may lead to the implementation of different learning outcomes for various students.
- An effective IEP provides for the utilization of many different instructional activities.
- IEP development should involve a cooperative planning model utilizing input from many different sources.
- There must be sufficient opportunity for effective implementation of many alternatives devised in the IEP. (pp. 52–54)

ENSURING THE ACQUISITION OF BASIC SKILLS

There is always the danger that the child who learns quickly will be given advanced material without having acquired certain basic skills essential for more complex learning. For example, children need word attack skills if they are to read more difficult materials independently. They may be able to discover some of these rules by themselves, but teachers must assess whether or not they have acquired them and provide specific instructions where needed.

Through observation and the use of assessment instruments, teachers must determine children's developmental levels to ensure acquisition of skills and knowledge specified in the regular curriculum. Although gifted youngsters will master this material more quickly than peers with lesser ability, the progress of the gifted must be monitored carefully to avoid gaps in learning.

A child's progress in mathematics, for example, is endangered if he or she fails to acquire certain basic mathematical skills before progressing to more advanced concepts.

There are various methods by which teachers may present basic information to gifted preschoolers. The method chosen depends on the needs and abilities of individual children. For the gifted preschooler who acquires basics fairly independently, the teacher may offer only occasional direct instruction and guidance, making a wide variety of materials available. Nevertheless, the teacher must be aware of the child's progress and intervene with direction at appropriate times. The teacher should keep in mind that a child who learns independently in one area may need direct instruction in another.

Passow (1982), on the other hand, has warned against penalizing the gifted child who has not acquired certain basic skills:

> We would argue . . . that gifted/talented students should not be barred from pursuing more advanced, complex, and sophisticated studies simply because they have not attained proficiency in all aspects of the basic or regular curric-ulum. Deferring the introduction and pursuit of advanced learning processes under such circumstances can be punitive, and can inhibit the development of individual potential. A youngster volunteering to write a poem or an essay who has deficiencies in spelling or grammar should be encouraged to write creatively, expressing his/her unique ideas, while at the same time being helped to master the necessary basic skills in the context of the task in which he/she is engaged. (p. 11)

Then, too, there are likely to be discrepancies of growth in the acquisition of cognitive and physical skills. A child may be able to develop a complicated story at age 4 but be unable to print. It would be ridiculous to suggest that the story cannot be recorded until the child learns to write. The teacher or an assistant may do the writing, or a tape recorder may be used.

In developing an individualized education program for a gifted/talented handicapped child, there must be a plan in the area of the handicap or hand-icaps and a plan in the area of giftedness or talent. It may be necessary for the teacher to concentrate on helping the child ameliorate, compensate for, or minimize the effects of the handicapping condition before the gifts/talents fully develop. In general, the principles in differentiating a curriculum for the handicapped child who is also gifted are the same as for the nonhandi-capped child who is gifted.

PROVIDING FOR HIGHER-LEVEL THOUGHT PROCESSES

Much has been written about learning models that stress the process of think-ing: Guilford's Structure of the Intellect, Bloom's Taxonomy of Educational Objectives, Williams' Cognitive-Affective Interaction Model, and Renzulli's Enrichment Triad Model, to name only four. (See Chapter 3 for more detailed descriptions and references.) These models recognize the complexity of the thinking process and furnish means to foster that process. A note of caution is in order, however, for a curriculum that exists for the sole purpose of teaching thinking processes is bound to fall short. The results tend to be artificial. If, for example, divergent thinking is being stressed, the teacher must recognize that ultimately the child's divergent responses must be evaluated to determine their merit. Similarly, information that the gifted child acquires is crucial in problem-solving, but the teacher should not be overly concerned with filling the child's mind with facts—and the temptation will be strong, since most gifted children learn facts easily. In short, if educators desire the gifted to be the producers of knowledge, they need to provide them with tools for systematic thinking, discovery, and evaluation.

Most educators agree that an important goal for any curriculum is to assist children in becoming active inquirers, and teacher-directed curricula have been criticized for making children comfortable with ''spoon-fed'' knowledge. When children are more active learners, more involved in learning and in making choices and decisions, their motivation increases. In addition, a more active approach allows gifted children to explore their own interests and learning styles. According to Treffinger (1974), ''most research on the personal characteristics of gifted, talented, and highly creative individuals suggests that they are critical, independent of thought and judgment, self-starting and perseverant'' (p. 47).

Discovery Method

The approach which encourages active inquiry is referred to by some as *self-directed learning* (Feldhusen & Treffinger, 1980; Treffinger, 1974, 1978) and by others as the *discovery method* (Gallagher, 1975). Kagan (1967) set forth the following argument for the discovery approach:

1. Discovery learning requires more involvement on the part of the child and therefore greater attention to the component materials being presented. Since the discovery strategy creates maximum attention and involvement, it should lead to more efficient learning.
2. Discovery learning requires the child to make an intellectual effort, and this effort leads to an increase in the value of the task.
3. Inferential learning is likely to increase the child's expectancy that he is able to solve problems autonomously.
4. The method of inferential learning requires and promotes a more independent attitude on the part of the child. (p. 160)

Freedom to explore the environment, of course, does not mean that the child is given complete license. The teacher must assume the role of facilitator, a stance that requires a great deal of insight and organization. Treffinger (1978) has detailed important considerations in fostering active inquiry on the part of young learners:

1. Admonitions are inadequate. [Help children to act independently; don't just tell them to do so.]

2. Don't assume. [Do assessments to determine the children's strengths and weaknesses; don't assume they have certain basic skills.]
3. Don't smother self-direction by doing for them things they can do (or can learn to do) for themselves.
4. Adults must have or develop an attitude of openness and support for self-directed learning.
5. Learn to defer judgment.
6. Emphasize the continuity of problems and challenges.
7. Provide systematic training in problem-solving and the skills of independent research and inquiry.
8. Treat difficult situations at home or school as opportunities to use creative problem-solving techniques, not merely as problems requiring the unilateral wisdom of an adult.
9. Be alert to audiences that are appropriate for sharing children's efforts or for opportunities to create such audiences.
10. Help students learn how to direct their own learning gradually—don't expect it to happen all at once.
11. CREATE! Be a model of self-directed learning in your own life. (pp. 15–19)

In short, teachers can assist by helping children define problems, locate resources and information, and evaluate their work.

When gifted children enter elementary school, they, like their average peers, are generally placed in a relatively highly structured, teacher-directed classroom. Preschool gifted children, however, are more likely to be placed in a classroom where they can explore their environment, ask questions, and solve problems. Their teachers frequently provide opportunities for choice, which Treffinger (1974) has claimed is the first of three steps toward self-directed learning. The second is for the teacher to involve children in creating options. In a preschool setting this might be done by assisting children in the investigation of problems that interest them. Third, when the children control their own choices, the teacher's role as facilitator fully emerges. The preschool is an opportune place to begin to develop the skills for inquiry and problem-solving that children need in later life.

Higher-level thought processes are also affected by the sort of questions teachers ask children. Taba (1966) showed a relationship between the cognitive operations in which children engaged and the questions and teaching strategies employed. Narrow questions (e.g., "What are we having for snack today?") produce answers that require a low level of thinking. If the teacher asks instead, "What are all the things we could have for snack?" the question is open-ended within the set of edible items. After snack, the teacher might ask, "What might a monster eat for snack?" Here the responses need not be restricted to a single set, and children are encouraged to think more divergently. Such questions also reinforce the idea that there can be several solutions to one problem. Asking what is the best item for snack requires children to evaluate the choice using their own criteria. It is crucial that teachers be cognizant of the types of questions they ask children and incorporate those that tap higher thought processes.

CONSIDERING SOCIAL AND EMOTIONAL DEVELOPMENT

The curriculum for the gifted preschooler should not be restricted to the cognitive domain. Williams (1970) argued that affective learning is inseparable from cognitive learning. It is safe to say that the two are of equal importance and that the interaction between them makes for a fully functioning individual. Included in the affective domain are self-concept, interpersonal skills, task commitment, and risk-taking.

Self-Concept

The development of a positive self-concept is vital if the gifted child's full potential is to be actualized (Sisk, 1976), and gifted children with poor self-concepts are often underachievers (Fine, 1977). Teachers can help in the development of the gifted child's self-concept by listening attentively and providing encouragement. They can also use techniques as role-playing to lead the child toward a self-concept that is realistic. Since the self-concept develops early, it is essential that the gifted preschooler receive support in this area.

Interpersonal Skills

To function productively as a member of a group, the gifted preschooler needs the interpersonal skills of cooperation and communication. Developers of the Seattle Child Development Center, which serves gifted preschoolers, noted the importance of enhancing the gifted child's ability to interact in socially appropriate ways and stressed the development of an awareness of the needs of others (Roedell & Robinson, 1977). Interpersonal skills can be fostered through a variety of activities. For example, children can work together classifying insects and making a collection, with each child responsible for a specific part of the project. Sharing information is essential in order to complete the task. Another suggestion is to help children solve real-life problems as a group; for example, resolve a dispute when half of the class votes to go to the zoo and the others vote to go to the park. With assistance from the teacher, the class considers both options and decides which is more appropriate.

Task Commitment

Persistence, the ability to work for a sustained period of time, is crucial to learning and success. It is especially important to encourage task commitment among gifted preschoolers, since success is strongly related to high levels of task commitment in gifted adults (Renzulli, 1977). Task commitment can be fostered through motivation and reinforcement. Studies have suggested that when the task commitment of gifted children is not reinforced by their parents, the children tend to become underachievers (Newman, Dember, & Krug, 1973; Zilli, 1971). Parents can help build task commitment by asking children about school projects, by modeling task commitment themselves, and by offering encouragement. Teachers as well as parents can provide reinforcement and should be supportive, positive, and enthusiastic in their general attitudes. In addition, teachers and parents should offer verbal praise freely to children displaying task commitment and encourage them to praise each other for accomplishments. Finally, teachers should present intriguing and challenging materials and provide ample time—days or weeks—to complete projects. After a youngster develops a sense of task commitment, the trait can become self-reinforcing.

Risk-Taking

Another important affective behavior to be nurtured in the gifted preschooler is risk-taking. Williams (1970) stressed that the ability to take risks is necesary in the development of creative potential. Risk-taking at the preschool level can be fostered by providing a nonthreatening atmosphere and by rewarding children for risk-taking, regardless of success or failure. Preschoolers should be encouraged to work independently, to state ideas and hazard guesses, and to defend positions. Preschoolers will take risks first in subject areas where they feel comfortable and should be encouraged to do so in other areas.

NURTURING CREATIVITY

It is essential that preschool curricula for gifted children develop creativity. Starkweather (1971) cited the importance of nurturing creativity as early as infancy on the grounds that it can be stifled by the age of 5 years. Feldhusen and Treffinger (1980) supported this contention:

> Early experience in creative thinking and problem solving paves the way, helps the children learn how to use divergent thinking capacities and creative problem solving. They should also become aware of the potency of creative thinking and problem solving as "mental tools" to achieve new heights of invention and production. (p. 10)

It has often been noted that teaching practices are profoundly important in nurturing creativity (Callahan, 1978). A basic component of a classroom that encourages creativity is an atmosphere that welcomes the generation of new ideas and opinions. The first step in establishing such an environment is to make children feel safe psychologically. A sure way to suppress creative responses is to be critical, to make children feel that their suggestions are inconsequential or silly. There needs to be an inherent respect on the part of the teacher for the ideas of children. In addition, the teacher must encourage children to attempt challenging problems, and it is here that motivation and task commitment come into play.

Feldhusen and Treffinger (1980) noted the importance of physical environment in enhancing creativity. The preschool classroom should be flexible enough for children to move from busy areas to quiet areas without the teacher's permission and should contain manipulable materials and other stimulating resources readily accessible to children. In such an environment teachers assume the role of facilitator. Without relinquishing control of the classroom, they allow children to engage comfortably in the creative process.

Both Passow (1977) and Gallagher (1975) have discussed the creative process in terms of three steps.

1. The child defines a problem, investigates it, and gathers information.
2. The child views the problem from as many different directions as possible.
3. The child brings the work to a conclusion.

Each step may involve a great deal of time, and teachers must have the patience not to rush children and the wisdom to assist them during periods of frustration.

Developing Divergent Thinking

Educators interested in the creative process should be particularly concerned with developing divergent thinking (Guilford, 1959, 1967a, 1967b). According to Guilford, the four basic abilities involved in divergent thinking are fluency, flexibility, originality, and elaboration. *Fluency* is the ability to produce a large number of ideas; the emphasis is on quantity, not quality. Teachers can encourage children to be fluent by saying, "Let's see how many answers you can give me," or by asking, "What else could you do?" *Flexibility* is the ability to produce a wide variety of ideas. Teachers should observe whether or not children are able to change directions in their thinking. They can ask, "Can you think of a different way of doing that?" The ability to produce novel, unusual ideas is *originality,* which can be observed by noting the unconventionality of responses. *Elaboration* is the ability to embellish or complete an idea. If a teacher wants a child to elaborate on a drawing, she may ask: "What else could you add to that picture?" or, "What can you add to keep that man warm in the snow?" Feldhusen and Kolloff (1979) have concluded that "gifted children need to expand their thinking skills to produce many possible ideas, different categories of ideas, unusual ideas, and well-developed ideas" (p. 9).

Teaching Techniques

Among the general techniques for stimulating creativity suggested by Callahan (1978) are the following:

1. Provide a nonthreatening atmosphere. An open, nonjudgmental attitude on the part of the teacher will allow freedom for divergent production.
2. Provide different and novel kinds of stimuli in the environment to stimulate curiosity.

3. Reward novel production of ideas. This will increase the likelihood that more unique ideas will be produced.
4. Provide opportunities to practice. Attempt to integrate questions that encourage divergent production and evaluation into as many content areas as possible.
5. Model creativity yourself as much as possible.
6. Provide children with many opportunities to ask questions. Children's ideas should be respected and encouraged. (pp. 71–72)

Creativity may be introduced into the classroom in two ways, either taught in its own right or advanced through the creative potential of all subject areas (Passow, 1977). Establishing an environment that nurtures creativity and using specific instructional techniques are important in the first case, but teachers must also be aware of the potentialities in mundane settings. For example, opportunities for the natural extension of a child's capacity for divergent thinking may occur during snack time. While passing out refreshments, the teacher might ask, "What are all the things we could eat that are cold and taste good?" If a child hears an unusual noise outside the classroom, the teacher might ask, "What are all the things that could have made that sound?" Another example of an everyday occurrence is dressing for outdoor play. The teacher might ask, "What are all the things you can wear on your head? What are all the things you *can't* wear on your head?" Key questions include: "How many ways can you . . .?" "What other way can you . . .?" and "Tell me another idea." It is important when asking these questions to accept all answers. Occasionally children offer baffling responses. A teacher can say, "That's an interesting idea, but I don't understand how it will help us solve our problem. Will you explain it to us?"

Teachers can adopt more structured approaches to the development of creative thinking by allotting a portion of the school day to that purpose. Preschool programs commonly have a time when teachers meet with large or small groups of children, for example, story time or circle time. These are appropriate occasions to encourage divergency. One medium is fantasy. A teacher might ask children to name all the things they would want to take with them on a trip to another planet, or to draw a picture of how the world would look if they were small as ants. Another technique is brainstorming solutions to real-life problems in the classroom: "Some children are hitting other children. What can we do about it?" or "What can we do to improve the housekeeping corner?" After the brainstorming session is completed, the teacher can help the children develop criteria for evaluating the suggestions. If a child suggests that an appropriate way to deal with a hitter is to strike back, the teacher might ask, "What do you think would happen then? How would the child who was hit feel?" Ultimately, the teacher should function as a facilitator in assisting children to set criteria and to evaluate their own suggestions.

Another means of enchancing creativity that can be adapted to the preschool gifted child is *synectics,* a technique that uses analogies and metaphors to assist the child in analyzing problems from a variety of perspectives (Feldhusen & Treffinger, 1980). One form of synectics is the direct analogy. The teacher might ask the preschooler, "How many ways can you compare an apple with a ball?" Initially this task may seem too difficult, even for the gifted preschooler, but the teacher can assist by asking leading questions that analyze the component parts of an object. In comparing an apple with a ball, the teacher might ask questions about shape, size, color, texture, scent, and taste. The teacher might ask, "What happens if you drop it, roll it, cut it into pieces?" This line of questioning can also be the starting point for attribute listing, a method that promotes a sharper view of the characteristics, qualities, and limitations of a problem.

Personal analogy is another aspect of synectics. It requires the child to assume the role of another person or an object. Teachers can use a variety of forms of expression to demonstrate this kind of analogy: "Imagine you are seeds. Show me how small you would be. What color are you? What would happen if someone watered you? Show me how you would grow. Now you are fully grown. What kind of plant are you?"

The majority of creative activities require children to respond verbally. Since the gifted preschooler is more likely than the average-ability child to excel verbally, creativity should also be encouraged in a variety of media. The average child, as well as the gifted, expresses creative potential through art, music, and movement, and responses in all these media should be fostered.

Preschool teachers should be keenly aware of the manner in which they present creative activities. Feldhusen and Treffinger (1980) have cautioned that "even the greatest lesson plan will not be effective unless it includes some strategy for establishing a receptive attitude among the students" (p. 69). To capture and retain the attention of the preschool child, teachers should present attractive materials, provide visual demonstrations, and employ a game-like format (Roedell & Robinson, 1977). By showing enthusiasm, the teacher stimulates the child's interest in the activity.

RATIONALE FOR COMBINING CONCEPTUAL MODELS

As stated in the chapter on conceptual models used in developing curriculum for gifted children, Guilford's Structure of the Intellect, Bloom's Taxonomy, and Renzulli's Enrichment Triad Model have been found to be more readily adaptable than others, but often no single model seems adequate to meet all of the goals of a given program for gifted and talented children. Combining aspects of several models may help to achieve a more effective preschool curriculum.

Enrichment Triad Model

Briefly, Renzulli's Enrichment Triad Model proposes three levels of enrichment for gifted students. The aim of Type I, General Exploratory Activities, is to expose children to a number of areas of potential interest in an atmosphere of freedom. Type II, Group Training Activities, is designed to develop thinking and feeling processes. Teachers involve children in specific activities that foster creative and productive thinking, particularly the development of divergent thinking. Individual and Small Group Investigation of Real Problems, Type III, is the focus of the model. The child becomes an active investigator of real problems—analyzing information, drawing conclusions, and communicating what has been learned. Renzulli and Smith (1978) pointed out that such activities should not consist of "writing ritualized reports about conclusions which have been reported by other people. . . . Real problem productivity, on the other hand, focuses on the identification and delimitation of problems that are similar in nature to those pursued by authentic researchers or artists in particular fields" (p. 27).

Renzulli's notion of Type I enrichment is particularly appropriate for the preschool child, since many opportunities can be provided that foster inquiry into the environment. The child can be immersed in experiences that foster creativity, curiosity, and interest in the environment. Teachers can provide interest centers, arrange exploratory field trips, and use parents or other adults as resource people. This experientially rich environment provides a backdrop against which a wealth of learning takes place.

Children attempting to solve real-life problems (Type III enrichment) often achieve their own understanding and interpretations of problems in an original manner; however, investigating problems with which adults are struggling may require an intellectual capacity beyond that of the gifted preschool child. Williams (1971) stated that "the young child may not be able to break new boundaries, at least in any sophisticated degree, by creating new concepts in the physical sciences; but he or she may be highly original and imaginative in dealing with their own discoveries and uses of already existing scientific concepts" (p. 224).

Structure of the Intellect Model

The Structure of the Intellect Model (SOI), developed by Guilford, is useful in proposing a theory that delineates and classifies intellectual factors. Intellectual ability is the combination of three factors: an operation or process, a content, and a product. The development of thinking processes is viewed as crucial in the development of creativity, and divergent production is considered a key element.

Bloom's Taxonomy

An advantage of Bloom's Taxonomy (Bloom, Engelhart, Furst, Hill, & Krathwohl, 1956) is that it can be used to organize teaching methodologies. There are six levels of objectives within the cognitive domain: knowledge, comprehension, application, analysis, synthesis, and evaluation. The Taxonomy is organized so that objectives in one level are built upon objectives in the preceding one. Leonard (1978) has stated that Bloom's model, "adapted to the preschool level, enables programming at higher cognitive levels and ensures that all activities will not be rote learning memorization at the knowledge level" (p. 48). The Chapel Hill Gifted-Handicapped Program (Bailey & Leonard, 1977) developed a unit approach to Bloom's Taxonomy. Within each unit, which was centered around a main theme or topic, educational objectives and activities were established at each of the six levels of the cognitive domain.

Although Bloom's Taxonomy includes creative thinking, it has been criticized for its placement of creativity within the hierarchy of thinking processes. Williams (1971) has argued that the Taxonomy follows a developmental sequence in which children must master lower thought processes before they are capable of learning the higher processes. Since the creative processes are high on the Taxonomy, they may remain undeveloped until the child is past preschool age, whereas most experts agree that creativity should be nurtured from an early age.

Bloom's Taxonomy has, however, an important asset: it can be applied to almost any content area or unit of study—and the unit is a popular way of presenting material in the preschool, whether that material be seasons, holidays, pets, or occupations. Another advantage is that the Taxonomy allows teachers to adapt content to the needs and learning abilities of individual children. One child may observe and explore sensually while another may experiment and investigate more systematically. Bloom's model, therefore, is appropriate for use with children who have a wide range of abilities.

One might argue that the synthesis level of Bloom's Taxonomy provides for divergent production and thus is sufficient to develop creativity. Divergent production, however, is conceptually different from the synthesis level of Bloom's Taxonomy. Synthesis requires the child to solve a problem by putting together information that requires original, creative thinking. As stated earlier, this occurs when lower thought processes have been accomplished. Guilford's notion of divergent thinking is more broadly based and requires the production of unanticipated responses. In addition, it does not restrict this aspect of thinking to a level that may not be attained by preschoolers.

Essential Components of Curricula for Gifted Preschoolers

In these three models for the development of curricula for gifted preschoolers, two essential components emerge. First, creative thinking is best developed in an environment that encourages exploration. Providing gifted preschoolers with a variety of experiences and opportunities to observe and interact with the environment is similar to Renzulli's Type I enrichment and encourages them to be active inquirers into their environment—investigating and evaluating their own problems. In close conjunction with an experientially rich environment are certain instructional techniques designed to foster creativity. Feldhusen and Treffinger (1980) and Callahan (1978) have described such techniques as brainstorming, attribute-listing, morphological analysis, synectics, and forced relationship. Initially, many teachers are disappointed in their efforts to use these and other techniques to stimulate divergent thinking. They often discover that the gifted preschoolers in their classrooms are limited in their responses. If teachers persist, however, they are likely to find a vast improvement in the quantity and quality of responses. Divergent thinking, like all skills, needs to be practiced on an ongoing basis.

The second essential component is provision for the development of higher-level thinking processes. Although taxonomies organizing intellectual processes (i.e., Bloom's Taxonomy and Guilford's Structure of the Intellect Model) have been used in designing preschool curricula, questions have been raised as to their appropriateness. Renzulli and Smith (1978) stated that "it is open for question whether the valid psychological concept of mental process has been a useful educational concept so far as curriculum planning is concerned" (p. 22).

The use of taxonomies such as Bloom's, however, can be helpful in structuring curricula to tap higher-level thinking processes and in organizing teaching methodologies. In addition, the flexibility, adaptability, and relative simplicity of Bloom's Taxonomy is a considerable advantage and helps to ensure a balance of process and content. For example, if the class is observing changes that occur in spring, gifted children might analyze and classify their observations in a relatively sophisticated manner. The skills of analysis they learn from that activity could then be transferred to other activities. Leonard (1978), in reporting the use of Bloom's Taxonomy with young gifted/talented handicapped children, stated: "Activities at the more basic levels are structured and more teacher-directed. As a student progresses past knowledge and comprehension, learning is more discovery oriented, drawing on the creativity and interests of the children and making use of interest centers" (p. 49). To some extent, however, learning should be child-directed regardless of the level of thinking involved.

In summary, then, a combination of more than one conceptual model may be the framework for the development of curricula to educate young gifted/talented children. Two essentials of such curricula are the enhancement of creativity through environment and teaching techniques and the development of higher-level thinking skills through specific content areas. In addition, involvement of gifted children in the investigation of real problems (Renzulli's Type III enrichment) is useful. Although Renzulli viewed his three types of enrichment as related, the investigation of real-life problems can be considered the backdrop against which creative and higher-level thinking occur; thus, the three models coalesce.

DIFFERENTIATED CURRICULUM FOR YOUNG GIFTED CHILDREN

Fostering Divergent Thinking

Lesson plans that stimulate divergent thinking using the SOI conceptual model have been developed and extensively field-tested by Karnes (1979, 1980,

1981, 1982). Although the lessons were intended to help children develop or define divergent thinking skills not necessarily tied in to a particular subject matter, they can be used to emphasize creative thinking within subject areas common to many preschool classrooms. Two lesson plans have been selected as examples. The first, Figure 5-1, encourages creativity through fantasy and exemplifies teaching creativity for its own sake. In the second, Figure 5-2, the study of shapes, a common component of the preschool mathematics curriculum, is expanded to encourage creative thinking. These lesson plans are followed by examples of divergent activities in subject matter areas.

FIGURE 5-1
Encouraging Creativity Through Fantasy

Classification: Divergence

Behavioral Objective: To list consequences of being only 2 inches tall.

Materials: None

Presentation:

1. Tell the following story to the children.

    "One day a little boy was walking down the sidewalk on his way home from school. As he walked, he looked down at the sidewalk to make sure he didn't step on any bugs. He was a very gentle little boy who didn't want to hurt anything. Suddenly he stopped. On the ground in front of him was a shiny new coin.

    "'Wow!' he said as he picked up the coin. 'Today must be my lucky day.' It was a beautiful gold coin with a picture of a tree on one side and a bird on the other. But the little boy did not know that he had found a magic coin. As soon as he put it into his pocket, he began to have the strangest feeling. He felt as if he were getting smaller and smaller, and he was right! This shrinking feeling didn't stop until he was only 2 inches high." [Indicate his size with your fingers.]
2. Ask the youngsters, "If you were that little boy, what would be your first thought?" Encourage each child to suggest at least one thought or feeling the little boy might have had upon discovering that he was only 2 inches tall.
3. Continue, "You've given me good ideas, and now I'll tell you what the story says about what the little boy thought. In the story, the little boy first wonders how he will get home, but the story doesn't say what he does to

Continued on next page

FIGURE 5-1 (Continued)

get home, so we have to help him. How can he get home? Remember, he is only 2 inches tall." List all suggestions on the chalkboard. Press for as many as possible.

4. Ask similar questions about the consequences of being only 2 inches tall, and encourage as many responses from each child as possible. Invent your own questions, but here are a few suggestions.

    a. What would happen when he got home? What would his parents think? His brothers and sisters? His dog or cat?

    b. What might be different at mealtime?

    c. What might be different at bedtime or when he woke up in the morning? Accept all answers, even if some are silly or improbable, but don't settle for only one suggestion from each child.

Criterion:

"You've given me quite a few good ideas about what might be different at home if the little boy were only 2 inches tall. Now, can you think of how things might be different at school?" Give each child two turns to suggest a consequence at school of being only 2 inches tall. To reach criterion, the child should be able to name at least two consequences.

Follow-Up:

Remind the children of the story of the magic coin and re-tell it briefly. Conclude by saying, "Today we're going to finish that story together. Well, after an entire day of being so small—only 2 inches tall—at home and at school, the little boy decided he wanted to be a boy-size again."

Interrupt the story and ask the children to suggest how the little boy might cause this to happen. Encourage a number of ideas. "Well, in this story the boy decided to try putting the magic coin back on the sidewalk; maybe then he would become his regular size again. He put it down with the tree picture facing up. The moment the coin touched the ground, the little boy could feel himself growing bigger and bigger. But the magic coin didn't know how tall the little boy had been, and so the little boy grew taller and taller and taller until he was 10 feet tall, and that's taller than this room."

Ask the children to list the consequences of being 10 feet tall. As before, encourage as many responses as possible.

"Well, the boy didn't like being 10 feet tall any better than being 2 inches high. He very much wanted to be boy-size again."

Interrupt the story and ask the children to suggest how he might cause this to happen.

"In this story, he decided to go back to the very spot where he had found the magic coin. This time he put it down with the bird side up. He felt again that shrinking feeling as he got smaller and smaller. But suddenly it stopped, and he was exactly the same size he had been before he found the magic gold coin."

Conclude by asking each child in turn to tell what he or she thinks the little boy did and said next.

FIGURE 5-2
Encouraging Creativity Through Study of Shapes

Classification: Divergence

Behavioral Objective: To name circular (rectangular, triangular) objects.

Materials: 1. Chalkboard.
2. Construction paper or oak tag to make a pair of goggles with circular "lenses" for each child.
3. A picture book for each child.

Presentation:

1. Hold up a pair of goggles and say, "This is a pair of magic goggles. I call them my magic circle goggles because when I put them on and look through them, I can see only things that are circles." Put the goggles on. "Oh, my! I see a lot of round things. I see one over there. Can you guess what I see?" Point to an area of the room in which there is something round (the doorknob), and encourage the children to guess the object you have in mind. Record their responses on the chalkboard.
2. Give each child a pair of goggles. Ask the children to wear them to look for round things in the room. "Remember, when you're wearing magic circle goggles you see only round things!" Add all contributions to the list on the board. If the children give incorrect responses, ask them to touch the objects they have named, to run their hands around the edges to determine if the objects are really round like circles. Representative responses: clock, wheels on toy cars, records, hole in records, cups, rings, watch face and knob, shoe eyelets, holes in wooden beads, paint jar lids.
3. Ask the children to close their eyes and imagine that they are wearing their magic circle goggles outside. Ask them to name circular objects they might see outside. Representative responses: car wheel, bike wheel, end of a log, parts of flowers, roller skate wheels, baseball, steering wheel, round cloud, round sign, bottom of a sand pail, end of a garden hose. Be sure to add these to the list on the chalkboard.
4. Ask the children to pick partners and to look at each other to find circles. Representative responses: mouth, nostrils, colored part of the eye, parts of the ears, buttons, bracelets, rings, earrings, shoe eyeletes, neckhole in a sweater, belt holes. Again, add each suggestion to the list.
5. If there is time, ask the children to wear their magic goggles and think about home. How many circles can they see there? Add these to the list: plates, glasses, cups, pots and lids, holes in a calendar, burners and knobs on the stove, ashtrays, pillows, radio knobs, kitchen table, drain hole, tin cans.

Criterion:

Give each child a picture book. Ask him or her to look for circles in the pictures while wearing the magic goggles. Ask each child in turn to show you the circles he or she has found. To meet the criterion, the child should find at least three circles in the pictures.

Continued on next page

FIGURE 5-2 (Continued)

Follow-Up:

Make goggles with triangular or rectangular lenses. Follow the same procedure, asking the children to look for rectangular objects (including squares) and, on a subsequent day, triangular objects. Again, they may look for these objects in the classroom, in pictures, or in their "mind's eye" view of home or playground.

Figure 5-3 presents examples of questions teachers can ask children to stimulate divergent thinking within subject areas common in preschool curricula (adapted from RAPYHT Project Materials and SOI lesson plans, Karnes, 1981).

FIGURE 5-3
Encouraging Divergent Thinking in Subject Areas

Subject Area	*Questions*
Science	Tell all the ways you can think of that we use water. Name as many things as you can that need electricity to run.
Language	What might have happened if Goldilocks hadn't run away? Describe the strangest space creature you can think of.
Math	Show all the ways a given set of objects can be classified and sorted (i.e., shape, color, size, edibility, inedibility, etc.). What are all the things you can think of that come in pairs?
Music	Produce all the different sounds you can with a certain instrument. List all the things a musical instrument could be saying.
Art	Make the same object (e.g., a tree, house) in different media. Given a set of materials, make a home for an imaginary creature. Create a new kind of bird with scrap materials.
Social Studies	Name all the people who help us travel, keep us from getting sick, fix things, and build things for us. Name different ways we could reuse empty egg cartons, paper bags, crayon stubs, pencil shavings.

Fostering Higher-Level Thinking Skills Using Bloom's Conceptual Model

One common approach to preschool curriculum that can be used to foster high-level thinking skills is the unit approach. Units generally center on broad themes that can be integrated into several subject areas. For example, in a transportation unit, a language activity might emphasize vocabulary associated with transportation: truck, train, boat, ferry, helicopter, glider. A math activity might involve classifying and sorting pictures of different forms of transportation according to specific criteria. An activity in social studies might compare forms of transportation in different cultures.

Bloom's Taxonomy is beneficial in developing the thinking skills of young children in a variety of units, and teachers can ask stimulating questions that carry over to other classroom situations. A sample unit on spring that relies on Bloom's Taxonomy is given in Figure 5-4. Each level of thinking is listed and activities appropriate to each level are given. Some of the activities at each level presuppose the completion of activities at the preceding level. For example, an activity on the application level asks the child to write or dictate stories or poems about changes in the spring. The child who undertakes this task must previously have observed those changes—activity at the knowledge level. Teachers of the gifted should concentrate on activities that develop higher-level thinking, but it is often appropriate for a particular child to start with lower-level thinking activities and gradually advance to higher-level activities.

FIGURE 5-4
Unit on Spring

Objective: Children will discover changes that occur in the spring.

Thinking Skill	Activities
Knowledge and Comprehension	Take spring nature walks. *Observe* spring signs of growth and change, e.g., buds on shrubs and trees, bulbs, new grass, insects, animals. Take along a magnifying glass.
	Listen to spring sounds. Bring along a tape recorder.
	Smell freshly cut grass, new flowers, rain on the pavement.
	Collect different kinds of seeds. Note differences in size, shape, texture.
	Plant a variety of seeds in the classroom. Observe growth in sunny areas, shady areas, and in different kinds of media, e.g., sand, blotting paper, cloth, sponge.
	Observe life cycles of certain insects, e.g., moths, butterflies.
	Discuss changes in clothing in the spring.

Continued on next page

FIGURE 5-4 (Continued)

Application	*Brainstorm* all the new things that appear in the spring.
	Germinate seeds and keep a record of their growth.
	Record spring changes by drawing a picture of what the outdoors looks like before and during the spring.
	Collect seeds that grow best in the sun/shade or in different media.
	Sort a group of objects according to such criteria as animals that hibernate in the winter and those that don't.
	Write or *dictate* stories or poems about the changes in spring.
	Compile a scrapbook of stories, poems, and pictures of spring changes.
Analysis	*Compare and contrast* the growth rates of different seeds.
	Tally the different things seen on a spring walk. For example:

Plants	(trees, grass, flowers)	Insects	(ants, earthworms, spiders)
1111	Total 4	111	Total 3

	Weigh cups of different seeds to see which is the heaviest.
	Classify birds according to what they eat.
Synthesis	*Design* a new kind of seed that would grow as tall as a house. What would it look like? Offer a variety of media.
	Pretend spring forgot to arrive one year. What would happen to plants, animals, insects, etc.? What would summer be like?
	Describe what kinds of changes you would see if you were as small as an ant.
Evaluation	After sprouting several kinds of seeds in school, *decide* which one you would prefer to sprout at home. Why?
	Observe different kinds of flowers/trees. *Decide* which is your favorite.
	Discuss the pro's and con's of caring for an animal in school.
	Decide which kind of animal would suit the class best.
	Select an appropriate name for the pet.

Following the unit on spring is one on insects (Figure 5-5). These units are followed by examples of how Bloom's Taxonomy can be used to differentiate curriculum for the gifted in three content areas. A chart of key words and phrases to use at each level of Bloom's Taxonomy (Figure 5-9) includes examples using this conceptual model.

The unit on insects, based on Bloom's Taxonomy, was developed by Chertoff (1979) for gifted kindergartners in a New York City District 26

FIGURE 5-5
Unit on Insects

Theme:
How do insects survive the winter? (Adaptation)

Problem:
Where did the ants go? (The children were curious about the disappearance of insects during the cold weather.)

Recall:
Located, identified, observed, and discovered the structure, function, life cycles, habitat, and environment of many insects.
Collected information from books and field trips.
Collected insects for the classroom, including an ant farm.
Joined "Ant Watchers Society."
Interviewed resource people.
Viewed photographs and filmstrips.
Read many stories and poems about insects.
Sang songs about insects.

Application:
Collected insects.
Recorded what was discovered.
Made dioramas, paintings, and drawings.
Reported on research findings.
Constructed a school-wide bulletin board to share information.
Taught and demonstrated at a school-wide science fair as experts on ants.

Analysis:
Compared insects from many aspects.
Contrasted how insects and humans adapt to seasonal changes.
Graphed a variety of ways insects adapt to cold weather.
Synectics: Thought of as many ways as possible to compare an ant with a truck.

Synthesis:
Combined information in order to create and design an insect (including habitat and environment) that might be found on another planet in the future. Hypothesized and predicted how this insect will adapt to its environment. Discussed characteristics of this insect.
Created stories and poems about "Insects that Bug You." (We won a *New York Times* award for this publication.)
Combined two insects into one.

Evaluation:
Discussed and evaluated all original work done by the children with the children.
Held a panel discussion about whether the insects created had a chance to survive in their environment. Children had to substantiate their reasons.

school and grew out of the interests of the children. The activities at each level of thinking were predicted upon the completion of the activities at the preceding level.

In Figures 5-6, 5-7, and 5-8 suggestions are given for fostering the skills of analysis, synthesis, and evaluation for three content areas—math, science, and language arts. Examples of application are also given, since this level may serve as a starting point for teaching higher-level skills. In addition, in a mainstreamed classroom the teaching of application skills is beneficial for the nongifted child.

Math

When higher-level thinking skills are brought into play, children are able to apply math to real problems, thereby making math a meaningful and dynamic experience. Concepts and topics appropriate for a preschool mathematics curriculum include numbers and numeration, addition, equivalence, measurement, geometric shapes, time, and money. The examples of application, analysis, synthesis, and evaluation shown in Figure 5-6 incorporate some of these concepts and topics.

FIGURE 5-6
Suggestions for Fostering Skills in Math

Application:
1. Help the child to see the practical implications of mathematical concepts. Ask how many pennies you need to buy a toy for a nickel. Request the preschooler to count how many days until an event such as a class trip or a holiday. You might ask, "Are there enough napkins for everyone sitting at the table?" Cooking activities offer opportunities to apply concepts of measurement, e.g., cups and teaspoons. You can say, "Tom, will you please cut the cookie in *half*?" or "Sally, pick up the mixing bowl that is lighter."
2. Help the children set up a store for the class to operate. Allow as much independence as possible in making decisions, e.g., what should be sold, what the prices will be, how purchases will be recorded, and what is needed to set the store up.
3. Encourage children to illustrate mathematical operations using a variety of objects—for example, using blocks to illustrate 2 + 2 = 4.

Analysis:
1. Make several puzzles that show patterns of geometric shapes in different colors and sizes. Have the child complete the sequence for each.
Example:
    "Draw (or point to) the shape that comes next."

$$\triangle \quad \bigcirc \quad \square \quad \triangle \quad \bigcirc \quad \square \quad \triangle \quad \underline{\quad}$$

Continued on next page

FIGURE 5-6 (Continued)

2. Give the child several cans in different sizes to arrange according to height. Then fill the cans with various objects and ask the child to order them according to weight.

Synthesis:

1. Ask the preschooler to invent a new money system, making examples of all pieces of money and explaining the system. As an extension of this activity, hold an auction in class. Have the child be the auctioneer and sell items using the new currency for payment.
2. Ask the child to invent a new shape and to give it a name. Ask why the name is appropriate. For example, the child might tell you that
is a combination of a square and a circle and is called a "squircle."
3. Tell children a robber has stolen *all* of the clocks and watches in the city. Ask them to think of ways we can keep track of time until new clocks can be ordered. Encourage each child to give more than one idea.

Evaluation:

1. (a) Ask the child whether it would be better to measure the following items with a ruler or with a yardstick.

an ant	your height
a log	your finger
your house	a car
a baby	a pencil

   (b) Ask the child to decide whether it would be better to measure the following ingredients for chocolate cake with measuring spoons or with measuring cups.

flour	water
salt	sugar
vanilla	cocoa

   (c) Now tell the child that you have a harder job. The class is to make breakfast for Paul Bunyan and his fellow loggers. Tell the story about the famous giant lumberjack. Then ask whether it would be better to measure the following foods (liquids and solids) with jugs or with boxes.

flour for pancakes	milk to drink
milk for pancakes	orange juice
oil for making pancakes	salt and pepper
syrup	eggs

Language Arts

Language arts combine listening, reading, writing, and oral communication. Language can be stimulated through riddles, poetry, folk and fairy tales, dramatic play, rhymes, and stories. Figure 5-7 provides suggestions for fostering skills in this area.

FIGURE 5-7
Suggestions for Fostering Skills in Language Arts

Application

1. If the preschooler knows the alphabet, help look up his or her phone number in the telephone book. Suggest that the child make a phone book with the names, addresses, and phone numbers of friends or classmates.
2. Make statements leaving out the last word. Ask the child to finish the sentence with a word that makes sense. For example, "I want to wear a _____," or "My favorite color is _____," or "Bill threw the _____." A more difficult version of this activity is to leave out a word in the middle or near the beginning of the sentence. For example, "Sally _____her baby brother," or "The _____rode a bike."
3. Ask children to think of rhyming words. For example, words that rhyme with car. Then have them make up a poem containing those rhyming words and dictate it to you.

Analysis:

1. If the child can read, make a puzzle out of his or her dictation. Cut the dictation apart evenly by sentences. Ask the child to order the sentences. You might also cut up dictated sentences by words:

The	house	is	red.

Ask the child either to reconstruct the original sentence or to rearrange the words in new sentences.
2. Designate a "Remember Your Favorite Villain Day." Have each child think of one mischievous deed, dress up as the villain, and act out the steps to pull off the crime.

Synthesis:

1. Have the child pretend that he or she is the greatest cook alive and demonstrate in a "television show" how to make the world's most delicious dish. Encourage the child to use any props or materials that he or she wishes.
2. Provide the child with four pictures that have no inherent order. Ask the child to arrange the pictures any way he or she wants and to tell a story that reflects the arrangement.
3. Set up a center for tape recorded stories without endings. Ask children to dictate or write their own endings.

Evaluation:

1. Bring copies of famous paintings and drawings to class. Ask the children to tell why they like or dislike a particular painting. If several examples of certain artists are available, have the preschoolers pick their favorite artists and tell why.
2. Have preschoolers dictate their own stories to you. After a lapse of time, read a story to its author and ask how it could be improved.

Continued on next page

FIGURE 5-7 (Continued)

3. Ask the children to pretend they are movie critics and to tell about movies they saw recently. Ask them to explain what they liked and disliked in the film. Then have one group of children role-play scenes from a movie or a story. Have another group of children act as movie critics and decide what they liked about the scene.

Science

There is considerable overlap between higher-level thinking skills and the skills needed for scientific inquiry. Typically, the science skills include observing, classifying, experimenting, and hypothesizing. Common topics at the preschool level are the five senses, weather, seasons, air, water, simple laws of nature, insects, plants, and animals. Figure 5-8 presents suggestions for fostering science skills.

FIGURE 5-8
Suggestions for Fostering Skills in Science

Application:
1. After studying about a particular animal, have the children apply the knowledge gained. For example, if the class has studied snakes, encourage independent projects that answer the following questions:
   a. What would you feed a pet snake?
   b. What kind of a house would you make for him?
   c. Where would you look for snakes outside?
2. Show the child how to make a balancing board by placing a long flat board on a fulcrum piece. Demonstrate how to balance two objects. Then let the preschooler experiment with varying numbers of blocks on each end.

Analysis:
1. Give the preschooler two containers of tinted water, an eye dropper, a sheet of waxed paper, and a magnifying lens. Let the child experiment with the materials. Ask the child to explain:
   a. What happened to the water when you dropped it on the waxed paper?
   b. What happened when two drops of water of different colors touched each other?
   c. What did the water do when you dropped it on your arm?
2. Help the child find an ant colony and examine it with a magnifying glass. Put some cookie crumbs nearby and ask the child to guess what the ants will do. After the ants have formed a trail, ask the child what will happen if he or she blocks the trail with a rock. Ask what will happen when you wash part of the trail away with detergent.

Continued on next page

FIGURE 5-8 (Continued)

3. Give the child some worms, water, soil, dark and light paper, a magnifying glass, and a flashlight. Have him take care of the worms for several days. Encourage the child to handle the worms and to use the different materials in experimenting with them. After the preschooler has had a chance to make observations, ask questions about what he or she has seen. "What do worms do in the light?" "How do worms react to water?" "How can you tell which is the front and back of the worm?" Allow the child to share other observations.
4. Help the child sprout alfalfa seeds by soaking them overnight and covering them with a wet towel. Each day have the child take polaroid photos of the sprouting process. Ask the child to describe the changes that have occurred. Use the same procedure to observe other growing processes: a sweet potato, flowers blooming, mold on a piece of bread.

Synthesis:
1. Ask the child to pretend that all the cows have suddenly lost their voices and can no longer moo. Challenge the child to think of a way the cows could communicate with each other. Remind the child that the cows no longer make any noises.
2. Have the child experiment with mixing colors to discover all the new colors he can make. This may be done with colored water, playdough, paints, or food coloring and white sand.
3. Suggest that the child invent a new "being" that is a combination of an insect, an animal, and a fish. Have the child describe this new creation— what it eats, where it lives, how it moves, etc. Ask the child to draw a picture of it.

Evaluation:
1. Ask the child to name his or her favorite food and to tell why he or she likes it better than all others. Do the same for animals, insects, fish, plants, etc.
2. Have the child pretend that a magic fairy will turn him or her into either a machine or an animal. Ask the child to decide which he or she would like to be and explain that choice.

Asking Questions to Stimulate Higher-Level Thinking

Figure 5-9 offers key words and phrases that teachers can use to stimulate thinking within Bloom's Taxonomy.

Challenging the Gifted Using an Eclectic Approach

The previous sections have given examples of how to stimulate divergent thinking using the SOI conceptual framework and higher-level thinking pro-

FIGURE 5-9
Stimulating Higher Level Thinking

Level Within Bloom's Taxonomy	*Key Words and Phrases*
Knowledge	Relate, list, tell, state, identify, describe, name
Comprehension	Tell in your own words, describe your feelings about, summarize, show the relationships, explain the meaning
Application	Demonstrate, show the use of, use it to solve
Analysis	Take apart, explain the causes of, compare and contrast, order, arrange, explain how and why
Synthesis	Design a new product, create, what would happen if, think of a new way, restate, think of another reason
Evaluation	Set standards for, select and choose, weigh the possibilities, criticize, choose your favorite, how do you feel about.

cesses using Bloom's Taxonomy. Figure 5-10 gives an example of how a teacher may draw from various conceptual models to differentiate curriculum for the gifted. An attempt has been made to suggest the types of questions or responses the teacher should solicit from the average child and from the gifted child. It was felt that teachers need to differentiate instruction for the gifted within a classroom made up of a wide range of abilities, especially since mainstreaming gifted children in regular classes is currently the most approved administrative plan.

FIGURE 5-10
Examples of Differentiated Curriculum

1. LIVING THINGS
Objective (Average): The child will give the two characteristics he or she believes are best for grouping objects as living and nonliving things and will give reasons for the choice.

Continued on next page

FIGURE 5-10 (Continued)

Objective (Gifted): The child will give as many characteristics as he or she can think of that can be used to group objects as living and nonliving things. The child will give reasons for the choices.

Materials for the teacher: Chalkboard, chalk, black construction paper, jars, turtle, worm, cat, grass, fish, pictures of animals.

Materials for the student: None.

TEACHER/CHILD INTERACTION	COGNITIVE PROCESS FOSTERED
"When we look around the room and outside on the playground we see many different things, and there are many ways we can group these things. Let's name some of those ways.	Fluency Flexibility
You can aid the average child by giving examples. For instance, "We could put everything green in one group and everything red in another and so on. Or put everything you can eat in one group and everything you cannot eat in another. Can anyone think of some other ways of grouping all the objects in the room and on the playground?"	Fluency Flexibility
For every child, encourage divergent thinking. For example, "Let's think of as many unusual ideas as we can. Be very creative."	Originality Creativity
"One way scientists group things is by seeing differences between living and nonliving things. Today we are going to learn how we can tell living things from nonliving things by discovering how all living things are alike. We will be studying their characteristics."	
"Who knows how we could discover the characteristics of living things?"	Originality
(A child answers: "By watching living things.")	
"That's one way. I've brought some living things to class so we can observe them. I have a turtle, a worm, a cat, a piece of grass, and a fish. Does anyone have anything to add to the group?" *(A student and a plant might be added.)* "In order to discover characteristics of living things, let's make a change in them and see how it affects them."	
"Bill, what is something we could do to all of the living things to see what effect it would have on them?"	Originality
"What is another way?"	Fluency
"Can you think of an entirely different way?"	Flexibility

Continued on next page

FIGURE 5-10 (Continued)

TEACHER/CHILD INTERACTION	COGNITIVE PROCESS FOSTERED
Examples of changes include depriving the living things of air, of food, and of water. For the gifted child you can ask what would happen if you deprived the living things of air, for example. For the average child you can actually make the change in the living things' environment. For example, you can put the plant in an air-tight container and watch the change in its behavior. For changes you cannot demonstrate (for example, depriving human beings of air), ask the child to imagine a situation where the change would occur. Examples are a swimmer caught in a rope at the bottom of the ocean and a man buried underground. Show the student a picture of the situation. For examples of the effect on the living thing, ask the student: "What would (or did) happen to the plant (man, fish, etc.)?"	Knowledge
Following all the examples, ask the child: "So what happened to all of the living things when they did not have any (air)?" "What do all living things need?"	Comprehension
After different changes have been applied, discussion about the characteristics of living things can continue, using some of the following questions to promote productive thinking.	
"What is another characteristic of all living things?" "Can you tell me of yet another characteristic?"	Fluency
"I like that idea, but can you tell me of another characteristic that is entirely different from the one you just gave?"	Flexibility
"Think of a characteristic that occurs when any living thing dies."	Synthesis
"Think of a characteristic of all living things that no one else has thought of before. Everyone give the most unusual idea you can."	Originality Creativity
"I like your idea but could you describe your characteristic in more detail?"	Elaboration
"Do you think your characteristic would be true for all living things?"	Evaluation
"What could you add to your characteristic that would make it true for *all* living things?"	Elaboration
"You believe that all living things move. Trees are living things. Do trees move from one place in the ground to another? In what way do they move? How do you know that is true? Is your evaluation based on actual observation, fact, or opinion?"	Critical Thinking

Continued on next page

FIGURE 5-10 (Continued)

TEACHER/CHILD INTERACTION	COGNITIVE PROCESS FOSTERED
EVALUATION	
''We were able to list many characteristics of living things. (*Read them.*) Now I want each of you to choose the two characteristics you believe are the best for grouping objects as living or nonliving and also to give your reasons for your choice.''	Evaluation Critical Thinking

The gifted child should choose characteristics under a specific restriction. For instance:
1. *The student has a short time to group the objects.*
2. *The student must sort the objects in the dark.*
3. *The student can only see pictures of the objects and will not have the objects themselves to group.*
4. *The student can choose only one characteristic.*

Have the gifted child give reasons for his or her choices.

FOLLOW-UP ACTIVITIES	
1. ''The 'Build Anything Engineering Firm' would like our class to construct a machine that groups objects into living and nonliving based on the characteristics of living things. Before our class makes the machine, I would like each of you to submit plans for it.	Originality
You may select any of the characteristics we discovered and as many as you wish. Be sure to draw in detail the part of the machine that would test each characteristic you selected. Label your parts. Color your machine and give it a name.''	Critical Thinking
After each child draws a machine, have the class decide on a plan for the machine to be constructed (it may be based on one child's drawing or on a combination of several children's drawings). Construct the machine out of materials decided upon by the class (cardboard, papier maché, etc.).	Evaluation
2. *Independent projects for the gifted include studying how a fish breathes through its gills and examining the food needed by plants.*	Independent Study Skill Critical Thinking
3. *Have the children study such invertebrates as anemones, list their characteristics, and compare them to the characteristics of living things.*	Analysis Synthesis Evaluation Critical Thinking Independent Study Skills Analysis Evaluation Observation Skills Class Reasoning

Continued on next page

FIGURE 5-10 (Continued)

VOCABULARY TO BE INCORPORATED INTO THE LESSON

Characteristics
Environment
Deprived
Divergent
Sort
Restrictions
Anemones

2. PETS

Objective (Average): When shown three pictures of pets and three pictures of nonpets (pictures that provide clues as to whether the animals are pets or nonpets), each child will give one correct reason for each picture why each animal is a pet or not a pet.

Objective (Gifted): Each child will be shown two sets of pictures containing two pictures each, one of a wild animal and another of a pet of the same species. The teacher will tell a story giving pertinent information about the animals. When asked to give two reasons why each pet is a pet and two reasons why each wild animal is not a pet, each child will give three-fourths correct answers.

Materials for the teacher: Pictures of pets that contain clues that they are pets; two sets of pictures containing two pictures each, one of a wild animal and another of a pet of the same species; and pictures of animals that are not pets, containing clues that they are not pets.

Materials for the student: None.

TEACHER/CHILD INTERACTION	COGNITIVE PROCESS FOSTERED
Have each child bring pictures of his or her pet to school. (If a child does not have a picture, have the child draw one. If a child does not have a pet, help the child select a picture of an imaginary pet.) Lay all of the pictures on the table and have the children say that the animals are pets.	Knowledge
Have each child tell about his or her pet—how big it is, how to take care of it, whether you can play with it, etc.	
After everyone has an opportunity to tell about his or her pet, talk about the characteristics of all pets.	Comprehension
"People have many different pets. Bill has a pet cat, Tom a pet snake, and Marianne has a pet worm. They are very	

Continued on next page

FIGURE 5-10 (Continued)

TEACHER/CHILD INTERACTION	COGNITIVE PROCESS FOSTERED
different from each other, but they are all pets. Let's list the things that make them all pets.''	
Have the children give their answers. The following questions may be used to help the children evaluate and analyze their answers.	
''Would that be true for a pet porcupine?'' (*The average child will need a picture of a porcupine.*)	Analysis
''Would that be true for Tommy's pet snake?''	Analysis
''Could you explain your answer in more detail?''	Elaboration
Encourage the children to be fluent and flexible. ''Bill, you have already thought of one trait of a pet. Can you think of another?''	Fluency
''Sally, think of a trait of a pet unlike any trait named so far. Be as original and creative as you can.''	Fluency Originality Creativity
In addition, the following questions can be used to help the average child think of traits of pets.	
''Could we tell by what an animal ate whether or not it was a pet?''	Analysis
''Could we tell by an animal's color whether or not it was a pet?''	Analysis
''Could we tell by where an animal slept whether or not it was a pet?''	Analysis
''How are a pet dog and a pet cat alike?''	Synthesis Direct Analogy
''How are a pet horse and a pet canary alike?''	Synthesis Direct Analogy
After all the children have the opportunity to answer, read the list of traits to the class.	
''We do have many traits. Are there any traits that you believe do not define a pet? Why?''	Evaluation Critical Thinking
Allow time for all the children to submit answers and give reasons and to disagree and tell why. Erase traits the class decides do not define a pet.	Evaluation Critical Thinking
''The traits we have left over make up a definition of a pet. Let's read them together.''	

Continued on next page

FIGURE 5-10 (Continued)

TEACHER/CHILD INTERACTION	COGNITIVE PROCESS FOSTERED
"Now let's each of us take turns giving the definition of a pet. State it in your own words."	Comprehension
The average child may have to recite parts of the definition after you.	Knowledge

EVALUATION

Average Child: Show the child pictures providing clues to whether an animal is a pet or not (for example, a boy playing ball with a dog, a lion crouching in the grass). When shown three pictures of pets and three pictures of nonpets, each child will give one reason for each picture why each animal is a pet or is not a pet.	Comprehension Analysis Synthesis
Gifted Child: Show two sets of pictures containing two pictures each, one of a wild animal and another of a pet of the same species. Tell a story about the two animals, depicting their lives. Ask each child to give two reasons why each pet is a pet and two reasons why each wild animal is not a pet. Each child should give at least three correct answers.	Synthesis Evaluation

FOLLOW-UP ACTIVITIES

"If you were a pet, what kind would you be? What about you would make you a good pet? What would you eat? How would you act? What would your master do for you? Where would you sleep? Tape a story of 'A Day and Night in the Life of a Pet.' Make a storybook about yourself."	Synthesis Personal Analogy
"You are a pet dog; however, one day some wild dogs come to your pen. You recognize your mother, father, and brother in the pack of wild dogs. They urge you to come with them on their roamings. What would you have to change to become a wild dog? Tell your story. Illustrate if you wish."	Synthesis Personal Analogy
"Pretend there were no pets for anyone in the world. How do you think people would feel? If persons liked walking their dogs, playing with their cats, playing ball with their pet monkeys, what could they do instead?"	Originality Creativity
"Do you believe a nonliving thing could be a pet? Why or why not? List three reasons why it could be a pet and three reasons why it could not be."	Critical Thinking
"Choose a nonliving thing to be a pet. List the advantages and disadvantages of having a nonliving thing for a pet."	Critical thinking

Continued on next page

FIGURE 5-10 (Continued)

VOCABULARY TO BE INCORPORATED INTO THE LESSON

Pet
Definition
Advantages
Disadvantages
Names of unusual animals
Traits
Creative
Original

SUMMARY

This chapter has highlighted the following points:

- A curriculum for gifted children is influenced by (a) characteristics, needs, and interests of the gifted child; (b) goals of the parents for the child and the extent of parent involvement; (c) the basic philosophy and goals that underlie a program; (d) attributes, attitudes, and values of the teacher; (e) breadth of instructional materials; (f) physical make-up of the classroom and the pupil/teacher ratio; (g) supportive services; (h) availability of community resources and the attitude of the community toward programs for the gifted; (i) financial allocations; and (j) supervisory and administrative support.
- Conceptual models that combine to form a framework for curriculum help teachers of gifted children to be more thoughtful in planning and assist in the development of ongoing educational objectives. There is no single best conceptual model to use in developing curricula for the gifted, and many teachers prefer an eclectic approach that relies on more than one conceptual model. Teachers, however, must be committed to whatever models are used.
- The gifted child may be superior in many respects; however, the gifted child is not equally accelerated in all aspects of development. A gifted child may be reading at the third grade level at age 4 but emotionally and socially may be more like children of similar chronological age. Thus, curricula objectives and goals must reflect knowledge of the child's stages of development and needs.
- Meeting the needs of the young gifted child is not equivalent to providing more of the same; neither is an appropriate curriculum for the gifted merely a sequence of tasks of increasing difficulty presented at a faster than normal pace. The curriculum must be qualitatively different.
- Care must be taken to prevent gaps in the gifted child's learning. It is essential that gifted children learn the basic skills so that they will be able to engage in higher-level thinking processes.

- The teacher of the gifted must be a good observer and match the stage of development of the gifted child with activities that are both challenging and of interest to the child and take into consideration the child's developmental stage and the likelihood of success.
- Teachers of the gifted must not overlook the importance of helping the child develop interpersonal skills and a healthy, positive self-concept. One of the goals of any gifted program is to enhance the social/affective development of the young gifted child.
- Critical to helping gifted children reach their potential is the development of attitudes and habits that ensure task commitment. Both teacher and family members play a significant role through encouraging and reinforcing the gifted child's efforts.
- Teachers of the gifted should help them acquire the skills needed to become independent learners.
- Teachers of the gifted must recognize that each gifted child is different: individualized programs such as those mandated for handicapped children are a valid procedure to use with gifted children. Parents of the gifted should be an integral part of the interdisciplinary team that designs the child's educational plan.
- Two essential curricular goals for gifted children are the development of creative thinking and higher-level thinking skills. Although it is essential to teach gifted children thinking skills, no curriculum should exist solely for that purpose. It is important that the content of learning be meaningful to the child and that it be explored in depth.
- It is not sufficient for a teacher of the gifted to set aside a block of time for promoting creative and productive thinking and higher-level thinking processes. These skills should be encouraged throughout the school day.
- It is especially important for parents of the young gifted child to be involved in differentiating a curriculum for their gifted child. As stressed in Chapter 8, when the school and home combine forces, the gifted child is more likely to maximize his or her potential.

REFERENCES

Bailey, D., & Leonard, J. A model for adapting Bloom's Taxonomy to a preschool curriculum for the gifted. *The Gifted Child Quarterly,* 1977, *21,* 97–103.

Bloom, B., Engelhart, M., Furst, E., Hill, W., & Krathwohl, D. *Taxonomy of educational objectives: The classification of educational goals.* New York: David McKay, 1956.

Callahan, C. *Developing creativity in gifted and talented.* Reston VA: The Council for Exceptional Children, 1978.

Chertoff, B. *Insect unit based on Bloom's Taxonomy.* Unpublished manuscript, 1979. (Available from Public School 221, District 26, Queens NY.)

Feldhusen, J., & Kolloff, M. Giftedness: A mixed blessing for the preschool child. In S. Loug & B. Batch, *Where there is crisis: Helping children cope with change.* Indiana Association for the Education of Young Children, 1979.

Feldhusen, J., & Treffinger, D. *Creative thinking and problem solving in gifted education.* Dubuque IA: Kendall/Hunt Publishing, 1980.

Fine, M. Facilitating parent-child relationships for creativity. *The Gifted Child Quarterly,* 1977, *21,* 487–499.

Gallagher, J. *Teaching the gifted child.* Boston: Allyn & Bacon, 1975.

Guilford, J. Three faces of intellect. *The American Psychologist,* 1959, *14,* 469–479.

Guilford, J. Creativity: Yesterday, today, tomorrow. *Journal of Creative Behavior,* 1967, *1,* 3–14. (a)

Guilford, J. *The nature of human intelligence.* New York: McGraw-Hill, 1967. (b)

Kagan, J. Personality and the learning process. In J. Kagan (Ed.), *Creativity and learning.* Boston: Houghton Mifflin, 1967.

Kaplan, S. *Providing programs for the gifted and talented: A handbook.* Ventura CA: Office of the Ventura County Superintendent of Schools, 1974.

Kaplan, S. *Curricular and programmatic concerns: Educating the preschool/primary gifted and talented.* Ventura CA: Ventura County Superintendent of Schools, 1980.

Karnes, M. *Lesson plans for promoting creative and productive thinking.* Unpublished field test versions. Urbana IL: University of Illinois, 1979, 1980, 1981, 1982.

Karnes, M., Shwedel, A., & Williams, M. Combining instructional models for young gifted children. *TEACHING Exceptional Children,* 1983, *15*(3), 128–135.

Leonard, J. *Chapel Hill Services to the Gifted/Handicapped: Program description of a demonstration project for preschool children.* A project summary. Chapel Hill NC: Chapel Hill Training Outreach Project, 1978.

Maker, C. *Curriculum development for the gifted.* Rockville MD: Aspen Systems, 1982.

Marland, S., Jr. *Education of the gifted and talented* (Vol. 1). Washington DC: U.S. Government Printing Office, 1971.

Newman, J., Dember, D., & Krug, O. He can but he won't. *Psychoanalytic Study of the Child,* 1973, *28,* 83–129.

Passow, A. Fostering creativity in the gifted child. *Exceptional Children,* 1977, *43,* 358–364.

Passow, A. *Differentiated curricula for the gifted/talented.* Ventura CA: National/State Leadership Training Institute on the Gifted and the Talented, 1982.

Renzulli, J. *The enrichment triad model: A guide for developing defensible programs for the gifted and talented.* Wethersfield CT: Creative Learning Press, 1977.

Renzulli, J., & Smith, L. Developing defensible programs for the gifted and talented. *Journal of Creative Behavior,* 1978, *12*(1), 21–30.

Renzulli, J., & Smith, L. A practical model for designing individualized education programs (IEPs) for gifted and talented students. In *Developing IEPs for the gifted/talented.* Ventura CA: Office of the Ventura County Superintendent of Schools, 1979.

Renzulli, J., Smith, L., & Reis, S. Curriculum compacting: An essential strategy for working with gifted students. *The Elementary School Journal,* 1982, *82*(3), 185–194.

Roedell, W., & Robinson, H. *Programming for intellectually advanced preschool children,* 1977. (ERIC Document Reproduction Service No. ED 151 094)

Sisk, D. A. Helping children know themselves. In B. Cherry (Ed.), *A handbook of bright ideas: Facilitating giftedness.* Manatee FL: Manatee Gifted Program, Manatee Junior College, 1976. (ERIC Document Reproduction Service No. ED 135 174)

Starkweather, E. Creativity research instrument designed for use with preschool children. *Journal of Creative Behavior,* 1971, *5*(4), 245–255.

Sumption, M., Norris, D., & Terman, L. Special education for the gifted child. In S. Kirk (Ed.), *The education of exceptional children.* 49th yearbook of the National Society for the Study of Education, Part II. Chicago: University of Chicago Press, 1952.

Taba, H. *Teaching strategies and cognitive functioning in elementary school children.* Cooperative Research Project No. 2404. Office of Education, HEW. San Francisco State College, 1966.

Treffinger, D. Teaching for self-directed learning: A priority for the gifted and talented. *The Gifted Child Quarterly,* 1974, *19,* 45–49.

Treffinger, D. Guidelines for encouraging independence and self-direction among gifted students. *Journal of Creative Behavior,* 1978, *12*(1), 14–19, 51.

Treffinger, D. Individualized education program plans for gifted, talented and creative students. In *Developing IEPs for the gifted/talented.* Ventura CA: Office of the Ventura County Superintendent of Schools, 1979.

Ward, V. *Differential education for the gifted.* Ventura CA: National/State Leadership Training on the Gifted and the Talented, Office of the Ventura County Superintendent of Schools, 1980.

Williams, F. *Classroom ideas for encouraging thinking and feeling.* Buffalo NY: DOK Publishers, 1970.

Williams, F. Models for encouraging creativity in the classroom. In J. C. Gowan, *Educating the ablest.* Itasca IL: F. E. Peacock, 1971.

Zilli, M. Reasons why the gifted adolescent underachieves and some of the implications of guidance and counseling to the problem. *The Gifted Child Quarterly,* 1971, *15,* 279–292.

CHAPTER 6

Affective Development

Kippy I. Abroms

Why devote an entire chapter to affective development? For many teachers this is a rhetorical question. The merits of affective education have been articulated by Dewey (1938), Krathwohl, Bloom, and Masia (1964), and others. Yet the implementation of affective education continues to receive low priority in the curriculum.

In the case of gifted preschoolers this is especially distressing. The extreme sensitivity of these children to their environment; their vulnerability to distortions of self-esteem; and the dynamic relationship between emotional status, adjustment, and academic achievement make affective intervention an unequivocal part of their education. Thus, it follows that affective education should be preventive as well as remedial.

What are appropriate affective goals for gifted preschoolers? Three goals are immediately apparent:

1. To develop an adequate self-concept and self-esteem.
2. To increase the child's awareness of and sensitivity to others.
3. To promote social competency.

Parents must assume a dual role in the attainment of these goals. They must realize that good parenting is good educating. Teachers have the same responsibility as they become "significant others" in the affective development of young children.

Feelings and emotions do not develop in a void. They evolve within a social context and are related to self, others, and things (Morse, Ardizzone, MacDonald, & Pasick, 1980). Thus, this chapter addresses the affective development of preschool gifted children in tandem with their social development, highlighting milestones that occur from birth through age 5. Parent and teacher behaviors, materials, and climates for promoting optimal affective development are juxtaposed against affective milestones, suggesting a developmental-sequential approach in preschool affective education.

EARLY CONTACT WITH THE SOCIAL ENVIRONMENT

The birth cry announcing "I'm here" is the infant's first affective contact. The cry sound "stimulates strong feelings and distinct reactions from almost everyone within earshot" (Ostwald & Peltzman, 1974). Just a few weeks later, the infant uses differentiated crying to communicate a variety of feelings to his or her primary caretakers—hunger, anger, distress, pain (Wolff, 1973). Among infants subsequently identified as gifted, differentiated crying may occur as early as 4 to 10 days after birth (Karelitz, Fisichelli, Costa, Karelitz, & Rosenfeld, 1964). These studies clearly illustrate a major premise concerning affective development: that affective behavior is socially learned through interactions with others.

Babies are equipped with other mechanisms that promote early interpersonal contact. Observations of 2-week-old infants suggest that infants discriminate between the faces of their mothers and those of strangers (Carpenter, Teece, Steckler, & Friedman, 1970). In the realm of auditory perception it appears that infants as young as 1 month are able to discriminate between adult phonemes of voiceless /p/ and voiced /b/ (Eimas, Siqueland, Jusczyk, & Vigorito, 1971). Rheingold (1961) has suggested that early perceptual contact may be the primary basis for social development.

At 6 weeks most babies start to smile, a behavior "so designed as to melt all but absolutely frozen hearts" (White, 1975). In essence, each of the developmental milestones mentioned thus far serves to bring about and sustain contact with primary caretakers. The contact is reciprocal: The child socializes the parents and the parents socialize the child! The warm, timely, nurturing behaviors that the infant secures from adults form the basis for attachment, a relationship that is generally expressed at about 6 months and maintains its intensity until about 18 months (Bowlby, 1969).

The construct of attachment is supported by the following examples of infant behaviors that occur during this period:

> Protest at separation from the parent, use of the parent as a secure base from which to explore the environment, approaching the parent, fear of strangers, smiling and vocalizing to the parent, and clinging to the parent. (Meyer & Dusek, 1979, p. 390)

It is presumed that responsiveness to the infant, the building up of a secure relationship between infant and primary caretaker(s), leads to infant feelings of security, well-being, and confidence. A number of studies demonstrating increased infant exploratory behaviors in the presence of the primary caretaker have been interpreted to support this premise (Ainsworth & Bell, 1970; Rheingold, 1969).

DEVELOPMENT OF SELF-CONCEPT AND SELF-ESTEEM

Expressions of "I," "Me," "Mine," "His," and "Hers," are presumed to serve as markers of an underlying self-concept. Most children express these revealing pronouns around the age of 2 years. Gifted children, often characterized by verbal precocity, tend to express such indicators at a younger age. In reality, the development of self-concept has been going on since birth both for children who are subsequently identified as gifted and for those who are not.

Selma Fraiberg (1959) has presented a delightful representation of the developing self-concept:

> . . . The infant is conducting a series of complicated experiments in sensory discrimination. We must remember that in the early months he does not discriminate between his body and other bodies. When he clutches the finger of his mother or his father he doesn't see it as someone else's finger and his behavior indicates that he treats it exactly the same as he does his own finger. It takes him some time, in fact, to recognize his own hand at sight and to acquire even a rudimentary feeling that this is part of his own body. In the first group of experiments he discovers that the object that passes occasionally in front of his eyes (which *we* know to be his hand) is the same as the object that he introduces into his mouth. It now becomes one object with visual and taste qualities that he can identify. In another experimental series he discovers that the sensations that accompany the introduction of *this* object into his mouth are different from those experienced when he takes a nipple in his mouth, or a toy, or his mother's or father's finger. . . . To us, this seems to be a commonplace observation. . . . But for the infant this has to be discovered. . . . Gradually he sorts out the data into two main categories which eventually become "me" feelings and "other" feelings. (pp. 43–44)

T. Berry Brazelton (1974) masterfully presented vignettes of 15-month-old Tony in play group. There is little doubt that interaction with peers contributed significantly to the development of Tony's self-concept:

> When it was time for juice and crackers, the children all sat around a table. The mothers ranged themselves at a distance, but watched this event. Mrs. Belew was horrified to see Tony grabbing all of the crackers, and jumped to intervene. Again, another mother stopped her and said, "Leave it to them." The boy seated next to Tony pulled Tony's juice cup away, leaving Tony with his hoard of crackers but no juice. When Tony protested and started to reach for his cup, the boy said "No" loudly. Tony seemed to interpret this correctly, shoved the crackers out toward the middle of the table, extracted his juice, and the party continued. (pp. 81–82).

With very little speech Tony clearly discerned peer perceptions of himself. Furthermore, his peers thrust knowledge upon Tony that he is separate and apart from other beings.

These narratives lead us to the question, "Specifically, what is self-concept?" Self-concept can be thought of as an integration of all of the child's experiences. These experiences form images, commonly delineated as follows:

1. Physical self, an image of one's body and its functions.
2. Social self, an image of how others perceive and respond to oneself.
3. Real self, an image of how one compares with others.
4. Ideal self, an image of the abilities, attributes, and relationships one values most and aspires to.

The composite of images and experiences leads to a sense of being, an awareness of self.

Numerous studies of academic underachievement (Gallagher & Crowder, 1957; Karnes, McCoy, Zehrbach, Wollersheim, Clarizo, Costin, & Stanley, 1961; Shaw & McCuen, 1960) have suggested the existence of a significant relationship between poor self-concept and underachievement. Cotter's (1967) study of first grade failures cogently indicated the importance of affective education during the preschool years. By age 2 many clever children experience a conflict between social self and real self due, in large part, to unrealistic expectations foisted upon them by adults.

Advanced verbal skills are often indicated in the distortion of adult perceptions of the gifted child's overall developmental level. For example, a gifted preschooler known by the author abandoned her neighborhood Halloween trick or treating activities because one naïve old lady expected this precocious child literally to perform a trick or to recite a poem as a prerequisite for her Halloween dole. Fortunately, our gifted youngster refused to sing for her supper.

In some cases knowledge of a child's giftedness can seduce parents to set unrealistic expectations and to use their gifted child as a vehicle for self-aggrandizement and fulfillment of previous disappointments (Freeman, 1979). Furthermore, the child's right to be a child can be at stake due to adult-imposed expectations that the child continue to achieve at successively higher levels.

Self-concept is derived, in great part, through interactions with other people. During the earliest years the development of self-concept revolves around "significant others"—parents or primary caretakers. Gifted 2-year-olds are characterized by their supersensitivity to the physical and social environment, enormous curiosity, risk-taking, and advanced cognitive and verbal skills ("When was yesterday?" "Where is tomorrow?"). When coupled with a high energy level they may innocently appear to push significant others to the limits.

It is not uncommon for a mother of a gifted preschooler to express physical and mental exhaustion after sustained contact with her child. "Some even are irritated by the child's persistent questioning and verbalization and they tend to react in ways that the child perceives as indifference or rejection" (Whitmore, 1980, p. 149). This type of parental behavior can lead to poor self-concept at an early age. The gifted child sees these behaviors as a negative reflection of himself and incorporates them into his self-concept.

Whitmore (1980) has contended that self-esteem exerts a greater influence upon behavior than does self-concept. She has defined self-esteem as "the measure of worth and accompanying feelings attached to the self-image one holds" (p. 177). Furthermore, Whitmore has expressed the belief that self-esteem is jeopardized by too great a discrepancy between the real self and the ideal self.

As stated earlier, young gifted children are highly vulnerable to distortions of self-esteem. An incident involving a precocious preschooler observed by the author serves as an example:

> Martha, age 3, was at the art table. "I'm gonna paste a triangle, a square, and a circle on here!" she exclaimed, waving a piece of construction paper for her teacher to see.
>
> Martha reached for a pair of scissors and strips of brightly colored paper. She diligently began cutting out the shapes for her project. Martha was deeply engrossed in the task when suddenly she cried out, "I'm stupid. Stupid."
>
> With that she threw her arms down in disgust and sobbed over to the nature table.

Martha was experiencing a discrepancy between her real self and her ideal self. Given Martha's advanced cognitive skills, she aspired to create a somewhat sophisticated collage. Unfortunately Martha's developmental level in fine motor skills, although quite adequate for her age, did not allow her to obtain her goal. Kirk (1972) has offered a valid summary statement:

> The child's intellectual abilities are growing nearly twice as fast as is usual, and it is too much to expect physical and emotional processes to keep pace with such rapid development. . . . Furthermore, the greatest deviation occurs at a time when he is least able to understand and handle it, that is, during the early school years. (p. 133)

Teacher Sensitivity to Self-Concept and Self-Esteem

Affective education is an ongoing process. Teachers must seize the teaching moment! In the case of Martha, there were a number of verbal and behavioral responses that the teacher could use to help to alleviate Martha's discomfort as well as stimulate discussion and provide insight for Martha. As Whitmore (1980) remarked, "All gifted children need adult assistance in learning to cope with the tendency to hold unreasonably high self-expectations" (p. 183).

> *"This is not what you had in mind, is it? How can we make this come out the way you wanted it?"*

If the child wishes to recover the project then the teacher's joint participation can remove some of the responsibility from the child or, if the project does not, in fact, turn out right then the teacher can assume some of the responsibility, again alleviating the enormous burden the child has innocently placed upon herself. However, a discussion of "How do you plan to do it next time?" is an important mediator for the future.

Another teacher response might be, "You really would like that to be finished perfectly, wouldn't you?" or "It just isn't quite the way you want it yet, is it?" By paraphrasing the child's convert concerns, the teacher indicates to the child that she is sensitive to the child's distress and also opens up avenues for discussion.

Parents and teachers can use other leading phrases that invite affective exploration following a variety of critical incidents. These include:

"How do you feel about it?"
"Tell me more about it."
"How does it look to you?"
"What do you think you would like to do about it?"
"What seems to get in the way most?"
"How would you go about it?"
"How would you go about it next time?"
"How do you suppose it will work out?"
"Why do you suppose you feel that way?"
"What was it like?"

Activities to Enhance Self-Concept and Self-Esteem

Not only is affective education ongoing, it is preventive and remedial. All preschool teaching requires careful structuring of the environment. Activities must be planned in terms of the growth and development of the whole child— not just in terms of cognitive functioning.

The following sequence of suggested themes, activities, and materials is by no means exhaustive. Rather, it is presented as a guide and a stimulus for teaching one aspect of affective education, self-concept and self-esteem.

Body Awareness

This basic level focuses upon teaching children specific parts of the body: names, movements, and functions. There are a number of songs ("The Hokey Pokey," "Head and Shoulders, Knees and Toes"), movement activities, and stories (*The Foot Book, The Ear Book*) to augment the initial presentation of body parts. Commercially prepared affective development programs such as *Know Me, Know You* by Merle Karnes (1983) and *Beginning Concepts* by Scholastic Magazine (1972) provide filmstrips on body parts accompanied by cassette narrations.

Understanding Self

Growth and individuality are stressed. Children are encouraged to bring in photos of themselves taken from birth onward. Changes in development are pointed out and discussed. Complimentary nature settings in the classroom (incubator with chicken eggs, ongoing metamorphosis of butterflies; frog eggs in "pond") provide for comparisons, synthesis, evaluation, and reinforcement. Individuality can be presented through the Mystery Box game (Elardo & Cooper, 1977), in which the uniqueness of each child is heightened by discovering a reflection of himself or herself in the Mystery Box. *Developing Understanding of Self and Others (DUSO)* by Don Dinkmeyer (1970) provides some excellent posters ("I am the only me in the world"; "I am glad that I am ME") as well as illustrated stories that point out unique attributes and differences among individuals.

It's OK to Be Me

This is a key theme for gifted children in light of their vulnerability to anguishing discrepancies among the various images contributing to self-concept and self-esteem. Gifted children need to know that it is alright to make mistakes. Injecting humor through absurdities in art and story (*Amelia Bedelia* is a superb example); showing examples of how society does, in fact, expect everyone to make mistakes (pencils with erasers, liquid paper, bumpers on automobiles); and discussing how people have both assets and liabilities (Sammy Davis, Jr., Walt Disney) allows children to identify with the humanness of imperfection. Children need to be reminded of patterns of growth that determine when certain things can and cannot be achieved.

Feelings

Children need to know that experiencing and expressing feelings are an integral part of self. There are a number of filmstrips that graphically introduce feelings (Anderson, Lang, & Scott, 1970; Dinkmeyer, 1970; Kindle, 1970) as well as books (*Let's Be Enemies, Where the Wild Things Are*). Group discussions pointing out comfortable and uncomfortable feelings and sensory experiences (hot soup, cold ice cream, wet clothes, dry feet) are an integral part of introducing feelings to children.

SUMMARY OF DEVELOPMENT OF SELF-CONCEPT AND SELF-ESTEEM

The development of self-concept begins at birth, with the infant gradually organizing his or her perceptions in a manner that culminates in the distinction between "Me" and "Not Me." Advanced verbal skills among the gifted typically provide for validation of the existence of self-concept at an earlier age than is demonstrated among average-ability children. The gifted are highly vulnerable to insults and distortions of self-concept because of their sensitivity to the social and physical environment and because of their advanced verbal and cognitive processing abilities. In many ways inconsistent expectations are held for gifted children, causing dissonance between the social self and the real self. Furthermore, young gifted children often appear to set high, perfectionistic standards for themselves, causing dissonance between the ideal self and the real self that may lead to low self-esteem. Research indicates that self-concept is pervasively related to a child's behaviors, including achievement in school. Overall, it appears that self-concept remains somewhat malleable during the preschool years and thus amenable to both preventive and remedial affective measures.

Affective education is an ongoing process. The climate of the classroom, provisions for individual differences, attitudes, verbal and nonverbal communication, and proximity and timeliness of responses all reflect examples of teacher participation in affective education. A number of leading questions and phrases to be used by teachers for promoting greater self-awareness and a sequence of themes for exploring self-concept in the classroom have been presented as ways of further implementing affective education in relation to the young gifted child's self-concept.

AWARENESS OF AND SENSITIVITY TO OTHERS

Social Cognition

The emergence of self-concept subsumes an awareness of others, separate and distinct from the self. Does this awareness include social cognition, a form of role-taking in which the child makes inferences about the thoughts, affect, intentions, and viewpoints of others?

Apparently by age 3 most children differentiate between happy and unhappy reactions in other people (Borke, 1973). There is some evidence suggesting that gifted 3-year-olds differentiate between afraid and mad when presented with laboratory tasks on the Borke Interpersonal Awareness Test (Abroms & Gollin, 1980). In this test the child is asked to identify, by pointing to one of four faces representing the feelings of happy, sad, afraid, or mad, how another child would feel under conditions narrated by the experimenter. For example, the child is told "Show me how Nancy would feel if you gave her some ice cream."

Other types of role-taking tasks assess the child's ability to (a) infer another's visual experience and (b) infer another's thoughts, knowledge, or needs. Piaget and Inhelder's three-mountain task (1956) is illustrative of paradigms used to assess the first level of role-taking, visual perspective role-taking.

Flavell, Botkin, Fry, Wright, and Jarvis' (1968) birthday tasks are illustrative of the second level, conceptual role-taking. In their paradigm the child is told to pretend that he or she is in a store. After the experimenter names a series of items on the "counter" the child is told: "Pretend it is the birthday of _____. What would you give him/her for a present?'' Pretend recipients include father, mother, brother (or friend who is a boy), sister (or friend who is a girl) and the child. Flavell et al. (1968) and Zahn-Waxler, Radke-Yarrow, and Brady-Smith (1977) found what they interpreted as evidence of conceptual role-taking in children 3 and 4 years old.

Prosocial Behavior

A study of upper middle class gifted 3-year-olds (Abroms & Gollin, 1980) suggested the presence of similar skills, with higher correlations in the spring than in the fall between performance on social cognitive tasks and IQ. When the relationship between social cognition and prosocial behaviors (spontaneously sharing, helping, responding to another's distress, providing physical affection during free play time at nursery school) was examined, the data indicated that, for this particular sample, gifted children showed trends in prosocial behaviors similar to those expressed by nongifted preschoolers in a naturalistic setting. There was a slight increase in the frequency of prosocial behaviors from fall to spring, probably due to increased play opportunities, play contiguity, and familiarity with peers rather than to advanced role-taking skills.

Roedell (1980) has suggested that despite precocious mental skills, many gifted 3- and 4-year-olds

> tend to hit and kick other children when frustrated, have trouble communicating needs and feelings to other children, lack the skill to initiate cooperative play or to join a group, have not learned to share and take turns, and so on. In short, these children are socially similar to three- and four-year-olds of average intelligence. At the same time, they think and reason much like much older children. (p. 15)

We have a highly imperfect understanding of the processes involved in social cognition. Perhaps the high performance levels on social cognitive tasks that gifted children exhibit reflect impersonal abstract reasoning abilities as well as elevated verbal skills and intimacy with the middle class ethos, with relatively little affect. The lack of a strong relationship with prosocial behaviors is reminiscent of the art historian who discerns a rare painting but, unlike the painter, seldom produces one. Cognitive understanding alone is not sufficient for behavior to occur. In other words, the child's cognitive behavior is out of step with his affective behavior.

Empathy

Another important form of interpersonal awareness, ''Empathy means feeling oneself into the feelings of another, absorbing those feelings in some fashion that lets the self feel what the other is feeling'' (Sears, 1975, p. 5). Thus, empathy appears to be a state of arousal, encompassing both physiological and cognitive components.

A primary form of empathy has been observed in 1- and 2-day-old infants who cry in response to the sound of another infant's cry (Sagi & Hoffman, 1976). Many a mother of a toddler, thinking of herself as being covertly in distress, has been surprised by a warm, reassuring pat from her youngster.

SOCIAL COMPETENCY

In 1973 a panel of child development specialists convened under the auspices of the Office of Child Development in an attempt to define "social competency" in young children. Their task was not new, but it had become more complex than ever. An increased number of child development projects, new research and evaluation data, rapidly changing technology, and shifting social mores all contributed to the enormity of the task. A total of 29 competencies were subsequently defined (Anderson & Messick, 1974). In the broadest sense these competencies represented the child's ability to deal effectively with the world.

In relation to affective development, the competencies represented a measure of quality in interpersonal relationships. Self-concept, self-esteem, awareness of different feelings, social cognition, and problem-solving skills were intimately related to this definition of social competency. Additional aspects of social competency related to affective development were advanced by the panel, including recognition of boundaries, regulation of antisocial behavior, competence motivation, and a sense of humor. Each of these will now be addressed in light of the gifted preschooler.

Recognition of Boundaries

Like all babies, gifted infants use people as resources. The infant's differentiated cry, mentioned earlier, serves as a primary example. The characteristics of the gifted toddler—keen awareness, supersensitivity, advanced cognitive processes, advanced verbal skills, abundant energy, curiosity, risk-taking, and a winning personality—all contribute to the gifted child's potential to manipulate his or her interpersonal environment in a precarious fashion. Why is the term *precarious* used? Brazelton's (1974) observations have provided a poignant reply:

> Without definite, firm, effective limit-setting from a parent, a child is pushed to find limits for himself. That's hard and often scary, for children seem to know instinctively when they are going too far. To me, a spoiled child demonstrates this kind of anxiety, constantly testing the system for limits which he knows are there somewhere, wanting them to come from the outside rather than having to find them for himself. It's no wonder that his response for being stopped is that of relief. (p. 76).

Brazelton (1974) contended that the second year is a period for establishing firm limits and that unless "parents can accept the responsibility for limiting the child and for using appropriate punishment where it is necessary, they are deserting the child. His new-found freedom is fraught with danger, and a child this age recognizes it'' (p. 225). Burton White (1975) fortified Brazelton's exhortations:

> Children in the first two years of life do not become detached from their primary caretakers very easily; even if you spank them regularly, you will find they keep coming back to you. This is very probably due to the absolutely vital need they have for close attachment to someone. . . . A child who has not been dealt with firmly during late infancy is considerably less well prepared to cope with life situations than one who has. (p. 140)

Gifted preschoolers continue to test their environment, and the need to establish boundaries continues. This is particularly true in relationships with parents and other caretakers. The child's command of alternative strategies, persistence, and adroit verbal skills can, literally, overwhelm some parents. However intimidated they may be by their precocious child, parents must define family rules and firmly uphold them. For example, a 7 o'clock bedtime must be adhered to and the child is told, ''In our family children are not allowed to ask another parent if they can watch more TV. The rule is 7 o'clock bedtime.''

By observing the play of young children teachers can see obvious expressions of the need children have for boundaries (Abroms, 1982). Gifted children tend to engage in complex dramatic play, with rigid structures invariably ascribed to a number of subthemes. Symbolically, gifted preschoolers are often dealing with their own needs for boundaries. For example, Brandt (father) was intransigent as he emphatically said to Brooke (baby), ''Baby, you cannot go outside until you pick up all of your toys. I've been working hard all day and I will not tolerate this mess. Do you understand me? Do you?''

Other joint activities among children can be effective in establishing boundaries. ''No,'' a solitary utterance from a peer, produced immediate respect for boundaries from 15-month-old Tony, as recounted earlier. The same scenario is often repeated among older children.

Sometimes the gifted child needs teacher assistance in the establishment of boundaries. For example, in group games gifted children are often frustrated by playing the game the same way each time. They see flaws in the rules of the game and want to make changes in a way that is destructive to group harmony. The sensitive teacher can respond by saying, for example, ''You thought of a better way to play. I can't let you play the game that way because the other children are in bounds.''

Neil, a clever 5-year-old, complained that nobody wanted to play trucks with him. Previously he had insisted, ''The trucks *have* to go this way because this is a one-way street!'' Unfortunately the other children in the group were not prepared to deal with the complexities of a one-way street. In this case the teacher marked off a section of the truck corner with masking tape and said, "This is Neil's corner. When the game comes here, we can play Neil's way." Thus, the teacher indicated respect for the clever lad's awareness while at the same time providing the other children with an opportunity to gradually assimilate and ease into Neil's cognitive structure. In a few minutes the advancing truck convoy approached Neil's corner and turned down the one-way street.

Boundaries are typically manifested in overt, finite ways and provide a source for the resolution of tension and for ultimate comfort among young children. Not all boundaries are explicit, however. As the child realizes that adults and children assume somewhat different roles in different situations, he must adjust to more symbolic boundaries.

Gifted 3-, 4-, and 5-year-olds tend to be attracted to peers of similar mental ages. Within the context of mainstream child-care settings gifted youngsters are faced with a range of interpersonal boundaries that accompany interactions with children of varying abilities and stages of development.

Expressive language is a salient example. The gifted 3-year-old who proclaims, "I have a handful of sand granules!" quickly loses her compatriots in the sandbox. Studies of nonexceptional children ages 3 through 5 have suggested that young children alter their speech according to the role of the listener. Specifically, mean length of utterances, intonation, content, and explicitness vary with the age, physical size, handicapping condition (if present), and linguistic and cognitive capacities of the listener (Maratsos, 1973; Shatz & Gelman, 1973).

Extrapolation from these studies of normal child development, coupled with knowledge of the characteristic sensitivity and advanced social cognitive skills of the gifted, suggest that young gifted children are likely to infer and respond to these symbolic boundaries through adaptations in expressive language. Social development is bidirectional. Each interaction affects each participant. It is hoped that the gifted preschooler, through social experiences, will readily perceive symbolic boundaries and temper his interactions accordingly.

Regulation of Antisocial Behavior

There is no doubt that physical extremes in aggression and competition occur among young gifted children. In observations of their free-play activities, however, teachers are immediately struck by the adroit use of verbal skills in the service of aggression and competition.

Antisocial aggression (temper tantrums, overt physical aggression, quarrels, and destructiveness) among children not identified as gifted increases between the ages of 2 and 4 (Hartup, 1970; Walters, Pearce, & Dahms, 1957). There is evidence that a shift from antisocial to more socialized forms of aggression (i.e., verbal insults) begins to occur at around age 4 (Jersild & Markey, 1935; Sears, 1961). Advanced cognitive and verbal skills may facilitate an earlier appearance of socialized aggression among the gifted. Recently, the author overheard the following conversation, illustrating verbal aggression, between two precocious 3-year-olds.

> Bob was angry with Tom. "Ya know what? You're gonna come to my house and ring the doorbell and I'm not gonna be there, but a snapping turtle is!"

Two common themes of verbal aggression are: "If you don't do this I won't like you any more," and "I'm not going to invite you to my birthday." In each case the intent to do harm is abundantly clear.

There are a number of conditions in child-care settings that increase the potential for aggression to occur. These include large group size, paucity and improper placement of materials and equipment, limited physical space, poorly planned activities, and undependable weather. The teacher can exert control over all but the last variable. In planning activities for the children it is important that the teacher allocate space wisely and not place too many children in a group; this helps to avoid pushing, shoving, and careening. Placement of moveable equipment in the play yard within proximity of stationary equipment also reduces the chances of aggressive behavior. Of course, the availability of age- and cognitive-appropriate activities is good practice under any circumstances.

Informal observations of gifted 3-, 4-, and 5-year-olds in self-contained settings clearly indicate the presence of competition. Again, this tends to be a highly cerebral and verbal form of behavior among the gifted. Two examples of competition shared by the teachers at Newcomb College Nursery School of Tulane University are illustrative:

> Anna and Jane had wanted to play alone with Jennifer in the tree house. "Get out Anna," said Jane. "You get out," Anna retorted. Anna climbed down the stairs, ran to the teacher and said, "Miss Bussie, please write us a sign saying 'This house is only for Anna and Jennifer.'" (Abroms, K., personal observations, 1979)
>
> At juice and cookie time in the nursery school the teacher passed the cookies on a tray. The rule is that each child is allowed one cookie until the tray is passed a second time. Garth took two cookies when the tray went round the first time. "Hey, he has two," Jeffrey shouted. "But I want it for a sandwich," Garth quickly replied.

Apparently competition is a developmental phenomenon, increasing with age. The issue of teacher intervention is a controversial one since the merits of competition as well as cooperation appear to be related significantly to socio-cultural factors. Informal observations by the director of the PIPPI preschool gifted program (largely composed of Hispanic children from low economic backgrounds in New York City) (Goldman, 1980) suggested a paucity of competitive behaviors and substantial expression of cooperation, particularly among girls. On the other hand, teachers of preschool gifted children from middle and upper class families note a strong sense of competition, particularly among 4- and 5-year-old boys (Johnston, 1980).

Competence Motivation

Competence motivation in the affective domain is interpreted to mean self-initiated improvement of social skills and the pursuit of new interpersonal skills. Mastery is typically associated with this construct.

In a classic observational study done in the late 1920's, Mildred Parten found that social participation changed quantitatively and qualitatively between the ages of 2 and 5. Parten (1933) reported that the amount of social participation is correlated with chronological age; thus, among older children the frequency of onlooking behavior, isolated and solitary play, decreases whereas the frequency of parallel associative and cooperative play with age-mates increases relative to amounts shown by younger children. Parten's paradigm has subsequently been replicated by a number of researchers.

Two comments are appropriate regarding the gifted. First, participation in solitary play is characterized by sustained, goal-directed, cognitive activities among 3- through 5-year-olds. Working with puzzles, cutting and pasting, drawing, painting, writing, and reading are examples. Second, comparisons of gifted children in self-contained programs with nonexceptional children in a regular preschool program have indicated that gifted children engage in associative and cooperative play earlier than their age-mates.

The gifted child in the mainstream may have difficulties establishing successful play patterns. All too often the gifted child asserts himself or herself as the organizer for cooperative play in ways not appreciated by nongifted peers. His or her advanced organizational patterns, rapid changes in thought, multiple directions, and extended verbal commands as well as individual temperament all contribute to the occurrence of the "Nobody likes me" syndrome.

Teachers can respond to this common complaint in several ways. The following vignette is a useful example:

Child: "Nobody likes me. I don't have any friends."
Teacher: "What can you do about that?"
Child: "I don't know."
Teacher: "One of the best ways to learn to become friends is to sit and watch other children and listen to what they have to say. That way you can *hear* how they got to be friends."

The gifted child sat and observed the other children in the yard for several minutes. Then he approached a popular age-mate.

Child: "I don't know how to dig a hole. Would you show me how?"

Teachers should be instrumental in promoting social competency by arranging situations and activities in ways that foster associative and cooperative play. Choosing congenial classmates to frost cupcakes with the gifted child is one example. Placing role-playing props that suggest a common theme in a neutral corner of the room is another example.

Cooperative arrangements between preschool teachers should accommodate occasional placement of a child with advanced organizational skills in classes for either younger or older children where he stands a good chance of meeting with success and acceptance as a leader. Cross-age free play activity time in the yard is also helpful.

A number of studies of popularity ratings among older children (Gottman, Gonzo, & Rasmussen, 1975; Hartup, Glazer, & Charlesworth, 1967; Jennings, 1975) have indicated that giving verbal reinforcement to peers is positively related to popularity. Gifted 3-, 4-, and 5-year-olds are usually acutely aware of their peers ("How come he gets two?") and should be encouraged to channel their observations and verbal skills toward the establishment and maintenance of interpersonal relationships ("I like it when you play with me.").

Like other children, the gifted care about satisfying peer relationships. The gifted have a variety of skills that can be employed in a proactive fashion toward establishing successful play interactions. Examples of how teachers can facilitate self-initiated peer relationships among gifted and nongifted children have been presented.

Sense of Humor

Apparently what is and what is not funny to young children is somewhat dependent upon their cognitive level. For example, gifted 3-year-olds find it hilarious to hear the name"Tiki Tiki Tim Bo No So Rim Bo"uttered, and they delight in repeating it in cadence. In this case retentive memory obviously plays a part in the enjoyment of the absurd. On the other hand, gifted 3-, 4-, and 5-year-olds, like other children, greet epithets of "Poo poo boy" and "Dung girl" with gales of laughter. Around age 4 the gifted begin to show an interest in riddles ("When is a door not a door? When it's ajar!"); 5-year-olds tend to enjoy play on words, and their jokes often reflect the type of exposure they have received ("What is a Beethoven fruit? Ba-Na-Na-Naaa!"). Humor often embraces a variety of feelings and may reflect the child's view of people, things, and self.

Social Competency Summary

The promotion of social competency is a major goal of affective education. At times parents and teachers need to establish unequivocal boundaries for young children. In the socialization process children are confronted with a variety of interpersonal situations in which boundaries are inferred. It is presumed that through socialization with nongifted children the clever child discerns symbolic boundaries and adapts his or her expressive language to the needs of the listener much in the same way that other children do.

The behavior of gifted children is not without aggression and competition. However, aggression and competition are typically expressed in more socialized forms through verbal mediation. Gifted preschoolers tend to engage in complex play patterns earlier than other children. They also experience conflicts in their play. Disparities may be heightened in a heterogenous child-care setting, and teachers may need to facilitate the development of additional social opportunities and skills for the gifted. Finally, young gifted children express and appreciate humor that is typical of their own age and that of older children.

ROLE PLAYING

Role playing appears to be well suited to the development and enhancement of empathy. There are several reasons for this. Most preschoolers have been at it for a good part of their young lives! Early forms of role playing are seen when the toddler symbolically pushes a truck across the room as he goes "Beep! Beep!" Props (dress-up clothing, cash register, typewriter, etc.), ample time and space plus a full-length mirror foster spontaneous role-playing.

Gifted children seem to be involved in rich dramatization by age 2½, with their abundant verbal skills and experiences facilitating a range of intricate subthemes and interpersonal nuances. Plasticity is one of the most attractive features of role playing, because it provides for joint participation by children of varied cognitive and physical abilities (Abroms, 1982).

When role playing is used to develop and enhance empathy the teacher serves as a facilitator, structuring opportunities for children to act out and process feelings accruing to themselves and others. By actually experiencing affect in the nonjudgmental milieu of role playing, and by acting out emotions in the context of a theme, children are better able to sort out emotions, understand their meanings, and label them correctly. As one gifted 4-year-old remarked, "When I can't have a turn it feels like a buffalo hit me. That's how I feel when I'm frustrated."

By taking the role of another and expressing one's own similar feelings at the same time, children experience empathy. However, role-playing activities must be practiced in order to achieve lasting clarity and attainment of empathy. Typically, young children view role-playing sessions as enjoyable experiences, and these sessions serve as an example of affective rather than didactic learning.

Teacher Facilitation of Role Playing

There are a number of social learning programs that include prepared role-playing themes and scripts. Many teachers prefer to develop their own. In either case, the basic steps suggested by Dinkmeyer (1970) are applicable.

1. *Preparation.* The teacher selects and reviews an appropriate theme and script. Examples of topics include feelings associated with sharing, how

it feels to be left out, and feelings of fear in new situations. The teacher may choose to use props such as photopictures, posters, audiocassettes, or chairs.

2. *Introduction.* The teacher briefly tells the children that the class is going to do some pretending and what the pretending will be about. A pantomine activity serving as a "warm-up" is presented to the total class. Typically it involves physical activity such as climbing or reaching. This type of group participation can be helpful in eventually bringing shy or withdrawn children into role-playing activities. Next the teacher briefly presents the actual role-playing situation to the class and asks for volunteers to take various roles. It is usually wise to begin with children who have a firm understanding of the characters and are comfortable in role-play.

3. *Enactment.* The teacher verbally assists the children in visualizing the setting, briefly reviews the scene, and tells the actors when to begin. When the scene appears to have been played out the teacher tells the children to stop.

4. *Discussion.* The teacher poses a number of provocative questions to the entire group: "Has anything like that ever happened to you?" "Would you have been angry if the car were yours?" "Would it help to cry?"

Puppetry is another form of role playing. In some cases children feel more comfortable in expressing themselves through inanimate figures. Both a theme and a script are used in puppetry, and it is recommended that the teacher use facilitative behaviors similar to those previously suggested for role playing.

INTERPERSONAL PROBLEM SOLVING

Conflicts among young children are inevitable. For the gifted child, difficulties in maintaining and establishing successful peer relationships may be exacerbated by advanced verbal skills and staggering cognitive leaps that quickly set the gifted child apart from his peers. Differences are quickly recognized; subsequent name-calling and expulsion from cliques are not uncommon among preschoolers. Sometimes the gifted child withdraws and becomes an isolate. Other times he or she protests, using highly cerebral, although inappropriate, tactics to gain social acceptance.

Shure, Spivack, and Jaeger (1971) found that a particular type of role-play among 4-year-old children from disadvantaged families was related to their social adjustment in school. The researchers named this phenomenon *problem-solving ability,* the ability to conceptualize alternative solutions to real-life interpersonal problems. They subsequently developed the Preschool Inter-personal Problem-Solving (PIPS) test as a measure of this ability. The test calls for verbal responses to the following types of hypothetical problems, which are accompanied by visual props (Shure & Spivack, 1974):

"Let's pretend that Pam just broke her mommy's favorite flower pot and she is afraid her mommy might be mad at her."

"What did Pam do?"

"What can Pam do so her mommy won't be mad at her?" (p. 28)

"Tom was playing ball. The ball hit a window, and the window _____."

"Yes, the window broke."

"He was afraid his mommy might be mad."

"What can Tom do so his mommy will not be mad at him?" (p. 24)

Behavioral adjustment ratings administered by child care workers and scores from the PIPS were significantly related. Another test, What Happens Next?, measures alternative consequences to solutions. Scores on this test and behavioral adjustment were also positively related.

Based on these results, the researchers developed a training program with an emphasis on teaching young children *how* to think, not what to think, in coping with everyday problems.

The seven fundamental principles of the training program are:

1. To teach prerequisite language and thinking skills before teaching problem-solving strategies.
2. To teach new concepts in the context of familiar content.
3. To base program content on people and interpersonal relations rather than objects and impersonal solutions.
4. To teach generally applicable concepts rather than correct grammar.
5. To teach the habit of seeking solutions and evaluating them on the basis of their potential consequences rather than the absolute merits of a particular solution to a problem.
6. To encourage the child to create his own ideas and offer them in the context of the problem.
7. To teach problem-solving skills not as ends in themselves but in relation to the adaptiveness of overt behavioral adjustment. (Spivack & Shure, 1974, p. 29)

At this juncture note must be made regarding the first principle, particularly as it relates to preschool programs for bilingual and culturally different gifted children. Spivack and Shure (1974) found that many of the 4-year-olds in their program did not have a basic mastery of words such as "or," "not," "before," "after," "now," "later," "why," "because," "maybe," and "might." Thus, it follows that teachers cannot blithely assume that just because a child has been identified as gifted he or she has mastery of linguistic concepts typically held by white middle class children.

The script in the Spivack and Shure training program incorporates items similar to those illustrated on the PIPS test. These items are used to teach alternative solutions. Other items are used to teach thought processes related to alternative consequences to solutions.

Evaluation of the Spivack and Shure training program indicated that children who began the training program well-adjusted remained so, while significant gains on measures of behavioral adjustment were made by children identified as having behavior problems at the beginning of the training program (1974, pp. 91–107).

Little doubt exists that the intent of the Spivack and Shure program, developing interpersonal problem-solving, is a valid one. The notion of using the training program as a preventive measure is also appealing. However, Roedell (1978) has suggested that the PIPS test may be an ineffective predictor of behavioral ratings among gifted 3- through 5-year-olds with a mean IQ of 138. Since the PIPS and the training program were developed using a Head Start sample, perhaps greater effectiveness of the Spivack and Shure program will be demonstrated among low-income gifted groups.

Another program predicated upon social cognitive skills and dedicated to interpersonal problem-solving is AWARE (Elardo & Cooper, 1977). The pilot study for this preventive program was conducted upon children ages 5 through 9 from low-income families. There were no significant effects after 1 year.

The revised version of the program addresses itself to children ages 8 through 11 and represents an ecological model in which AWARE activities are taught on a daily basis as an integral part of the curriculum. The goals of the AWARE program are:

1. To increase each child's ability to understand the thoughts and feelings of self and others.
2. To increase each child's ability to be more understanding and accepting of individual differences.
3. To improve each child's ability to solve interpersonal problems by learning (a) to define a problem, (b) to formulate alternatives to the problem, and (c) to understand the consequences of each alternative for all people involved.
4. To increase each child's respect and concern for others.

(Elardo & Cooper, 1977, p. vii)

There are four units in the AWARE program, each unit interfacing one of the listed goals. "Developing Social Living Behaviors" addresses the third goal, interpersonal problem-solving. Each lesson in this unit has a script with "Objective," "Overview," and "Activity and Discussion."

Examples of objectives include the following:

The children will understand the meaning of problem, alternatives, and consequences.

The children will understand the importance of considering everyone's thoughts and feelings in solving problems.

The children will define self-control and then give examples of self-control.

The children will be able to understand how others feel when they are interrupted.

The children will analyze the causes and consequences of conflicts.

The children will suggest alternatives for solving problems where two conflicting promises have been made.

The activities and discussion questions appear to be quite reasonable for gifted 4- and 5-year-olds, many of whom have mental ages of 8 years or older and levels of social cognition equivalent to those attained by older children. Evaluation of the revised AWARE program is in process.

Although AWARE was also developed using low-income children, its major purpose is not remedial, unlike the Spivack and Shure program. Overall, the AWARE program appears to have face validity as a preventive measure for use among 4- and 5-year-old gifted children.

Summary of Interpersonal Problem Solving

It appears that preschool gifted children show advanced awareness of others as measured by laboratory tasks of social cognition. As with nongifted children, the relationship between social cognition and measures of behavioral sensitivity remains inconclusive. Empathy has been described as another measure of people perception. Role-playing techniques appear amenable to the development and enhancement of empathy. A training program in interpersonal problem-solving strategies, developed by Spivack and Shure, holds promise for use in the classroom as a preventive measure and possibly as a remedial measure in social adjustment among young gifted children.

Another program, AWARE, includes interpersonal problem solving as part of a more inclusive approach to affective development. The majority of activities in the AWARE program appear well suited for use with bright 4- and 5-year-olds.

THE CLIMATE FOR AFFECTIVE EDUCATION: AT SCHOOL AND AT HOME

The teacher is the single most important variable in promoting affective development in the context of a preschool setting. Hildebrand (1980) has listed 16 qualities the teacher should have as a "significant other" in the lives of young children:

1. Being knowledgeable about children's development.
2. Being a nurturing person.
3. Being a model.
4. Being a perceptive observer and listener.
5. Being skillful in selecting and using guidance techniques.
6. Being self-confident.
7. Being dedicated.
8. Being confident of basic goodness in people.
9. Being strong, healthy, and energetic.
10. Being knowledgeable about children's curriculum.
11. Being effective with your voice.
12. Being able to set and enforce limits for children.
13. Being alert to health and safety.
14. Being a teacher instead of a supervisor.

15. Being a decision-maker.
16. Being scholarly and professional. (pp. 358–359)

The responsibility for nurturing affective development cannot exist solely in the teacher and the school. Parent involvement is essential to its fulfillment—a two-way process from the home to the school and from the school to the home. Teachers need to communicate this philosophy to parents and can do so through parent conferences, class meetings, home visits, or the mail.

In working with parents of gifted preschoolers teachers have frequently observed the following:

1. Parents tend to make assumptions about what a child will or will not do by virtue of the fact that he or she is gifted. For example, one morning the preschool teacher noticed that George was out of sorts. Soon after, he said, "I'm mad. I've had a terrible morning." George's parents simply assumed that their gifted child would inform his teacher that the heating system at home had broken during the night and George and his family had remained awake, cold, and uncomfortable, until morning. Fortunately the teacher maintained a benevolent attitude toward George's behavior. Had the parents informed the teacher of George's sleepless night the teacher would have been in a position to respond to George's very real needs.
2. Parents often expect too much from their gifted child! They expect the child to be as socially advanced as he or she is cognitively. Teachers must remind parents that a gifted 3-year-old who falls down and skins a knee has the right to cry like any other 3-year-old.
3. Parents have difficulties in communicating to their gifted child at various levels. In essence, many parents are poor at role-taking when it comes to dealing with young children. They consistently approach the child at an adult level and forget that this is not always the most appropriate way to reach the child. Teachers would be wise to share with parents some of their own special communication techniques as examples.
4. Parents tend to over-program their gifted children. Sometimes parents are seduced by their young child's enormous cognitive capacity and feel that it is incumbent upon them to challenge this capacity at every step of the child's development. Gifted children need time just to be children! They need not have every hour filled with dancing, piano, gymnastics, and swimming lessons. Teachers should share the richness of the preschool program with parents and encourage them to come to school and observe. This may help parents feel more comfortable in cutting back on their child's extracurricular activities.
5. Parents sometimes use their gifted child as a vehicle for their own aspirations and unfulfilled accomplishments. They place the child on center stage where he or she receives adulation for remarkable feats of memory and verbalization. At the same time the child is placed in the uncomfortable

position of being met with indifference upon mastery of other behaviors, such as learning how to skip, a feat the child views as equally wondrous. Many parents are naïve about child development. The teacher can support the child by recommending reading materials to the parents and by impressing upon the parents the worthiness of the child's other behaviors.

6. Parents often cast the gifted child into the role of star of the family, to the detriment of the child and the distress of his or her siblings. Parent conferences often provide teachers with opportunities to point out the uncomfortable feelings a stellar position may create among siblings, the invidious comparisons, and the ultimate friction between the gifted child and the family.

7. Parents may indiscriminately confide in their gifted child about family conflicts, or they may indiscriminately allow the gifted child to be privy to family tensions. Teachers must remind parents that while a young child is cognitively capable of understanding aspects of adult conflicts, he or she is not emotionally sophisticated enough to handle them. This may be particularly so for the gifted child who processes information at great depths, including future implications and how they relate to himself or herself. Teachers should impress upon families the important role the school can play in helping a child deal with family conflict and the need for parent-teacher communication to bring about this helping relationship.

Just as a newsletter is sent home recounting cognitive activities accomplished to date and outlining forthcoming ones, the same should be done for the affective domain. Parents need to be reminded, through newsletters and direct contact, of the young child's developing self-concept and the effects the family has upon the child's self-esteem. If interpersonal problem-solving techniques are being learned in school, then parents should be encouraged to provide follow-up opportunities in the home. If new boundaries are being defined and implemented in either the home or school, this information should be conveyed to the appropriate caretaker. If a traumatic event or change has occurred in the family, the school needs to be on the alert for indicators in the child's behavior. If the child is experiencing discomfort in peer relations at school, the family needs to be made aware as well. The multitude of events impinging upon the child's affective development are ongoing. In order to provide the gifted child with optimal support during this delicate process, communication between the home and school must be ongoing.

Guidelines for Affective Development of Preschool Gifted Children

The following synopsis highlights the content of this chapter and provides guidelines for promoting the affective development of preschool gifted children:

1. Affective intervention is important for all children, but it is particularly important for gifted/talented children, who are likely to be more sensitive and thus more vulnerable to distortions of their self-esteem.

2. Teachers and parents should keep in mind the importance of helping the gifted/talented child to develop an adequate self-concept and self-esteem, to become more sensitive to the feelings and needs of others, and to become more competent socially.

3. Affective behavior is learned through interactions with others and has its beginnings in infancy. It is important, therefore, for the significant adults in the gifted child's life to be aware of the impact their interactions with the child have on his or her affective development.

4. There are certain adult behaviors and certain climates that promote optimal affective development. It is important for adults interacting with the child to know how to maximize the child's affective development.

5. The relationship between a poor self-concept and underachievement has been well documented by research. Unrealistic expectations for the young gifted child can be damaging to self-esteem.

6. There appears to be a segmental character to the development of affective behavior. In providing the young gifted/talented child with the appropriate affective education, the adult must be able to assess where the child is developmentally and provide him or her with the experiences, interactions, and climate that will enable the child to progress to the next milestone.

7. While gifted children tend to be generally superior in all respects, they are not necessarily at the same stage in all facets of development. For example, they may be far more advanced cognitively, especially in expressing themselves verbally, than they are in affective development. Adults must not set unrealistic expectations for the gifted child in the affective area merely because the child is precocious mentally. Teachers must differentiate instruction among young gifted children in affective development as well as in cognitive and other facets.

8. While gifted children tend to show advanced awareness of others, deliberate effort should be made to facilitate this kind of behavior.

9. Role playing activities have been found to be a good technique for enhancing empathy in young children.

10. Social adjustment among young gifted children may be facilitated by providing them with activities that train them to acquire interpersonal problem solving strategies.

11. Gifted children, as is true of children in general, need limits set for them. Well-selected boundaries make the child feel more secure and tend to reduce tension and aggressive behavior.

12. Gifted children can engage in associative and cooperative play at an earlier age than their peers with average abilities and should be encouraged to do so, but they must be guided in such a way that they develop the social competence to be successful in their play patterns. Otherwise they may experience rejection by their peers.

13. Parents of the gifted are key adults in promoting their affective development. Teachers and parents need to work closely together on this aspect

of the child's development as well as others. This working relationship must be an ongoing one.

REFERENCES

Abroms, K. Classroom interaction of gifted preschoolers. *TEACHING Exceptional Children,*1982,*14,*223–225.Abroms, K., & Gollin, J. Developmental study of gifted preschool children and measures of psychosocial giftedness. *Exceptional Children,* 1980, *46,* 334–341.

Ainsworth, M., & Bell, S. Attachment, exploration, and separation: Illustrated by the behavior of one-year-olds in a strange situation. *Child Development,* 1970, *41,* 49–67.

Anderson, J., Lang, C., & Scott, V. *Focus on self-development stage one: AWARENESS.* Chicago: Science Research Associates, 1970.

Anderson, S., & Messick, S. Social competency in young children. *Developmental Psychology,* 1974, *10,* 282–293.

Beginning Concepts. New York: Scholastic Magazine, 1972.

Borke, H. The development of empathy in Chinese and American children between three and six years of age: A cross-cultural study. *Developmental Psychology,* 1973, *9,* 102–108.

Bowlby, J. *Attachment and loss: Separation.* New York: Basic Books, 1969.

Brazelton, T. *Toddlers and parents.* New York: Dell, 1974.

Carpenter, G., Teece, J., Steckler, G., & Friedman, S. Differential visual behavior to humans and humanoid faces in early infancy. *Merrill-Palmer Quarterly,* 1970, *16,* 91–108.

Cotter, K. First grade failure: Diagnosis, treatment, and prevention. *Childhood Education,* 1967, *44,* 172–176.

Dewey, J. *Experience and Education.* New York: Macmillan, 1938.

Dinkmeyer, D. *Developing understanding of self and others (DUSO).* Circle Pines, MN: American Guidance Service, 1970.

Eimas, P., Siqueland, E., Jusczyk, P., & Vigorito, J. Speech perception in infants. *Science,* 1971, *171,* 303–306.

Elardo, P., & Cooper, M. *AWARE.* Menlo Park CA: Addison-Wesley, 1977.

Flavell, J., Botkin, P., Fry, C., Jr., Wright, J., & Jarvis, P. *The development of role-taking and communication skills in children.* New York: Wiley, 1968.

Fraiberg, S. *The magic years.* New York: Charles Scribner's Sons, 1959.

Freeman, J. *Gifted children.* Baltimore: University Park Press, 1979.

Gallagher, J., & Crowder, T. The adjustment of gifted children in the regular classroom. *Exceptional Children,* 1957, *23,* 306–312.

Goldman, N. The PIPPI program: A program for gifted preschoolers and their parents. Paper presented at The Annual Meeting of The Council for Exceptional Children, Philadelphia, 1980.

Gottman, J., Gonzo, J., & Rasmussen, B. Social interaction, social competence, and friendship in children. *Child Development,* 1975, *46,* 709–718.

Hartup, W. Peer relations. In T. Spencer & N. Kass (Eds.),*Perspectives in child psychology.*New York: McGraw-Hill, 1970.

Hartup, W., Glazer, J., & Charlesworth, R. Peer reinforcement and sociometric status. *Child Development,* 1967, *38,* 1017–1024.

Hildebrand, V. *Guiding young children.* New York: Macmillan, 1980.

Jennings, K. People versus object orientation, social behavior, and intellectual abilities in preschool children. *Developmental Psychology*, 1975, *11*, 511–519.

Jersild, A., & Markey, F. Conflicts between preschool children. *Child Development Monographs*, 1935, No. 21.

Johnston, C. Personal communication. New Orleans LA, 1980.

Karelitz, S., Fisichelli, V., Costa, J., Karelitz, R., & Rosenfeld, L. Relation of crying activity in early infancy to speech and intellectual development at age three years. *Child Development*, 1964, *35*, 769–777.

Karnes, M. *Know me, know you*. Allen TX: Developmental Learning Materials, 1983.

Karnes, M., McCoy, G., Zehrbach, R., Wollersheim, J., Clarizio, H., Costin, L., & Stanley, L. Factors associated with underachievement and overachievement of intellectually gifted children. *Exceptional Children*, 1961, *28*, 167–175.

Kindle. *All kinds of feelings*. Englewood Cliffs NJ: Scholastic Filmstrips, 1970.

Kirk, S. *Educating exceptional children*. Boston: Houghton Mifflin, 1972.

Krathwohl, D., Bloom, B., & Masia, B. *Taxonomy of educational objectives, Handbook II: Affective domain*. New York: David McKay, 1964.

Maratsos, M. Nonegocentric communication abilities in preschool children. *Child Development*, 1973, *44*, 697–700.

Meyer, W., & Dusek, J. *Child psychology, a developmental perspective*. Lexington MA: D. C. Heath, 1979.

Morse, W., Ardizzone, J., MacDonald, C., & Pasick, P. *Affective education for special children and youth*. Reston VA: The Council for Exceptional Children, 1980.

Ostwald, P., & Peltzman, P. The cry of the human infant. *Scientific American*, 1974, *230*, 84–90.

Parten, M. Social participation among pre-school children. *The Journal of Abnormal and Social Psychology*, 1933, *27*, 243–269.

Piaget, J., & Inhelder, B. *The child's conception of space*. London: Routledge & Kegan Paul, 1956.

Rheingold, H. The effects of environmental stimulation upon social and exploratory behavior in the human infant. In B. Foss (Ed.), *Determinants of infant behavior* (Vol. 1). New York: Wiley, 1961.

Rheingold, H. The effect of a strange environment on the behavior of infants. In B. Foss (Ed.), *Determinants of infant behavior* (Vol. 4). New York: Barnes & Noble, 1969.

Roedell, W. Social development in intellectually advanced children. In H. Robinson (Chair), *Intellectually advanced children: Preliminary findings of a longitudinal study*. Symposium presented at the annual convention of the American Psychological Association, Toronto, 1978.

Roedell, W. Characteristics of gifted young children. In W. Roedell, N. Jackson, & H. Robinson (Eds.), *Gifted young children*. New York: Teachers College Press, 1980.

Sagi, A., & Hoffman, M. Empathic distress in newborns. *Developmental Psychology*, 1976, *12*, 175–176.

Sears, R. Relation of early socialization experiences to aggression in middle childhood. *Journal of Abnormal Social Psychology*, 1961, *63*, 446–492.

Shatz, M., & Gelman, R. The development of communication skills: Modifications in the speech of young children as a function of listener. *Monographs of the Society for Research in Child Development*, 1973, *38* (Serial No. 152).

AN: ED235645
CHN: EC160802
AU: Karnes, Merle B., Ed.
TI: The Underserved: Our Young Gifted Children.
CS: ERIC Clearinghouse on Handicapped and Gifted Children, Reston, Va.
SP: National Inst. of Education (ED), Washington, DC.
RN: ISBN-0-86586-147-1
CN: 400-76-0119
PY: 1983
AV: The Council for Exceptional Children, Publication Sales, 1920 Association
Dr., Reston, VA 22091 ($15.00, Publication No. 273).

NT: 238 p.
PR: EDRS Price - MF01/FC10 Plus Postage.
DT: Books (010); Guides - Non-classroom (055); Information Analyses - ERIC
IAP's (071)
AF: U.S.; Virginia
LA: English
PG: 238
DE: Affective Behavior; Creativity; Inservice Teacher Education; Models;

Shaw, M., & McCuen, J. The onset of academic underachievement in bright children. *Journal of Educational Research,* 1960, *51,* 103–108.

Shure, M., Spivack, G., & Jaeger, M. Problem-solving thinking and adjustment among disadvantaged preschool children. *Child Development,* 1971, *42,* 1791–1803.

Shure, M., & Spivack, G. *The PIPS test manual.* Philadelphia: Hahnemann Medical College & Hospital, 1974.

Spivack, G., & Shure, M. *Social adjustment in young children.* San Francisco: Jossey-Bass, 1974.

Walters, J., Pearce, D., & Dahms, L. Affectional and aggressive behavior of preschool children. *Child Development,* 1957, *28,* 15–26.

White, B. *The first three years of life.* Englewood Cliffs NJ: Prentice-Hall, 1975.

Whitmore, J. *Giftedness, conflict, and underachievement.* Boston: Allyn & Bacon, 1980.

Wolff, P. The natural history of crying and other vocalizations in early infancy. In L. Stone, H. Smith, & L. Murphy (Eds.), *The competent infant.* New York: Basic Books, 1973.

Zahn-Waxler, C., Radke-Yarrow, H., & Brady-Smith, J. Perceptive-taking and pro-social behavior. *Developmental Psychology,* 1977, *13,* 87–88.

CHAPTER 7

Creativity and Play

Andrew Gunsberg

The teacher who is interested in promoting creative behavior in the classroom must first grapple with questions of what creativity is and how it is made manifest, before considering ways to encourage it. The first part of this chapter pertains to relationships between creative behavior and play behavior, followed by descriptions of specific techniques for encouraging divergent thinking and problem solving during the play period. Each suggestion is illustrated by an anecdote taken from the author's experience in the classroom and is followed by a brief discussion of the techniques illustrated in the anecdote.

DEFINITION OF CREATIVITY

The definition of creativity used in this chapter agrees with Fromm's: "The capacity for wonder, the capacity to face incongruity and tension, to orient oneself toward the new, to be aware of experience and to respond fully to such awareness" (1959, p. 48).

Creativity considered in such a light does not depend on the quality of the product but rather describes characteristics and processes that are thought to result in creative productivity. There is ample precedent for employing this definition when speaking of work with young children. Curriculum theorists in language arts, social skills, mathematics, and science stress the importance of process, experimentation, and involvement over the insistence on a finished product to be judged according to its quality.

Preschool education purports to develop social, language, and other skills and judges achievement of its goals in relation to children's previous behavior. Each child is evaluated in light of his or her particular abilities, and educators consider themselves successful if children are able to do something they were not able to do before. Many educators, however, seem to view creativity as a fixed quality possessed by a select few and unavailable to the broader population of students. Their view is based upon qualitative judgments of students' products in relation to the products of the general population. While this criterion is useful in distinguishing "more" creative individuals from the general population, it is less useful in encouraging creative behavior among students at school. If educators confine their definition of creativity to the relative quality of products, they can never begin to consider the antecedent behaviors to creating these products, and hence never reach an understanding of the ways children achieve creative productivity.

In contrast to conceptions concerned with products in relation to other products, the view of creativity favored here, based upon the humanistic approaches proposed by Fromm, Maslow, May, and Rodgers, sees it in relation to the individual. This view is also derived from the environmentalist perspective of Torrance, who sought to isolate and examine those situational antecedents that foster and reinforce creative behavior. Research by Wallace and Kogan (1965) found that the manipulation of environmental variables can increase or decrease those behaviors deemed creative by the various researchers. Such variables as freedom from criticism, low stress situations, and evaluation-free situations were associated with improved levels of performance on creative and intellectual tasks.

When speaking of educating young children to be creative, we mean developing the capacity and the propensity to engage in behaviors that will result in a creative product. But what are these behaviors teachers are attempting to develop? Has anyone identified those behaviors that lead to the creation of a product deemed "creative" by peers and adults in a preschool classroom? It is this author's belief that research on the creativity of young children should concentrate on discovering those molecular behaviors observed in children during their activities in the classroom that lead them to discover new ways of approaching and interacting with their environment.

RELATIONSHIP BETWEEN PLAY AND CREATIVITY

The situation at school in which children can best be observed in self-directed activity is the play period. Play has been the focus of several studies aimed at investigating hypothesized relationships between play and creative behavior. Investigators hypothesized that because play is a process- rather than a product-oriented activity in which subjective states of the individual determine the rearrangement of the external environment, often producing novel results, allowing children to engage in play behavior would perhaps be associated with increases on measures of creative behavior. Dansky and Silverman (1973) investigated the relationship between play with objects and ideational fluency. The results showed that children, when allowed to play freely with a set of small common objects, produced significantly more nonstandard responses for the use of every object than did children who were not allowed to play freely with the objects. Feitelson and Ross (1973) found that children who were exposed to adults modeling pretend play behavior engaged in significantly more interactive play than children who were not play tutored, and achieved significantly higher originality scores on the picture completion subtest of the *Torrance Thinking Creatively with Pictures Test*. These studies lend support to the hypothesis that pretend play in some way facilitates novel and creative responses.

Difference Between Play and Exploration

Play researchers have stated that play is a process-oriented activity that involves a child's arranging the environment according to his or her subjective ideas. The difference between "play" and other forms of exploration behavior occurring during a play period has been examined in the research of Corrine Hutt (1971). Hutt presented nursery school children with an apparatus providing varying degrees of complexity in sound when a lever was pulled. The apparatus was presented to children in an alternative choice situation involving five familiar toys. Hutt's analysis of the children's behavior with the novel object pointed up important differences between exploration and the more diversive forms of behavior that Hutt calls "play."

> As investigations of the object decreased, other activities involving it increased. When analyzed, these consisted of repetitive motor movements, manipulations of long duration accompanied by visual inspection of other objects, and the sequence of activities incorporating both the novel object and other toys, in other words a "game." Examples of these were respectively: patting the lever repeatedly, leaning on the lever making the bell ring continuously while looking around the room, and running around with a truck ringing the bell each time the object was passed. There is another group of responses which can be termed "transposition-of-function"—those responses which resulted in the object explicitly fulfilling another function, e.g., something to climb, a bridge or a seat. All these activities (i.e., repetitive movements, games, and transposition of function responses) are those which an observer would recognize and label as play. (pp. 240–241)

Hutt summarized the distinction between play and exploration in the following terms: "In play the emphasis changes from the question 'What does this object do?' to 'What can I do with this object?' While investigation is stimulus referent, play is response referent" (p. 246).

Hutt's research implied a sequence in the occurrence of exploration and play in the child's behavior. Exploration occurs first as the child's attention is directed toward the novel object or aspect of the environment. It is only after the child has investigated the novel object that his or her exploratory behavior is gradually replaced by the diverse repetitive behaviors that Hutt equated with "play."

Hutt's description of the kinds of behaviors observed in children's play revealed that play involves children's initiating various "games" with objects, using them as they see fit, in a variety of ways that are both repetitive and liable to change suddenly. Play is characterized by a fluidity of response, a rapid shift from one idea to another as the play progresses. The child uses materials in various ways, often utilizing one aspect of the object, such as the lever to ring the bell, and then another—the surface of the object as a "bridge"—as the occasion and the need arise. This self-initiated process of creating enjoyable games for oneself by manipulating the environment as one sees fit resembles in many ways the characteristics associated with divergent thinking. It is this resemblance that has led researchers to hypothesize that ideational fluency and other traits associated with creativity can be developed through play.

Role of Play in Developing Divergent Thinking

The four basic abilities inherent in divergent thinking—fluency, flexibility, originality, and elaboration—have been discussed in Chapter 5, but not in relation to children's behavior during play. Dansky and Silverman's (1973) research testing the assumption that preschool-aged children would be able to come up with more nonstandard uses for objects that they were allowed to play with than would children who were allowed to look at but not play with the objects lends support to the notion that play can increase both ideational fluency and originality of response. It is important to note here that preschoolers reach their nonstandard responses by actually using the objects in play, by experimenting with the different things they can do with the object. This approach seems well suited to work with preschoolers, whose thinking is often better stimulated by actual handling of a concrete "referent" than by questions such as "How many things can you do with a cup?" that are unaccompanied by experience and force a child to rely upon a fund of experience with the object that he or she may not possess.

Opportunities for a child to increase his or her flexibility and ability to elaborate on ideas are inherent in the nature of play. Children playing a pretend game must elaborate the theme of the play in order for the play to progress, for example, a doctor must have patients, the patients a sickness, the sickness a cure, the cure some special apparatus, and so on. Children in the course of their play confront problems that they must solve by coming up with different ways of doing things and by elaboration on the theme of the play. The children may use an old blanket as a stretcher to carry the "patient," the "doctor" may construct an X-ray machine out of giant tinker toys, chairs may be put together to make an ambulance. The ability to play well requires children to be both flexible and able to elaborate on their own ideas and the ideas of others.

Another advantage that play possesses as a means to increase children's creativity is that it is an intrinsically motivating activity. Children are engaged in play because they enjoy the process of playing. A teacher who is cognizant of play's potential for developing divergent thinking abilities in children can harness this enjoyment and high level of motivation to guide children gently toward richer and more creative forms of play activity.

THE TEACHER'S ROLE IN GUIDING PLAY

Once an educator has concluded that play can be a valuable approach to increasing divergent thinking abilities in preschool children, the next problem is to understand his or her role as teacher during the play period. At one extreme a teacher can simply provide materials and administer social praise for appropriate behavior. At the other extreme the teacher can so totally control the course of the child's play that it no longer is play but rather another classroom exercise in which the teacher is contributing all the ideas and the child becomes a passive spectator. Neither of these extremes is desirable or reflects adequate knowledge of what the teacher's role should be in attempting to develop children's creative abilities through play.

Providing a Nonthreatening Atmosphere

Callahan (1978) suggested some general guidelines for stimulating creative behavior in a classroom setting. These can serve as a useful starting point for discussing the role of the teacher during play. She encouraged teachers to provide a nonthreatening atmosphere and suggested that an open, nonjudgmental attitude on the part of the teacher will allow freedom for divergent production. In order to follow this suggestion and provide a nonthreatening atmosphere, the teacher must first feel unthreatened. Beginning teachers may have the misconception that play period means not enforcing general classroom rules or not interfering with children's behavior if the noise level becomes unacceptable or if there is too much clutter or running about in the room. The teacher should approach the play period as a special time in which all the children are free enough from interferences to initiate and follow through on their own ideas for play. This means that the noise level should not be distracting, that intrusive movement must be curtailed, and that materials must be kept together in such a manner that they are available to all the children and do not interfere with play. The teacher's first role during the play period is to monitor the environment and make sure that both the children and the teacher can function effectively. It is especially important for the teacher to feel in control and comfortable, because this will determine the teacher's freedom to concentrate on observing and interacting with the children. A comfortable teacher is likely to be a better observer and better able to model creative behavior.

An anecdotal record of a play sequence involving play with movement will serve to illustrate how confusion over rules in the classroom during play can force the teacher onto the defensive and prompt the teacher to cut short an activity that has potential for child-initiated creativity.

A group of children are playing with a rope that the teacher's aide has brought into the classroom. Two of the children are holding onto the rope while others pull them along. Several are making train noises. They are moving around the classroom when they lurch against a table at which several children are doing puzzles. The puzzles fall on the floor and the teacher says, "Okay, that's it. Now let's put the rope away." The teacher takes the rope from the children, who scatter to other activities in the classroom.

The children involved in the rope activity were intruding on the space of others in the classroom by lurching around close to the table. The teacher might have solved the problem and preserved the rope play by bringing their movement under control. A statement such as "Hey! a train needs a track!" catches the children's attention. "You can't just move around with a track. Let's see. How can we make a track?" The teacher enters into the game of train by presenting the players with a problem they must solve that is part of the game they are playing. The teacher expands upon the idea of a train. "What can we use for tracks?" This allows the children to present their solution. The teacher should allow the children to brainstorm the problem and then lead a discussion aimed at evaluating which idea is the most desirable. "Let's see now, if we lay the wooden blocks down for tracks, will we be able to walk on them with the rope? Which would be easier to walk on, blocks or tape?" In this fashion the teacher brings the activity of the group under control and limits their play to an area away from the table while at the same time giving the children the opportunity to come up with a creative solution to a problem. The teacher is able to maintain the desirable group spirit of the rope play by insisting on adherence to rules of the game.

The teacher described in the anecdote took away the rope and broke up the children's play. Peace and quiet were obtained at the expense of the children's train idea. The teacher who is able to bring the children's behavior under control by expanding upon their idea and challenging them to solve a problem that grows out of the play is able both to establish control and to help extend and elaborate their play. A track may lead to a stoplight and a stoplight to a station before the play is through.

Introducing Novel Stimuli and New Behaviors

The second item of general advice Callahan has offered teachers interested in stimulating creativity is that they provide different and novel kinds of stimuli to encourage curiosity. The introduction of new materials into the classroom, such as netting, strips of rubber, corregated boxes, and other interesting items, will stimulate children to experiment in their use. A less commonly thought-of aspect of novel stimuli involves the teacher's introducing new behavior as well as new materials into the children's play. The following anecdote will illustrate this point.

The children have just finished a unit on air during which the teacher brought in an inner tube and a bicycle pump. Each child had an opportunity to pump air into the inner tube, and later that week, outside on the playground, the teacher pretended to be a flat inner tube by lying collapsed on the deck of the climbing structure. A child pretended to "blow" the teacher up with the bicycle pump. As the child "pumped," the teacher rose to a sitting position, spread his arms, took deep breaths, and puffed his cheeks as though he were an inner tube full of air. The children kept pumping until the teacher "burst," making a loud exploding noise and sinking back into a collapsed position. The children observing this laughed, and all wanted a turn to pump. After several children pumped the teacher up, other children volunteered to be the inner tube, and the game continued without the teacher.

Novel stimuli combined with new forms of behavior introduced by the teacher, as shown in the anecdote, can involve children in a creative game that promotes transfer of learning from one medium to another. The teacher follows Callahan's suggestion by bringing to class two novel objects, a bicycle pump and an inner tube, in order that the children may observe the qualities of air, in this case how air can be used to make something expand. The teacher extends the idea of air filling space and making things expand by introducing a novel behavior. He makes his body the inner tube and enacts the processes of being filled with air. What was learned through experimentation with new objects is now learned by experimentation with one's own body.

This introduction of a new behavior by the teacher may lead children to elaborate on the game, by pretending to float when they are full of air, or pretending to rush about when air is let out of them, the way a balloon does when air is suddenly released. It is important to note here that the children's play is based on experience. The teacher had brought in balloons and filled them with air and released them. He had let the children play with balloons and encouraged them to think of as many things to do with them as possible. The teacher then took the idea of introducing novelty one step further by introducing novel behavior in relation to the concept of air, in this case by pretending to be an inner tube being filled.

Children have a much greater chance of being able to elaborate their play creatively if they have actual first-hand experience with the objects and concepts being represented in play. A useful approach to follow is to allow time to experiment with novel objects and other forms of stimuli introduced in the classroom, then brainstorm alternative approaches to the use of these objects, and then introduce a novel form of play behavior involving use of the concept you are teaching and encourage the children to elaborate upon the new behavior you have introduced. This procedure follows the sequences of behavior observed in the play of young children by Corrine Hutt (1971), moving from concentration on what an object is to what can be done with an object. It also encourages flexibility in that the teacher introduces new ways of dealing with the concept, in this case by showing how a body can represent an inner tube and enacting the process of filling up.

Using Intrinsic Rewards to Encourage Elaboration

Once a teacher has introduced new forms of behavior aimed at enlarging a child's repertoire and enriching play, the teacher hopes that these new ideas will stimulate imitation and then elaboration on the theme. The question confronting the teacher at this point is how one encourages children to come up with their own ideas. When Callahan suggested that teachers reward the production of novel ideas, because rewards will increase the likelihood that more will be produced, her term "rewards" was ambiguous. What does rewarding a child's idea consist of? Which rewards are best, and how does a reward serve to increase the likelihood that more ideas will be forthcoming? The following anecdote will illustrate the effects of a teacher's use of intrinsic rewards to promote elaboration on ideas presented in play.

Billy and the Blocks

The teacher and three children are playing with cylindrical blocks on the floor. The teacher has just shown the children a game in which he used the cylindrical blocks as bowling balls to knock down other blocks that are standing up. The children attempt the game but aren't having much success because it is difficult to roll the cylindrical blocks in a straight path toward the standing blocks. One of the children takes two of the cylindrical blocks and puts them on his head like horns and starts saying "Moo, moo."

Realize the Value of Children's Ideas

The teacher in this anecdote could insist that the boy stop being silly, that he take the blocks off his head and get back to the business of attempting to knock down the blocks. The teacher would be insisting that his idea of what to play is more important and more valuable than the idea the child has expressed. If the teacher actively discourages children's ideas about what can be done with objects, in favor of his ideas, he is teaching that the children's ideas are not as good as the teacher's. It is the teacher's goal as an encourager of creative behavior to reward novel ideas about the use of materials in the classroom. Insisting that children conform to the teacher's idea of what a play episode should be does not encourage children to express their ideas. A more useful approach is described in the following conclusion to the block play episode just described.

The teacher observes the boy putting the two cylindrical blocks on top of his head like horns and hears him say "Moo." The teacher says, "Hey, look at what Billy is doing, he has turned into a cow." He calls the attention of the other two players to Billy's new idea, moves close to Billy, and pats him on the back. "Hello, cow. Hello. Are you a milk cow? Do you give milk?" Billy, still holding the blocks on his head, or horns, answers "Yes." The teacher then says, "Well, I need some milk. I'm going to milk you. Where's the pail?" One of the observing children hands the teacher another cylindrical block to use as a pail. The teacher pretends to milk Billy by reaching under his stomach and making squeezing motions with his hands. The teacher then says, "The pail is full," and gives it back to the observing child. The observing child drinks the milk. The teacher says, "Hey, you drank my milk. Now you milk the cow." The other child comes over and starts to milk Billy. The child then suggests they put Billy in the barn for the night. The teacher says, "What can we use for a barn?'' The children offer several suggestions and they decide that under the table would be a good barn. "What are we going to feed him?'' asks the teacher. A fourth child, who had not been playing previously, picks up two cylindrical blocks and holds them in front of her nose like an elephant's trunk, moves her head up and down, and trumpets through the trunk. "Oh, no,'' says the teacher in mock worry, "now we have an elephant, too!'' The teacher asks the children what other animals can be made with blocks and put in the barn. The children make a rattle snake, a bird with a beak, and so forth.

In this conclusion to the anecdote, the teacher is using several techniques of intrinsic reinforcement that possess distinct advantages over merely telling a child to stop being silly when he or she presents an idea different from the one the teacher presented. The first thing the teacher does to encourage novel production of ideas is to realize that Billy's pretending to be a cow is a good idea, that in fact it could be a better idea than the teacher's game of bowling with the cylindrical blocks, which was not going well. The teacher then calls attention to the idea. He directs the classmates to Billy's idea by saying in an interested voice, "Hey, look at what Billy is doing!'' This makes Billy cognizant of the fact that he is doing something of interest. The next step in the reward process is then taken when the teacher responds to Billy's idea. The teacher asks Billy if he is a milk cow. When Billy says yes, the teacher uses the idea to begin a game. The teacher begins to milk Billy, elaborating on the idea of "cow'' by providing another idea, that of "milking.'' The teacher then begins to involve the observing children by asking them to provide a needed play prop, in this case a pail to hold the milk. When the observing child gives him a block, the teacher accepts it, fills it, and gives it back to the observing child. The observing child then initiates an idea. He drinks the milk from the pail. The teacher then tells the child to milk Billy, getting the observing child more involved. New problems arise when they must decide where to put the cow, and a new dimension is added when an onlooking child, using the blocks, invents an elephant and adds that to the play—which leads all the other children to start inventing animals with the blocks as body parts.

Call Attention to Ideas

Realizing that children's ideas are valuable, no matter how silly or inappropriate they may seem to you, is the first step in increasing the flow of creative ideas in the classroom. The second step is to call attention to these ideas when they occur, with the exception of those behaviors that are totally inappropriate in a classroom setting. The teacher should view himself or herself as a person who facilitates the flow of ideas between children, and in order to do this the teacher must know when to direct children's attention to a good idea. Oftentimes children may be absorbed in their own play and not act upon what they see their peers doing, but at least it will be reinforcing to the child presenting the idea to know that it is valuable enough for the teacher to call attention to.

Respond to Ideas

The third step in the process of encouraging creative ideas is to *do* things with these ideas when children present them: respond to them by getting involved, offer an idea in response, play with what the child creates, use the idea. If the idea is used, it becomes dynamic, it changes, children can elaborate upon it, just as in the anecdote the idea of milking led to the barn and the creation of other animals to go into the barn. Merely saying, "That's a good idea," and doing nothing with it does not further the creative process as much as reacting to the idea as another player and involving other children in it.

Allowing children to model creative behavior for their peers by calling attention to it, and responding to it by incorporating their ideas into play, shows children that their creative behavior is intrinsically valuable because it has an effect on the environment. The teacher must decide how often to call attention to new ideas and how far to go in encouraging elaboration.

Providing Opportunity for Practice

There are occasions in the classroom when children are best left alone to pursue their own ideas in solitary or group play, even if these ideas seem to the teacher at first to be limited and repetitious. Play as a form of behavior is characterized by much repetition. Children find an effect they like and repeat the associated actions over and over until they discover a new behavior that changes the effect; then they practice this new behavior. Callahan's suggestion that teachers provide children opportunity for practice is relevant here. She characterized practice as the integration of questions encouraging divergent thinking into as many concept areas as possible. This author suggests that preschool children should have the time to practice in play those behaviors they have discovered to be pleasurable, because with practice will come further evolution of the idea and elaboration of it, either in solitary play or in play with other children. An anecdote will clarify this point.

> Chad is building with the giant tinker toys. He is making bridges connecting two upright pieces with a bar across. The teacher observing Chad suggests that he use the bridges as hurdles and try to jump over them. Chad shakes his head no and keeps building bridges. After a time the teacher suggests that Chad use the bridges to make a tunnel and crawl through them. Chad again ignores the teacher's suggestion and continues building. A few minutes later, the teacher feels someone tapping him on the shoulder. He turns around and sees Chad holding a large, elaborate tinker toy construction. "Wow," says the teacher. "It's a four," says Chad. He has added two upright pieces to the bridge to form a giant number four.

Chad's creation illustrates how children who are involved in play will often reject new ideas because they are busy practicing their own ideas or acting on ideas that are still forming. Teachers should not insist that children follow suggestions for elaboration of an idea. The child may not be ready to leave the original idea yet. A good rule of thumb regarding when to introduce new ideas is first to allow children time to practice their own ideas, then to observe and notice when the children begin to look about for new things to do. This would probably be the best time to provide suggestions or introduce an elaboration of the original idea. Timing is important. Often children are capable of producing many ideas on how to elaborate their own play but need to be allowed time to interact with materials so that their ideas can develop. Chad was still involved in the building potential of the giant tinker toys and accordingly rejected the teacher's suggestions to leave his building play and use the bridges in a game involving jumping and crawling. He was more involved in building, and the result of letting him follow his inclination was that he elaborated his own play and came up with an original product, a giant number four built out of tinker toys.

Modeling Creativity

Callahan's fifth suggestion on how to stimulate creativity in the classroom was that the teacher model creativity as much as possible. Teachers can use modeling as a stimulus to prompt children to engage in behaviors they have not previously tried. The following anecdote illustrates how teacher modeling can prompt children to attempt new forms of behavior.

> The teacher is sitting at the table drawing a picture of a shark with crayons on paper. Several children are sitting around him. The teacher finishes his shark and must leave the table to mediate a problem in the block corner. When he returns, one of the children sitting at the table holds up a picture. "Look at my sharks," he says. On the paper are two sharks representing different views of a shark, a front view and a side view.

This anecdote reveals an interesting aspect of modeling. Children observing a model progress from pure imitation to initiating new behavior of their own. Modeling has a disinhibiting effect; that is to say, observing a model somehow makes it easier for individuals to come up with their own ideas, oftentimes elaborations of the model's initial behavior. This occurred when the child observing the teacher drawing a shark came up with his own interpretation of a shark but expressed with different perspectives.

Teachers may sometimes be afraid to engage in activities with children such as modeling clay, building blocks, drawing, or making music, either because they are afraid of making the children feel inadequate or because they themselves feel inadequate in some of these areas. It is this author's opinion that these fears stand in the way of a teacher's contributing expertise and enthusiasm to classroom activity. It does not take much music skill to beat a drum or experiment with percussion instruments, nor will children feel inadequate if their teacher draws an interesting picture. Children will be attracted to the teacher's efforts and will emulate them. When this happens, the teacher and students are partners in a mutual creative endeavor, and the teacher can gain more insight into particular problems children may encounter when working with various materials.

Another reason for the importance of teacher modeling is that shy children may need to see the teacher engaged in an activity before they will attempt it. Doing an activity with the teacher is rewarding, and when children are engaged in activity the teacher can gradually fade out when necessary. Teachers will learn when to pull back from an activity and observe how the children are progressing, and then re-enter the activity with suggestions or elaborations as they gain experience from being a participant in play as well as an observer.

Providing Opportunity for Questions

Callahan's final suggestion was that teachers provide children with many opportunities to ask questions. Perhaps an addition to this suggestion should read, "and to answer as many of their own questions as possible." Often children, and also adults, ask questions that they are already in the process of answering in their own minds. A teacher, when asked a question by a child, might do well to give the child a bit of time to answer the question himself or herself.

> The children have been making Lone Ranger masks out of construction paper, but the masks keep ripping when the children wear them. A child approaches the teacher and says, "Teacher, these are no good, what are we going to do?"

The teacher could say, "Well, we could mend them with tape, or we could staple them together, or we could make masks out of scrap cloth." The teacher would then be doing the children's thinking for them. A response that might encourage more problem-solving behavior would be to restate the problem. "Those paper masks are no good. Let's think about what we can do." Given the opportunity, the child may come up with ideas the teacher never thought of.

If a child cannot come up with an answer to his question, the teacher can provide a starter. The teacher can say, "Well, maybe we could fix things." This may start the child thinking of how to go about fixing the masks. If the child still cannot respond, the teacher can go a bit further with help. "What could we use to fix it?" or "What other things could we make masks of?" The principle here is that the teacher does only the bare minimum to answer the question, giving the responsibility, and hence the feeling of satisfaction when the question is answered, to the child. The teacher must see to it that the child comes up with an answer, and then act on the answer. If the answer is not feasible, the teacher can help the child evaluate his answer by saying, "Do you think paste would hold it?" If the child insists it would, then the teacher should provide materials to give the suggestion a try. Children will gain feelings of competence and independence if they can solve many of their own problems.

RESOURCES FOR CREATIVE PLAY

The teacher interested in encouraging creative behavior in gifted children through play should be aware of the resources at his or her disposal. A playful orientation toward language, movement, social roles, and use of materials connotes a willingness to experiment, to engage in behavior for the sake of the pleasure it gives the player and his companions. Creative behavior often involves making connections between dissimilar elements to form a new whole. Seemingly unrelated elements are brought into a new relationship to each other through the vision of the creative individual. Children at play can be encouraged by the teacher to combine materials, language, motion, and other media in new ways to form an original product.

> The children are playing lions, roaming and making clawing motions. The teacher helps them make manes of curling construction paper and staples the manes to strips of cloth the children tie around their heads. One of the children finds a hula hoop. The teacher suggests one child be the "lion tamer" and the "lions" jump through the hoop. The children do this for a while. Then they change roles. The lions hold the hoop, and the lion tamer crawls through. The teacher brings out a tambourine and shakes it and hits it every time a lion crawls through the hoop. The children start moving to the rhythm of the tambourine, doing a lion dance.

This anecdote illustrates how diverse elements and materials such as construction paper, a hula hoop, the idea of a circus, music, rhythm, and language are combined in an activity that results in an original product, a circus act in which the lion tamer and the lion switch roles! The combining of media, art with music, music with movement, movement with language, leads to surprising new developments. The teacher might have taken the activity one step further by having the children make up a story about what they were doing and tell it into a tape recorder, and then playing the recording back for the children to hear.

A good training procedure to develop flexibility of thinking is to take a concept, any concept, such as heaviness, and brainstorm how many different ways the idea of heaviness could be played with in the classroom, using various media, such as language, movement, social play, art work, and/or any other medium a teacher can think of. This practice will provide the teacher with a backlog of ideas that could come in handy during play.

SUMMARY

The primary goal of this chapter has been to provide teachers of young potentially gifted children with suggestions as to how to encourage creativity during the blocks of time allocated to play.

Stress was placed on the importance of process, experimentation, and involvement as opposed to a finished product judged to be of quality by an adult. The message of this chapter is that creative behaviors can be increased or decreased by the behaviors of the significant adults in the child's environment. Therefore, it is important for these adults to recognize what they can do to foster creative productivity. Not being critical of a child's production, safeguarding him from excessive amounts of stress, and refraining from evaluation during creative production are some positive behaviors of adults that enable a child to behave creatively.

Children can increase their flexibility in play and their ability to elaborate on ideas if they are given ample opportunities. Since play seems to be an intrinsically motivating activity, it has great promise for increasing children's creativity, especially those children who are gifted.

Callahan's (1978) guidelines for stimulating behavior in a classroom setting can be useful to teachers in clarifying their role in promoting creativity among children through play. The real-life anecdotes presented in this chapter were cited to bring to life Callahan's guidelines.

It is the author's hope that these suggestions will serve to interest educators in the potential of play as a possible avenue toward encouraging creative behavior in the classroom and provide teachers with some useful techniques for initiating creative play in their own classrooms during the school year.

REFERENCES

Callahan, C. *Developing creativity in gifted and talented*. Reston VA: The Council for Exceptional Children, 1978.

Dansky, J., & Silverman, I. Effects of play on associative fluency in preschool-aged children. *Developmental Psychology*, 1973, *9*, 38–43.

Feitelson, D., & Ross, G. The neglected factor—play. *Human Development*, 1973, *16*, 202–223.

Fromm, E. The creative attitude. In H. Anderson (Ed.), *Creativity and its cultivation*. New York: Harper & Row, 1959.

Hutt, C. Exploration and play in children. In R. Herron & B. Sutton-Smith (Eds.), *Child's play*. New York: Wiley, 1971.

Wallace, & Kogan. *Modes of thinking in young children: A study of the creative intelligence distinction in young children*. New York: Holt, Rinehart & Winston, 1959.

CHAPTER 8

The Role of the Family

Merle B. Karnes

As teachers and parents begin to recognize the special problems and needs of gifted children, both socially and educationally, and as they work together toward solutions, using patience, commitment, and understanding, gifted children will benefit. What these children need from teachers and parents are understanding, a more positive perspective gleaned from the adults' experience, and the freedom to learn creatively. When gifted children see themselves as part of a team, respected by adults and given choices in their education, they will gain more confidence and become self-directed learners in their education and their lives. (Sherman, 1982, p. 44)

Nearly two decades ago, Hunt (1961) and Bloom (1964) stressed the importance of the first 5 years in the development of the child, noting especially the crucial role of the family. Schaefer (1975) suggested "that the family has more influence on child development than other social institutions and that programs which supplement family care and education are less cost effective than programs which strengthen and support the family" (p. 138). Thus, researchers have confirmed what practitioners believe: that family members must be an integral part of the team who educate the young child, whether that child is of average ability, handicapped, or gifted/talented. Indeed, the authors of this publication hold that family involvement is as critical for gifted/talented children as it is for handicapped children.

Parent involvement was an integral part of Head Start from its inception in the mid-1960's. Parents were employed as staff members in many programs, and only projects committed by the proposals to parent involvement received funding. The same held true for First Chance programs initiated by the Bureau of Education for the Handicapped in 1969. In addition, the federal government has funded numerous research projects in which low-income parents were to become "change agents" in the lives of their young children.

Among the researchers who received funds from such federal offices as the Office of Economic Opportunity, the Office of Child Development, and the Office of Education were Gordon (1969); Karnes, Studley, Wright, and Hodgins (1968); Karnes, Teska, Hodgins, and Badger (1970); and Levenstein (1971). Other researchers included parent involvement in center-based programs but were unable to evaluate its impact because of confounding variables.

Public Law 94-142 has had a profound effect on parent involvement. Although focused on the handicapped, this law has influenced practice in programs for gifted children because it recognizes that parents have rights in the education of their children and that these rights entail making decisions about the appropriateness of educational programs. Public Law 94-142 also provides legal ways for parents to protect these rights. The implications of this law for parents of gifted children were suggested in a recent article by Callahan and Kauffman (1982) entitled "Involving Gifted Children's Parents: Federal Law Is Silent, but Its Assumptions Apply" (p. 50).

Few programs for preschool gifted youngsters exist, but among those with published reports are two for gifted/talented handicapped youngsters funded by the Bureau of Education for the Handicapped (one in the public schools of Chapel Hill, North Carolina, the other at the University of Illinois); one for the highly intellectually gifted at the University of Washington; one for the gifted/talented handicapped at Coeur D'Alene, Idaho; and another University of Illinois program for the gifted/talented funded by the Office of the Gifted and Talented. A sixth was funded by the Astor Foundation in New York City. Since so few programs for gifted/talented preschoolers have been reported in the literature and since information describing parent involvement in these programs is limited, data obtained from work with low-income families and with parents of handicapped children have been relied upon in the discussion that follows.

RATIONALE FOR FAMILY INVOLVEMENT

La Crosse (1982) had this to say about the important role parents play in the lives of their children:

> Being a parent implies becoming an advocate, a preacher, a lawyer, an accountant, a teacher, a nurse, and much more. Parents hold their children's guardianship, their proxy, their power of attorney, their custody, and their care. They are the child's representative in an adult society and the protectors of their legal and human rights. Parents have the responsibility for their children's care and development 24 hours a day, 365 days a year for as long as they remain dependent. (p. 1)

Being a parent is an awesome responsibility; being a parent of a young gifted child is even more challenging and potentially overwhelming.

There are a number of valid reasons why school and home should work closely together. These reasons hold true for all children, but some have particular relevance for gifted children.

The gifted child needs a manager of his or her educational program throughout the school years. The family is the sustaining influence on the gifted child; teachers and other professionals come and go, but the family, especially the parents, ultimately are responsible for the identification of the child's gifts/talents and for the provision of an appropriate and challenging educational program. This means that parents must establish a positive, ongoing relationship with the school. The quality of interaction that is needed, however, is seldom found, and few models for effective school/home relationships exist.

Not everyone is sympathetic toward special programming for the gifted, and it is the parents, therefore, who must make sure that their gifted children receive placement and programming that develop potential to the fullest. To fulfill this role, parents need to acquire the skills to work effectively with school personnel and to avoid being labeled as "fault finders," "meddlesome," and "pushy." Regardless of the risk, however, parents must approach professionals when they feel the needs of their gifted children are unmet.

The home is the institution that has the major influence on the child's values, attitudes, and behavior; parents must therefore help determine the child's educational program. In some cases, parental aspirations are not compatible with a child's abilities; in others, child-rearing practices may be inappropriate for the full development of the child. Such dissonance between home and school must be recognized and a plan developed whereby parents can gain insights that will close the gap between school and home. But it is not always parents who need to change, for some teachers also inhibit rather than enhance the development of gifted children. In such cases, parents can tactfully bring teachers to see their point of view in such matters as management of the child or setting goals compatible with ability.

In discussing the influence of the family on the child's values, Khatena (1978) pointed out that in some instances a gifted child's behavior does not reflect the family's values: "The gifted child is often dominated by the inner forces of his creativity that make him do things sometimes beyond his control" (p. 13). This kind of behavior makes it even more important for the home and school to work closely together in understanding the child and setting goals for him or her.

Parental attitudes can increase the drive for perfection and cause distress for the gifted child who is unable to achieve standards set for him or her.

> Parents may place very high expectations on advanced children and expect perfection. These children may be very fearful of making a mistake because mistakes are not tolerated at home, or at any rate, they are always "put down for an error." (Meyers, Ball, & Crutchfield, 1974, p. 27)

Thus, it can readily be seen that good communication between the school and home is a must. Both institutions need to share problems and determine cooperatively the action that should be taken to alleviate such.

The family usually knows a great deal about the interests and needs of the gifted child and should share this information with teachers. A child's behavior at home and at school is not always the same, and this information is valuable to teachers. Parents may have discovered certain management techniques that are effective with their child, and the teacher may find them equally useful at school. Knowing the interests of a child is particularly helpful to the teacher in planning specific learning activities. Teachers also need to know about physical problems, especially if special attention needs to be given.

Parents are reliable in identifying giftedness in their young children. Thus, professionals can rely on parents to share with them information that will lead to more accurate identification. Jacobs (1971) found them to be 76% effective and 61% efficient as compared to teachers, who were only 9.5% effective and 4.4% efficient in identifying gifted children. The ability of parents to identify their children as gifted has been corroborated by Ciha, Harris, and Hoffman (1974).

Family members can learn a great deal from teachers or caretakers of the gifted/talented child and can reinforce school learning at home. Parents cannot, however, keep abreast of the child's instructional program merely by participating in a limited number of conferences. How parents can become more intimately involved in educational programs is discussed later in the chapter.

Parents have a right to expect professionals to help them work more effectively with their gifted child. Research indicates that parents need help especially in disciplinary and instructional methods. They also need to become more knowledgeable about child development. In response to these needs, teachers can instruct parents in the use of developmental guidelines so that they can become better observers of their child's behavior. When both teachers and parents observe the child, they can share valuable information from two settings. Oftentimes, the teacher does most of the talking during parent/teacher conferences, but trained parents soon become active conference participants.

Home and school programs can be compatible when there is a close working relationship between parents and teachers. The young gifted child may become confused when expectations at home and at school differ radically. Sometimes parents expect too much, sometimes too little. In addition, gifted children are sometimes clever manipulators of adults, playing teacher against parents or vice versa. When school and home work closely together, what is taught in school can be reinforced and extended at home.

Fisher (1981) reported that a parent education study group conducted by a Westchester County, New York, public school provided parents with information on successful home environments. Some of the kinds of modeling behaviors discussed included overcoming fears of risk-taking, use of leisure time, sensitivity to individual differences in ability, and independence.

Gains made by the gifted child during the school year can be sustained and enhanced over the summer. Teachers often worry about loss of skills and other learnings over the summer, while parents of the gifted complain that their young children do not have enough to do during the summer. The gifted child can sustain and extend learning if parents and teachers map out a challenging summer plan that the parents can supervise. If a parent association for the gifted is organized, summer enrichment programs in various talent areas can be financed through parent fees.

Parents learn more readily from other parents if they are involved in the school program. Parents of gifted children have problems, too, and sharing these problems with other parents of gifted children is helpful. An organized school program for young gifted children fosters interaction among parents.

Involving family members in the educational program tends to make them less anxious about their role with their gifted child. A precocious child who far excels his or her peers—or other family members, for that matter—creates anxiety within a family. Several problems may arise when other siblings in the family are not gifted. For example, parents may unintentionally compare the gifted child with his or her siblings, thereby creating competition (Peterson, 1977). Almost all parents express concern about child-rearing adequacy, but parents of the gifted/talented are even more likely to question their abilities to do what is best. They are often troubled by the relationship of their young gifted child with other siblings and with the children of relatives, neighbors, and friends. Support and assurance from knowledgeable professionals working with their child helps them realize that they are capable of managing their child's experiences so that he or she will grow up to be happy and productive.

Parents who are involved in the gifted/talented child's educational program are its best advocates. It is always difficult to get public support for programs designed to meet the needs of gifted children. The common belief is that those with talent will succeed without special help, so why spend money on them when schools are faced with so many financial problems. Niro (1978), in a pamphlet published by The Council for Exceptional Children on securing funds for gifted education, put it this way:

> In a nation sold on the idea that equal education means the same education for all students, advocates of special education for any exceptional group must work to convince the rest of the community of the need for different educational programs.
>
> Advocates of programs for the gifted and talented frequently must act as persuasive salesmen in communities that spend their money on other products. This includes convincing them to pay the bill for services. (p. 1)

Who is in a more strategic position to convince others that gifted/talented children need special programming than the parents of these children? Without the leadership of the parents of handicapped children many of our most important legislative measures would never have passed. The more parents understand the unique needs of gifted children and the more they understand how these needs can be met, the better prepared they are to convince others that programs for the gifted are worthy of development and maintenance.

Parents involved in the educational program of their gifted child are in the best position to form local action groups. Parents of the gifted must realize that the budgets of public schools, private schools, Head Start, and day care centers that serve young gifted children in mainstreamed programs do not offer unlimited financial resources. A local association, however, can spearhead the development of after-school and summer programs for the gifted. Parents of young gifted children are frequently concerned about providing their children with challenging activities and are often willing to pay fees for the opportunity to enroll their children in classes where they can enhance skills and knowledge in particular talent areas. Niro (1978) has offered excellent suggestions for forming local parent associations for the education of gifted and talented children.

Children of parents who involve themselves in the educational program are higher achievers than those whose parents are uninvolved. Research and good sense suggest that when parents demonstrate interest in education and give their time and energy to help the school in various ways, children are likely to value education more and to achieve at a higher level than children of uninvolved parents. Parents are models for their children. If they demonstrate that they value educational achievement, so will their children.

The school can put parents in touch with resources in the community, county, or state that meet the special needs of the gifted child. The director of programs for the gifted in a school system or staff members who have demonstrated interest in gifted children are aware of resources available to families of gifted children and willing to explore possibilities and suggest alternatives. Making use of community resources for gifted children is particularly important, and parents play a prominent role in this endeavor.

RELEVANT RESEARCH

Although research is sparse, studies have indicated that parents of young gifted children do indeed need special support. Hackney (1981) noted that parents may feel personally and financially inadequate to meet their perceived obligations as parents of gifted children. They may feel inadequately educated and not intelligent enough to be responsible for the guidance of gifted children (Bridges, 1973). Some fear that their children may become misfits unable to enjoy the activities of childhood and to relate to children of similar age (Dettmann & Colangelo, 1980). Then, too, some parents wonder how others perceive them; often they are concerned that others may regard them as "snobbish" or setting themselves apart (Hackney, 1981). In addition, gifted children are often more demanding than children with lesser abilities and may tax their parents' time and energy. Problems may also exist between siblings (Bridges, 1973), especially because of the verbal skills of gifted children. There is, however, a body of related research that highlights the importance of the family, and parents in particular, and that has significant implications for those working with families of the young gifted/talented. These research findings are discussed under three headings: effect of parental attitudes, values, and behavior on the child; effectiveness of parent involvement; and concerns of parents of the gifted/talented.

Effects of Parental Attitudes, Values, and Behaviors on the Child

There is no doubt that the gifted child's attitudes, values, and behaviors reflect to no small degree those of his or her parents. This influence begins in the early years and is well established during the elementary school years—and with the gifted, perhaps even earlier. Flanagan (1964) identified the gifted among a population of 400,000 high school pupils in grades 9 through 12. Only 13% of the gifted students planned to go to college after graduation from high school. (Some did plan to attend vocational schools.) Information from the parents revealed that fewer than one-fifth of them aspired to have their children go to college. Thus, student aspiration accorded with that of parents. These findings imply that gifted children should be identified as early as possible and that parents should be provided with information regarding the capabilities of their children so that they can set expectations and aspirations in keeping with those abilities.

A number of studies have found a significant relationship between the attitudes and values of parents and the academic achievement of their children. Moss and Kagan (1958), for example, found that parents who value achievement and verbal expression transmit these values to their children, who in turn achieve in these areas. According to Thiel and Thill (1977), parental perceptions of children's abilities have a direct influence on achievement, self-concept, and aspirations. They found low school achievement was significantly correlated with discrepancies between fathers' perceptions and their sons' self-reports. Staples and Baer (1978) and Bloom and Sosniak (1981) have verified that when parents demonstrate that they value education and work closely with the school, children transfer and generalize learning to a greater degree.

Hess, Shipman, Brophy, and Baer (1968) investigated interactions among Black mothers and their young children. One group of mothers completed 4 years of college, and their husbands were employed in professional or managerial positions; another group completed high school, and their husbands held white- or blue-collar jobs; the third group terminated formal schooling no later than tenth grade, and their husbands had unskilled or semiskilled jobs. None of the mothers worked. A fourth group of mothers were on welfare and had no more than a tenth-grade education; no fathers were in these homes. All of the children were nearing their fourth birthdays.

Findings indicated that the more education the mother had, the more confidence she had in controlling what happened to her through her own attitudes and efforts. The more highly educated mothers perceived themselves as influential in helping their children attain certain goals. Mothers who were less educated saw themselves in a more passive role. Less educated mothers also tended to be more punitive in disciplining their children, while more educated mothers provided their children with more information and explanations about what was expected. In general, more educated mothers gave their children more specific information and feedback when they made mistakes; this information helped youngsters to correct mistakes. Better educated mothers provided more cognitive stimulation for their children, while less educated mothers were less likely to help their children focus on the important elements in the environment or to make valid judgments and discriminations. Terman and Oden's earlier study (1959) had comparable findings.

It is often assumed that gifted children have gifted parents. The assumption is false, and even if the parents are gifted it is wrong to conclude that they will have the knowledge and skills to facilitate their children's development (Passow, 1979; Robinson, 1977).

The importance of setting high standards of excellence for children was found by Rau, Mlodnosky, and Anastasiow (1964) and by Rosen and D'Androde (1959). Bloom and Sosniak (1981), in their study of parents of the gifted, found that the home plays a very important role in supporting and fostering talent development when parents consistently monitor the practice of the child and encourage and correct him or her.

Language development is critical for the full development of the academically talented child. Among the researchers who studied ways of promoting language development are Bing (1963), Milner (1951), Dave (1963), and Wolf (1964). They found that including children in activities and conversations with adults was important to language development and that parents who deliberately set about to enhance a child's vocabulary did promote language development. In recent years much more knowledge has been generated regarding language acquisition and how to promote language development, which is admittedly broader than acquisition of vocabulary.

Children who do well in school usually have parents who keep informed of how they are doing (Wolf, 1964), show interest and concern about school progress (Bayley & Schaefer, 1964), offer assistance in school and nonschool activities (Dave, 1963), make books available to them and read to them often (Bing, 1963), demonstrate warmth and provide support (Baldwin, Kalhorn, & Breese, 1945), and convey to them that they have a high regard for their competencies (Rosen & D'Androde, 1959).

In working with gifted 3- to 6-year-olds and their parents, Dwinell (1977) found that parents need to interact with other parents of gifted children. O'Neill (1978) reported on the help parents give each other in her parent involvement program.

Hess, Block, Costello, Knowles, & Largny (1971), summarizing the findings of a series of studies conducted at the University of Chicago, suggested eight aspects of parental behavior that affect the development of the young child in positive ways: consistency of discipline, explanatory control, expectations of success, sense of control, verbal interaction in the home, parental self-esteem, warmth, and independence training.

Milner (1971) found that children who are achievers are those whose family and school values are in harmony. In fact, he found that the high-scoring children were from middle class homes. Parents read to these children more often, engaged in conversation at mealtime more often, and administered less harsh physical discipline. According to the findings of Groth (1971), men derive their inspiration to achieve primarily from their warm mothers.

Walsh (1956), in a study of elementary-age underachieving boys, found that they felt less well accepted by their families than did achievers. Walsh explained that the reaction of the parents toward the gifted boys who were underachievers influenced them to reject the values of the family as well as those of society. Another study found fathers to be more influential in the lives of achievers than in the lives of underachievers (Pierce & Bowman, 1960). Dwinell (1977) suggested that the self-concept of parent and child are critical. She explained that when the parents gain self-confidence they are more likely to provide their gifted child with love and the emotional support they need.

Dewing (1970) found that the factors that appeared to be most influential in promoting creativity in the gifted child were discipline that was nonauthoritarian, encouragement of intellectual interests, and a parent/child relationship that was not overly dependent.

A study by Karnes, McCoy, Zehrbach, Wollersheim, Clarizio, Costin, & Stanley (1961) with gifted children in grades 2 through 5 investigated differences between underachievers and overachievers. Assessment of parental attitudes revealed that high achievers perceived themselves as more accepted by their parents than did underachievers. High achievers had more realistic self-concepts and a higher degree of creative ability. Another finding was that fathers of high achievers were significantly less hostile and rejecting than fathers of underachievers.

Mothers low in authoritarianism had daughters who were underachieving, according to the findings of Pierce and Bowman (1960). High-achieving girls had mothers who were highly dominant. Drews and Teahan (1957) offered comparable findings.

Gallagher and Crowder (1957) investigated the adjustment of 54 pupils with Binet IQ's of 150 or higher; approximately two-thirds of the group were underachievers. The causes of underachievement (lack of motivation and personality problems) were found to have their genesis predominantly outside of school.

While most studies seem to indicate that the home climate and parents play a major role in causing underachievement, Whitmore (1979) found that classroom conditions play the major role in contributing to underachievement.

In a book on underachievement, Fine (1967) made this statement based on his own observations:

> My observation as headmaster of a school that extends from nursery grades through high school fully supports the thesis that many parents inadvertently and unknowingly prepare the child for underachievement and then make the problem worse during the early and crucial school years. (p. 42)

Pringle (1970) reinforced Fine's observation:

> Since the basis of all learning is laid in the home during the earliest years of life, the chances are high that the roots of underachievement are also to be found there. Parental attitudes to the child, to achievement in general and to scholastic success in particular, as well as their own level of education and the cultural stimulation they provided during the preschool years and thereafter, play a major part. The child's own personality and how it interacts with and is influenced by that of his brothers and sisters further affects progress. Emotional relationships within the family, between the parents and between them and the child also have a vital role. And none of these operate in isolation but in their unique combination they affect emotional and intellectual development, and hence the child's readiness, adaptation, and responsiveness to the school situation. (p. 106)

Most studies of underachievers have been conducted with children in the middle grades and older. There is reason to believe, however, that the beginnings of underachievement occur at an early age, thus making a strong case for parent involvement. Pringle (1970), after studying able misfits in England, had this to say about the prevention and rehabilitation of underachievement:

> Much remains to be learned about how best to promote the development of able children. But enough is known already to justify taking action now. It needs to be on two fronts simultaneously, preventive and rehabilitative, and in each case the earlier it is attempted the higher the chance for its success. Preventive action would aim at the early identification of able children to ensure the optimal environment for the development of their potentialities. Rehabilitation would aim at an early detection of able misfits so that appropriate help can be given before the difficulties have become too intractable. (p. 127)

Abroms' chapter on affective development elaborates on the importance of self-concept and self-esteem in maximizing abilities. Pringle (1970) reinforced the important role parents play in the child's attitudes toward self and toward learning.

> The self has been defined as "reflected appraisals," which implies that whether a child develops a constructive attitude to himself, and subsequently to other people, depends in the first place on his parents' attitudes toward him. The more cherished he is, the more he comes to feel himself to be a worthwhile person. Similarly, being loved he learns to give love and trust. Thirdly, and perhaps most important for the achievement of his potential, the pleasure of his parents in his progress provides the main incentive for his learning. (p. 92)

The work of Terman and Oden (1959) on underachievers is probably the earliest and most extensive. In a longitudinal study with a population sample of 700 men, they compared the 150 most successful gifted men with the 150 least successful. Their findings revealed that the key to success was not so much IQ score as personality characteristics. They obtained ratings from the subjects, their wives, and their parents. The following four attributes differentiated the unsuccessful from the successful.

1. Lack of self-confidence.
2. Inability to persevere, to stick to a task, to tolerate frustration while finishing a task.
3. Lack of integration of goals; uncertainty about where they are going.
4. Inferiority feelings.

Data obtained from school records indicated that the two groups could have been differentiated as early as age 10. Further, the study found that these behaviors were consistent over time. These results have implications for early identification and programming with a strong emphasis on parent involvement.

More recent research on underachievers has reinforced the findings of Terman and Oden. For example, Bachtold (1974) compared the personality traits of achievers and underachievers in the fifth grade. Underachieving girls were found to lack self-confidence, to have less self-control, and to become excited more easily than high achievers. High-achieving males tended to be more stable, to manifest more sensitivity, and to be more serious than low achievers. Perkins (1965) found that achievers spent more time in work tasks involving peers and that underachievers tended to withdraw from academic tasks. In fact, underachievers in this study exhibited behavior that was incompatible with effective learning. A study conducted with gifted children in grades 4, 7, and 10 by Shaw and McCuen (1960) identified 1,000 achievers and 628 underachievers. On personality tests underachievers indicated a poorer self-concept and greater hostility than did achievers. Typically, underachievers looked more negatively on life than did achieving peers with like ability.

To prevent underachievement, Pringle (1970) suggested that four general psychological needs of the gifted must be met: need for love and security, need for new experiences, need for achievement and recognition, and need for responsibility and independence. "The basis of stable and enduring motivation lies in the satisfaction of the above four psychological needs" (p. 94). If these needs are met, underachievement is likely not to occur. If the child is underachieving, the best remedy is early detection and an all-out effort to see that the basic psychological needs are met.

Effectiveness of Parent Involvement

There are no longitudinal studies of young gifted children whose parents or other family members were involved in educational programs. Most intervention programs with children below the age of 5 have focused on children from low-income families, and only a few of these programs were home-based, where mothers were trained to be the primary change agents. One such program was the Mother Training Program at the University of Illinois (Karnes et al., 1968). Mothers met for 2 hours weekly and were trained to teach their 3- to 4-year-old children. In a period of 12 weeks the children whose mothers were being trained achieved a 7-point Stanford-Binet IQ gain. There was no IQ change in a comparable group of control children. In language development, as assessed by the Illinois Test of Psycholinguistic Abilities, the experimental children made 8.6 months' gain and the control group 4.3. Another study conducted with infants at the University of Illinois (Karnes et al., 1970) trained mothers over a 2-year period to intervene with their infants. The experimental group scored higher by 16 points on the Stanford-Binet as compared to a matched control group. On the Illinois Test of Psycholinguistic Abilities the experimental group scored 5 months ahead of the control groups at age 3. A sibling comparison yielded a 28-point difference on the Stanford-Binet and a total language-age difference of 7 months in favor of the experimental subjects.

Levenstein (1971) trained mothers to work with their 2- and 3-year-old children. The experimental group made significantly greater gains on standardized measures of intellectual functioning than did the control groups. Weikart (1969) also worked with mothers to enhance their teaching skills. While there was no control group, the infant subjects made significantly greater gains on the Bayley mental scales than would be expected over the treatment time.

The research mentioned here has endorsed the training of mothers to work with their young children. Whether or not significant gains could be obtained by working with mothers from middle and upper income groups is yet to be investigated.

There are some organized efforts to enhance the role of parents of the gifted and through parent involvement to facilitate change in schools. One such program is located at the University of Wisconsin in Madison in the Guidance Institute for Talented Students (GIFTS). While this program involves parents of older gifted students, there is reason to believe that such a program for parents of preschoolers would be equally effective.

While no research projects have been reported on the effectiveness of parent involvement on the development of the young gifted child, Callahan and Kauffman (1982) have stated: "There is little evidence that parents are systematically involved in the schooling of their gifted children; and much expert opinion suggests that parents of gifted children are not often involved" (p. 53). This does not imply, however, that parents of the gifted should not be involved in their child's educational program.

Concerns of Parents of the Gifted/Talented

The concerns of parents of gifted youngsters as indicated by research have implications for what professionals need to do to involve parents and other family members. Parents' concerns range from their child's educational options to anticipated problems of boredom and maladjustment. Counseling services to the parents of the intellectually advanced children can address these concerns.

In a 1978 study (Debinski & Mauser), questionnaires were sent to 200 (105 returns) parents of gifted children ages 4 to 20 who were enrolled in private or public school programs for the gifted. The major purpose of this study was to obtain recommendations from the parents to professionals regarding the essential aspects of the parent-professional relationship. The following recommendations were made to the professionals as interpreted by the researchers:

> *Parents request information on their child's social as well as academic behavior.* The recommendation suggests that parents are becoming aware of the possible implications giftedness may have for a child's social adjustment. Professionals should consider not only the unique skills of a child but also the child as a whole.
>
> *Parents emphasize receiving immediate relevant advice, e.g., how to teach children to do things, suggestions for enrichment activities, and information regarding current academic and social progress as opposed to long-term recommendations regarding future educational and vocational outcomes.* Federal legislation (PL 94-142) stipulates the development of individualized educational plans for the exceptional child. This regulation should contribute to the realization of this recommendation. Educational objectives and corresponding intervention techniques developed by school officials will be shared with parents, thus providing them with a source of direction and assurance.
>
> *Parents strongly recommend receiving copies of reports written about their children.* Mandatory legislation has included a provision which realizes this particular parental need.
>
> *Parents overwhelmingly disapprove of the use of professional jargon.* The language used to communicate between professionals is not appropriate for communicating with the lay person. The de-emphasis on jargon should facilitate the development of a comfortable, supporting atmosphere in which parents are free to ask questions and pursue topics or issues of concern to them.
>
> *Parents of gifted children strongly recommend that teachers keep them informed of their child's academic progress.* It appears that parents of gifted and learning disabled children are alike in their efforts to sustain progress and arrest deterioration in academic and social skills. (pp. 12–13)

Malone (1975) investigated the needs of parents of the gifted and discovered that they wanted more counseling and a knowledge of teaching methods to use with their children. They particularly sought help with discipline, with how to help their children develop their strengths, and with how to enhance their sensitivity. They were also concerned about their rights as parents. Another concern was how to provide their children with a home atmosphere conducive to child development. They were also aware that children have different learning styles and were interested in how to facilitate the learning styles of their own children.

In investigating the characteristics parents of the gifted want for their children, Bachtold (1974) found these to be most desired: health, sense of humor, self-sufficiency, sense of beauty, independence in thinking, curiosity, courage in convictions, self-confidence, affection, independence in judgment, receptivity to the ideas of others, sincerity, consideration of others, and self-starting ability. (These are not ranked in order of parental preference.)

Colangelo and Dettmann (1982) reviewed the literature on families of the gifted and pinpointed the critical needs expressed by parents:

1. Need for knowledge of characteristics and definitions of giftedness;
2. Need for knowledge about ways to promote and respond to achievement, since parental emphasis on achievement is controversial and has been associated with both academic successes and failures;
3. Need for knowledge of discipline techniques that work with bright and creative children;
4. Need for knowledge of techniques that alleviate sibling rivalry;
5. Need for reassurance to counteract fears about gifted children's social maladjustment;
6. Need for reassurance to counteract feelings of being inadequately prepared to deal with a gifted child;
7. Need for clarification of their own roles and those of the school in taking responsibility for helping a gifted child develop. (p. 59)

The Chapel Hill Project for the gifted/talented handicapped (Leonard, 1978) conducted a survey in which parents were asked to rank activities in the program that they felt were most helpful to them. The following four were found to be the most helpful: individual parent-staff conferences, classroom observation, printed materials regarding the child's special needs, and staff assistance with individual requests for the location of community resources.

Mathews (1981) reviewed the concerns of parents of gifted children regarding educational placement and programs (Debinski & Mauser, 1978; Malone, 1975) and offered suggestions for parent-teacher communication: (a) informational materials (program, placement options, teacher's background, bibliography of gifted materials, and questionnaire), (b) parent newsletter, (c) parent-awareness meeting, and (d) parent-teacher conferences.

At the close of each year, the parents of children in the Astor Program completed a questionnaire-evaluation of the program. A significantly high proportion of the parents were consistently well pleased with the effects the program had on academic progress, cognitive skills, attitudes, interpersonal relationships, and interests (Ehrlich, 1978).

At the end of the 1977 school year, the Astor Program became a part of the local school districts. A follow-up questionnaire was sent to parents whose children were enrolled in the Astor Program during 1974–1977 to determine how parents viewed the program. The following is a list of the benefits parents noted in approximate order of frequency (Ehrlich, 1978);

- "Love of learning"—"A comfortableness with learning"
- Increased self-assurance
- Positive self-esteem—acceptance of self as different and "Knowing it's O.K."
- Introduction to a variety of subjects
- Broadened interests
- Opportunity to acquire bright and talented friends
- Being among intellectual peers is "expansive"
- Increased sociability
- Development of an open and spontaneous curiosity
- Exposure to exceptional teachers
- Ability to read fluently
- Awareness of and excellence in mathematics
- Increased vocabulary
- Joy in teaching and learning from peers
- Ease in communication with other people
- Interest in nature and science, or art, or music
- Ability to work independently and to follow directions
- Capacity to follow through on projects and complete tasks
- Increased sense of responsibility
- Admiration and respect for abilities of others. (p. 165)

While there were some parents who had reservations about and objections to various aspects of the program, it would appear that parents in general viewed the Astor Program positively.

OPTIONS FOR FAMILY INVOLVEMENT

The success of a family involvement program is contingent upon a staff trained in early childhood, knowledgeable about the gifted, adept at working with parents, and genuinely committed to parents; yet success also depends to a great extent upon flexibility. Families need a number of options, and some of those have been outlined by Karnes and Zehrbach (1972): attending large or small group meetings and conferences, working on a class newsletter or on instructional materials, directly teaching in the classroom or at home, working with another parent, taking field trips to other programs with other parents, and taking field trips with the children. Additional alternatives in family involvement according to these authors include observing in the classroom, interpreting the program to visitors, enrolling in an organized course, participating in identification procedures, assisting in evaluation, and collecting data.

Colangelo and Dettman (1982) recently reported on their research regarding the role of parents in the education of their gifted child. Extending their investigation of who has primary responsibility for educating gifted students, these authors established a parent-teacher model that differentiates four types of interaction:

Type I (Cooperation)—A sharing of information and concern for educational programming.

Type II (Conflict)—Parental concern for specialized programs versus teachers' reserving such programs for learning disabled and handicapped children.

Type III (Interference)—Parents' concern about "labeling" versus the school's desire to provide special programs for the gifted.

Type IV (Natural Development)—Passivity on the part of both parents and teachers.

The authors felt that such a model can provide an important basis for determining the role that exists and the role that is preferred by both parties.

Another author who has addressed parent involvement is Cassidy (1981), who also stressed the importance of parent involvement in gifted education and defined five roles parents can perform: advisor/advocate, parental guide, mentor, classroom aide, and materials developer. "All parents should assume at least two of them; and teachers of the gifted should encourage maximum participation in all five roles" (p. 287).

Kroth (1980) has identified four levels of involvement which can be applied to all parents. The first level is informational from the standpoints of both teachers and parents. At the second level, parents participate in school-related projects, attend IEP conferences, and assist in class placement decisions. The third level involves assistance in the planning of educational experiences. The highest level of involvement, level four, is parents working together as a group organizing workshops and the like. Further suggestions for parent involvement have been discussed by Nolte and Dinklocker (1981) and McQuilken (1981).

In a tour of 15 school districts in a large midwestern metropolitan area that provides for elementary gifted and talented children, Newman (1981) found that less than 20% of the parents were involved at the classroom level and that 20% of the building administrators considered parents of gifted children *persona non grata*. On the other hand, "parents in all districts showed a strong concern for supporting programs and maintaining two-way communication with teachers and program coordinators" (p. 116).

Needs Assessment

One of the first steps in determining options for a parent involvement program is to conduct a needs assessment wherein parents are made aware of some options open to them and have opportunities to add others. (One such assessment instrument, developed at the University of Illinois, is shown in Figure 8-1.) Without such suggestions, the professional puts parents at a decided disadvantage by merely asking, "How do you want to become involved in the program?" Parents usually have only their own school experience to fall back on, when parent involvement may have meant attending a conference with the teacher once or twice a year—and then only if a child had serious problems. Alternative plans for meeting the needs of individual

FIGURE 8-1
Family Needs Assessment Form

FAMILY NEEDS ASSESSMENT

University of Illinois Program for Preschool Bright and Gifted Children

Name of Family Member: _____

Name of Child in Program: _____

Date: _____

Please rank the following statements within *each* area according to your needs as a parent or other family member of a young gifted child. Use #1 to identify your area of greatest concern, #2 the area of next greatest concern, etc. The highest number will indicate the area of *least* concern.

I. Knowledge of Giftedness
   ____ Need for more understanding of the characteristics of gifted children.
   ____ Need for more information about my child's developmental profile and test results.
   ____ Need for more knowledge about early identification of giftedness in young children.
   ____ Other—Specify

II. Ways of Working with Your Child
   ____ Need for knowing how to stimulate creativity at home.
   ____ Need for knowing ways to manage my child's behavior.
   ____ Need for knowing ways to develop task persistence.
   ____ Need for knowing how to increase independence in my child.
   ____ Need for knowing how to extend my child's self-selected activities or projects.
   ____ Other—Specify

III. Please list 3 areas of concern you have as parent of a gifted child.

   _____

   _____

   _____

IV. Please list 3 goals you have for your child in this year's preschool program.

   _____

   _____

   _____

V. What do you consider the most important characteristics parents of gifted children need to have or develop? (Please list at least 3!)

   _____   _____

   _____   _____

   _____   _____

Continued on next page

FIGURE 8-1 (Continued)

VI. Do you think being the parent of a gifted child requires skills or abilities different from those required of the parent of a normal child?
Please explain:

_____

_____

_____

VII. Please feel free to make any other comments regarding parent activities for the program.

_____

_____

_____

NOTE: This instrument has been found to be most effective when it is used in a structured interview with individual parents. In no instance should it be sent by mail without previous personal contact and an explanation as to why the assessment is made and what will be done with the results.

parents can be made during individual conferences, but a group meeting might be an appropriate time to share the results of the needs assessment and to make decisions regarding future meetings. A committee might be charged with planning the details of such meetings.

Guidelines for Parent Involvement Program

The coordinator of the parent involvement program would do well to keep in mind the following guidelines when considering options for parent involvement.

No two members of a family have exactly the same needs or interests in working in the program. One needs assessment, therefore, is not sufficient for all members of a family. The father, for example, might decide to attend a study group to learn more about child development, but the mother might prefer direct teaching in the classroom; an older brother may decide to read a story to the child each night.

Goals for each family member should be developed before involvement begins. Procedures for assessing family needs and establishing goals have been found effective in preschool programs for the gifted at the University of Illinois. It is advocated that a number of alternative ways for family members to become involved in their child's program be shared with them, as well as suggested appropriate goals.

Records should be kept regarding what each family member does to foster the development of the young gifted child. The record-keeping system should not be time-consuming, but it should ensure that important information is retained.

Each family member should help to evaluate the work he or she does. Everyone needs feedback to maintain interested and informed participation; therefore, individual conferences with family members are a must.

Family participants should meet periodically with the coordinator and other staff members involved in the child's educational program. During these meetings the contributions of each family member should be reviewed and ideas for further programming developed.

Needs assessment is not a one-time activity but an ongoing one. Needs change over time.

Professionals should assist family members to extend their involvement as they gain greater knowledge and skill. At first a family member might feel more comfortable collecting data (language samples from the child, for example), but when the necessary competencies have been acquired, he or she may be ready to do direct teaching in the classroom.

Family members who do not wish to become involved must not be forced to do so. Instead, the coordinator should try to determine why that person does not want to participate. There may be other problems facing that person—pending divorce, problems with other children, financial problems—that interfere with participation at a given time. Support from another parent may help to involve a hesitant parent.

Family members should participate in the development of a plan to evaluate the parent involvement program. A representative group of parents may work with the coordinator and an evaluator to develop an evaluation plan. Family members may even be interested in helping collect and analyze data.

Parents should help decide how to improve the family involvement program. Their evaluation is useful in determining what areas need to be improved. Parents can be very creative in planning ways of improving a program, some of which may entail greater involvement on their part.

Professionals should from time to time evaluate themselves to determine where professional growth is needed. Working with parents is a challenge, and it may be an even greater challenge to work with parents who, like their gifted children, have many creative ideas and dare to challenge what the school is or is not doing.

Three Common Options for Parent Involvement

Karnes and Zehrbach (1972) have cited the three most commonly used options for involving parents in the school: large group meetings, small group discussions, and individual conferences. They have also provided suggestions for making these three alternatives successful.

Large Group Meetings

Typically large group meetings are used to convey information quickly, and they are usually limited to a given topic. Not all parents are interested in attending group meetings, but Karnes and Zehrbach (1972) concluded that successful meetings that are well attended tend to have certain characteristics. Among them are:

- Parent involvement in the selection of topics, speakers, and date and hour of meeting. Evening meetings are best for most parents.
- Monthly meetings. Parents are busy and too-frequent meetings discourage attendance. The length of the meeting should be set and maintained.
- Notification of the meeting through notes, newsletters, and telephone call reminders. Sending one notification of meetings for the year is not adequate. There should be an initial notice at least a month in advance and follow-up reminders 4 to 7 days prior to the meeting.
- Dynamic speakers and the use of visual aids. The speaker should be thoroughly familiar with the type of audience to whom she or he will be speaking.
- Arrangements for child care at the site of the meeting.
- Car pools or other transportation arrangements.
- Involving parents in committee work to support the group.
- A friendly atmosphere. There should be time for socializing with other parents during the course of the meeting.

Attendance records should be kept. Comments made by family members that give insight into their needs should also be recorded. This information is useful in planning and in determining the progress of the involvement program over time.

During an informal social gathering early in the year the staff should be introduced and the philosophy and content of the program discussed. A guided tour of the classroom is always appreciated. Slides of the children involved in their classrooms add interest to such a meeting and foster an understanding of how the goals of the program are being accomplished. Questions from parents should be encouraged.

Parents also appreciate having the names of all parents and children in the program as well as their telephone numbers early in the year.

This first meeting is a good time to discuss the purpose of the needs assessment. A committee can be appointed to serve with professional staff in the development of future group meetings.

Small Group Discussions

Small group meetings bring together parents with similar interests and needs. The size of the group should be under eight. These meetings should be informal and held at times most convenient to parents. They should deal with a given topic that meets immediate needs. Such groups may meet a limited number of times. When the needs of the group seem to be met, the small group meetings are discontinued. Over the year, small group meetings may be held on various topics, and their make-up changes according to the interests and needs of parents.

A typical subject for a small group discussion might be coping with sibling rivalry. This topic is very stressful to some parents, and the opportunity to talk with other parents facing the same problem is enlightening and helpful. Teachers also gain insights during these small group meetings that help them understand a particular gifted child. Then, too, teachers may be able to suggest how parents can handle difficult situations.

The following ways to ensure the success of small group meetings are adapted from Karnes and Zehrbach (1972):

- Meetings are held frequently, as often as once weekly, but are usually discontinued after a few weeks when group needs are met.
- Related or interrelated topics are chosen by parents.
- Responsibilities for planning and conducting meetings rotate among parents.
- Articles, books, or cassette tapes, reviewed during the week can provide the basis for meetings.
- Careful attention must be given to individual needs within the group—social, emotional, and intellectual. It is important for parents to have an opportunity to discuss and seek help for specific problems.
- The content of the meeting must be challenging, yet on a level where comprehension and assimilation are possible for all participants, even though the education levels of parents of gifted children are not always comparable. This is particularly important if the gifted child is mainstreamed and parents of children with lesser abilities are members of the group.
- Social amenities such as dress and language should be compatible with group customs.
- A relaxed but goal-oriented atmosphere must be developed.
- The teacher must participate but not be dominant or condescending. A first-name basis for interacting may be appropriate for one locale and inappropriate for another.
- The small group setting may offer an opportunity to plan ways of helping new parents or reluctant participants to become involved in activities suited to their needs. Focusing the group on this kind of problem enhances its cohesiveness.
- Meetings should be held for definite, predetermined periods of time, usually not exceeding 2 hours.
- The teacher should be alert to the growth and development of group members so that an individual who outgrows one group can be encouraged to shift to a more appropriate one.
- Group goals may need to be shifted to a higher level or different direction to meet the individual needs of members of the group.
- The teacher should be sensitive to the need for change and provide the necessary support and guidance. The teacher should view such changes as growth.

- Pertinent information that emerges during a meeting should be recorded by the teacher following the meeting for purposes stated previously.

Individual Conferences

Among parents of the gifted, the individual conference seems to be the most popular parent involvement strategy. Most parents appreciate an opportunity to interact with the teacher individually and generally feel freer to ask questions and to share concerns on a one-to-one basis. Teachers gain a great deal from such sessions, including more effective ways of interacting with a given child in the school situation and learning what parents do at home to reinforce or extend the offerings of the school. Problems emerging in the home that have not surfaced in the school may also come to light. The parent conference, then, is a time for sharing facts and feelings. Both parent and teacher have a special understanding of what the child is like, and this kind of sharing can be very gratifying and helpful to both parties.

The following suggestions to teachers can help make the parent/teacher conference a success.

- Set up the conference well in advance. Give the parents ample time to make arrangements for the care of other children. The time should be mutually agreeable to parents and teacher.
- Be prepared for the conference. Review the child's records. Think carefully about the questions you are going to ask the parents and the material you are going to share with them.
- Set a time limit for the conference and observe it. If the material being discussed hasn't been adequately dealt with, set up another conference rather than prolong the current one. Conferences should be no longer than an hour. Terminate the conference when interest is high.
- Help make the parents feel comfortable. Do not sit behind a desk, which tends to place you in a position of authority. An unhurried, friendly atmosphere gets the conference off to a good start. A cup of coffee may help.
- Be positive. No matter what problems the gifted child may manifest, the discussion can be conducted in an affirmative manner. The gifted child who is an only child, for instance, may hold center stage at home and have difficulty sharing the teacher with other children. Until rapport is established with the parents, the teacher should not introduce this problem. When the time is right, a constructive approach is to tell the parents, "One of our goals for Johnny is to help him learn to take turns and share my time with others."
- Respect the feelings and beliefs of the parents. You may not agree with how the parents are handling the child, but they should not be made to feel inadequate or guilty. Later, through participating in small group meetings, through observing at the school, through talking with other parents, the parents in question may discover better ways of interacting with the child.

- Be flexible. You may have planned to discuss certain materials at the conference, but the parents may need to discuss another topic. Shift gears. If the parents ask for help in an area in which you do not feel prepared, seek help from another professional and set a future meeting for the parents.
- Be a good listener. Teachers are prone to do all of the talking, but they can learn a great deal if they listen attentively. Praise the parents' efforts. Parents of the gifted may have self-doubts; they need encouragement and support.
- Let the parents know how vital they are in the development of the child. In no way should the teacher imply that the school has all of the "know how" about rearing gifted children. Convey instead that the school is supporting the efforts of the parents. Make clear that it is important for the school and home to work closely together for the best interests of the child.
- Be a good observer of the parents. Sometimes it is as important to note what the parents do not say as what they do say. Body language tells a great deal. Heightened color, restlessness, hesitation, and repetition convey messages.
- Don't expect the same responses from all parents of the gifted. It takes a long time for some parents to share their concerns or to become genuinely involved in their child's educational program. Take your cue from the parents. At what entry level do the parents feel most comfortable? What are their goals for themselves? Good relationships take time. Don't make timid or reluctant parents feel you are moving in on them.
- Don't compare a gifted child with other gifted children in the classroom. Help the parents determine where the child is developmentally and compare the child's present progress with past progress.
- Facilitate discussion by asking leading questions: "What does Bobby like to do by himself?" "What do you do when ____?" "Tell me some ways you discipline Mary." Use your comments to reassure and to encourage sharing.
- Refrain from telling parents what they should be doing. In other words, don't play the role of an "expert." Planning together with parents taking the lead is preferable. After all, the parent is the manager of the child over time and should be in the driver's seat.
- Near the end of the conference, summarize what has transpired and make joint plans for the next conference. Highlight the accomplishments and give the parents definite reasons to look forward to the next conference.
- Record salient aspects of the conferences immediately after the conference. Taking notes during a conference tends to make parents uncomfortable, but written records are invaluable for future planning and evaluation.

Naumann (1981) has listed the following questions as important focal points for parents of gifted children during teacher conferences:

(1) What is my child reading?
(2) How is my child's language development?

(3) What is my child's approach to problem-solving?
(4) What does my child do when his work is finished?
(5) What are my child's strengths and weaknesses?
(6) What are your goals for my child?
(7) What can I do to nurture my child's abilities? (p. 2)

Teachers may need inservice meetings to help them improve their skills in conducting parent-teacher conferences. Social workers trained in interviewing can be most helpful to teachers in acquiring skills in this area.

PROBLEMS IN INVOLVING PARENTS

Following are some of the many problems encountered when professionals try to involve parents in the educational programs of their young gifted/talented children.

A large percentage of the mothers of young children work outside the home. Over 50% of the women who have children under age 6 work outside the home. (It is not known what percentage of mothers of gifted children work outside the home.) Obviously, it is difficult for these women to come to school for conferences, to observe, or to participate in activities such as direct teaching in the classroom.

Some parents are reluctant to be involved. While the importance of parent involvement should be made clear, professionals should not put undue pressure on parents or make them feel guilty if they are hesitant to involve themselves. If the professional is patient and keeps in contact with the parents through notes or telephone calls, most parents eventually become involved. Parents shouldn't be forced to do what they do not want to do. While some parents of the gifted seem disinclined to involve themselves in the school program, parents of the gifted generally become involved more readily and more consistently than any other group of parents.

It is not uncommon for staff members who have spent a great deal of time and effort in planning for family involvement to become frustrated with parental responses (Israelson, 1980). Professionals who anticipate this response will not be dismayed when it occurs.

Other preschool children in the family make it difficult for mothers to become involved. In many programs babysitting arrangements are made at school or parents take turns keeping each other's children. In the needs assessment of the family, school personnel must take into consideration the various demands placed on parents' time.

Getting fathers and other members of the family involved is difficult. Mothers are the family members most frequently involved. Fathers sometimes do not become involved because they feel unwanted or awkward. An effort should be made to get fathers to visit the school, to observe, and to go on field trips. Some can arrange to take a couple of hours off from work. Most can find a night to attend a meeting. Older siblings should also be welcomed; they are with young preschoolers for long periods of time and have many teaching opportunities. They, too, can acquire improved skills of interacting with their younger brothers and sisters.

Lack of transportation can prevent parent involvement. This problem may seem trite; however, families with only one automobile may find it difficult to attend daytime meetings. Parents may find the cost of public transportation to meetings prohibitive. The coordinator can usually help parents work out car pools, which also help parents get to know each other better.

Activities sometimes do not meet the needs of the parents. Nothing undermines parent involvement more than programs in which speakers seem to focus on topics of little interest to parents or who do not have the expertise needed to interact with parents of gifted children. If a speaker is central to a meeting, he or she must not only be knowledgeable on the subject but must have the personality and interpersonal skills to interact with parents of precocious children. For the most part, parents of gifted children are themselves likely to be gifted or talented, and some teachers find it difficult to interact with parents who are markedly superior.

ENSURING THE SUCCESS OF THE PARENT INVOLVEMENT PROGRAM

How can professionals make sure the parent involvement program gets off to a good start? They must keep in mind that parent involvement is a relatively new concept. To many educators, parent involvement merely means having conferences with parents two or three times a year and telling them what they "should" know. While progress is being made in involving parents, it is not as intensive or widespread as one would hope. The following guidelines may help avoid failure:

Employ a mature, experienced person with above-average ability to coordinate the program. Parents of the gifted/talented are usually very capable themselves and can easily threaten even an experienced teacher. Parents cannot relate to a person who is uncomfortable interacting with them. If it is not financially feasible to employ a coordinator for the program, an administrator will have to decide who is best qualified to carry out that role.

Employ a coordinator trained in education of the gifted as well as in early childhood. To ensure the program's success, its leader needs expertise in both fields. The administration should plan ahead; if a well-trained person with experience cannot be employed, the administrator might consider hiring a person with good potential and related experience and then arranging for that person to receive the needed training.

See that parents of gifted children have opportunities to interact as a group. Since there are a limited number of gifted children in any one classroom, the coordinator should arrange meetings for the parents of the gifted to express concerns, to share ways of promoting talents, and to gain new knowledge about gifted children. This does not mean that parents of the gifted should not meet with parents of average-ability or handicapped children. In fact, through such meetings parents can become more cognizant of how gifted children differ from other children and can become more sensitive to their special needs.

Conduct a needs assessment among the parents of gifted children to discover how they want to be involved and what specific concerns they have. There is no meeting more doomed to failure than one in which professionals have tried to guess parent needs and to plan the meeting without parental input.

Develop staff commitment to working with parents. It is well known that many professionals do not want parents to be involved in the educational program. A study conducted in Connecticut has confirmed this impression (Yoshida, Fenton, Kaufman, & Maxwell, 1978). In fact, educators often convey to parents that they are not needed (Clements & Alexander, 1975; Kelly, 1974). While these studies were conducted with teachers of handicapped children, it is likely that teachers feel the same way about parents of gifted children.

Provide in the budget for the parent involvement program. There are two good reasons for the parent involvement program to have a line in the budget. One is to provide money to equip a parent meeting room and to begin a parent library. Initially, the budget may be modest, but the parents may take over much of the financial responsibility after the program gets started, including the raising of funds to supplement the budget. The other reason is that a line in the budget indicates a firm commitment from the administration to the parent involvement program.

Initiate the program on a small scale. If there has never been a parent involvement program for the young gifted child or if the coordinator has never coordinated such a program before, integrate parents into the program gradually. Initial involvement may be limited to the development of the individualized education program and to guided observation in the classroom followed by a conference. In several weeks or even months, workshops in the management of gifted children may begin. It may be 2 years before a full program is under way.

Establish good communication between the school and home. Parents need to know how their gifted children are progressing. Parents also need feedback on whether or not they are facilitating the development of their children. The professional has an obligation to help parents apply what they have learned in the parent involvement program and to evaluate their efforts to facilitate the growth of their gifted/talented children.

Individualize parent involvement. Parents of the gifted/talented are as varied as the children in the program. They come from a variety of socioeconomic backgrounds. Their needs and concerns are sometimes quite diverse. They have different levels of education. Even though some involvement will be in groups, there must also be differentiation.

WHAT PARENTS NEED TO KNOW TO HELP THEIR YOUNG GIFTED/TALENTED CHILD DEVELOP FULLY

Parents of gifted children vary on many dimensions, but the concern here is differences in knowledge and skills. The information in this section is based on research findings, the opinions of experts, and the experience of those who work with parents of the gifted/talented, especially parents of young children, and can be used as a guideline in developing a training program for parents. Gowan (1964) and Ginsberg (1976) have discussed the suggestions of parents, but the list that follows brings together suggestions from a number of practitioners.

Young gifted/talented children are first of all children, and they share the basic needs of all children. They need love, affection, and support, but at the same time they need limits. These limits must be fair, they must be understood by the child, and they must be maintained by parents. Young gifted children can be manipulative and will test limits, but ultimately they will feel more secure if they know that caring adults are strong enough to help them control their behavior. Young gifted/talented children should, however, participate in the decision-making process as early as they are able.

Young gifted children are quick to model the value systems of their parents, their attitudes, and their modes of behavior. Parents, therefore, must take a critical look at themselves. Are they modeling behaviors they wish their children to adopt? In addition, husbands and wives sometimes disagree about value systems. These differences should be reconciled and a compromise agreed upon to avoid confusing the child.

Young gifted children, like all children, need a happy, stable environment. Difficult problems may occur when parents divorce, a parent dies, or the family has to move. During such periods parents may need to seek counseling to determine how to maintain the most stable environment possible.

Consistency in managing young children is of utmost importance. The gifted child soon learns to pit one parent against another if he or she finds that parents are not in agreement or vacillate in their decisions.

Young gifted children need a stimulating environment in which to react. Toys that have more than one use encourage problem-solving and divergent thinking. Gifted youngsters need books that are compatible with their interests and level of development. They should be read to regularly and observe other members of the family reading. They should be taken to museums and historical sites and encouraged to watch special television programs; then parents should talk with them about what they have seen and heard.

Parents need to accept their gifted children for themselves, not for what they can do better than their age-mates. At the same time, parents should appreciate these talents and convey this feeling to their gifted children. They should let their children know that they value their achievements.

Building a healthy, realistic self-concept in the gifted/talented child is a major goal of school and home. The child should recognize that he or she is respected and valued and should be praised for accomplishments. At the same time, gifted youngsters need parents and teachers who can help them learn to get along with children of lesser abilities.

The curiosity of young gifted children should be nourished and their questions answered. Even at an early age these children should learn how to answer questions by going to the library or using an encyclopedia and dictionaries. The gifted child should be encouraged to seek knowledge, to formulate questions, to find answers.

A well-developed language system is crucial for young gifted/talented children. Parents should deliberately help these children enhance their vocabulary. They should include them in spontaneous conversations and set up situations in which they will have opportunities to express themselves.

Encouraging and challenging the gifted child facilitates development, but pressure tends to have the opposite effect. Parents should guard against trying to live through their child. The unfulfilled aspirations of parents should not be bequeathed to the gifted child.

Parents should not let their gifted child threaten them. Even a 4-year-old may have some knowledge an adult hasn't acquired; certainly he or she will ask questions a parent can't answer. Parents can learn to say, "I don't know the answer to that, but I can help you find it."

Parents should realize that it is damaging to gifted children to exploit them. Exploitation makes them less well accepted by their peers and by adults and encourages antagonistic attitudes. At the same time, the gifted child may develop in unacceptable ways, and the labels "conceited" or "smart aleck" may soon be justified.

Parents should recognize that family relationships can be undermined by comparing one sibling to another or for that matter by comparing the gifted child to any other child.

Setting standards of excellence in keeping with what the gifted/talented child is capable of doing should start in the preschool years because this is a value that must be internalized. The task might be simple: putting toys away on the shelf. At first the parent might help the child set the standard of what constitutes a good job. Later, the child should be expected to do the job well, but he or she needs to be given responsibility early.

Parents should avoid overscheduling the gifted child. When parents realize their child is gifted, they sometimes enroll the child in dancing classes, arrange for piano and violin lessons, schedule a library hour on Saturday, and take the child to children's plays or to adult performances. Some gifted youngsters don't have a moment to call their own. Talented children need independent time to choose their own activities.

While gifted/talented children tend to be superior physically, socially, emotionally, and intellectually, they are not always equally gifted in all areas, and parents should not set unreasonable goals. A gifted youngster may have the language of an 8-year-old, but when he falls down and cuts his knee he cries like the 4-year-old he is and wants the comfort and attention that his age-mates would receive in similar circumstances.

Parents of young gifted children should encourage them to be independent in appropriate ways—dressing and undressing, taking an active role in bathing, setting the table, putting away their toys, completing a puzzle or operating a record player without help. Encouraging gifted children to take responsibility is important for their future success; they should be given chores and monitored to see that they complete them. On the other hand, gifted children are sometimes more dependent on adults in certain ways than their less gifted peers; for example, gifted youngsters may be unable to obtain the information they want and need from books or to obtain the materials/experiences they need to learn what they want to learn.

Parents should take time to help their gifted children correct errors. It is distressing to any child to be told that he or she has done something wrong when the child has no notion of how to do it correctly, but gifted children are especially sensitive about and critical of their own efforts. They need the support of the significant adults in their lives to help them learn to accept failure and to benefit from mistakes.

Parents who do not have a good relationship with their young gifted/talented child should seek help immediately. Numerous research findings cited previously indicate that poor parental relationships are associated with the underachievement of gifted children. Parents of a gifted child, like all parents, are busy, but they should set aside time that belongs to the child. Special time together helps establish the reinforcing relationship the child needs.

Gifted children whose parents take an active interest in how they are doing in school and who become involved in the school programs do well in school. Parents should let the school know they are interested in progress reports. In fact, research suggests that parents want written reports on child progress and want to know about affective as well as academic areas.

Parents should arrange for their gifted child to have playmates of comparable age and ability even if that requires "car pooling." Parents of gifted youngsters might get together and work out a cooperative arrangement so that transportation can be organized and schedules planned in advance.

Talented children should be encouraged to think divergently and be rewarded for doing so. Some of their solutions to a problem may seem far-fetched, but parents should recognize that it is important for gifted children to think in original ways. Children whose creative responses are not appreciated will soon cease to express them.

Parents should investigate the possibility of organizing a parent association to support the school in developing and maintaining programs for the gifted. Such a group can promote, even help write, good legislation; it can work to obtain the help of community agencies in developing after-school and summer programs for the gifted; and it can help provide resources for such programs during the school year.

Parents should actively seek help in developing the skills that will enable them to be good advocates for their children throughout their education. If they leave educational programming to chance, their gifted children may never develop their potential to the fullest. Parents should not hesitate to ask the school staff for help in finding the parent training they need.

Parents need to grow in their abilities to understand and work with their gifted children. The better parents feel about themselves, the more effective they will be in promoting the growth, including the self-concept and self-esteem, of their children. Parents won't feel very good about their gifted children if they don't feel good about themselves as parents.

Unfortunately, relatively few publications have been written for the parents of young gifted children. Useful resources are Gowan and Torrance (1971), Malone (1975), and Ginsberg (1976). Ginsberg has offered parents of gifted children a list of sensible cautions, reasonable expectations, and useful actions:

1. Gifted children are children first and gifted second.
2. Enjoy your child's giftedness.
3. Listen to your gifted child.
4. Don't compare your gifted child to other children—in other words, do not place extra pressure on him.
5. Show your child the world.
6. Let your child specialize if he/she wants to.
7. Education is expensive—start to save now.
8. Let your child have time of his own—to daydream, to explore, etc.
9. Don't expect your child to live up to any of your own unfulfilled aspirations.
10. Give your child responsibility early.
11. Praise your child—help him build a *good* self-concept.
12. Discipline.
13. Recognize there are times to reach out and times to hold back. Knowing the difference makes you a gifted parent.
14. Be truthful and honest yourself to serve as an example for your child.
15. Make the home a place where knowledge is valued and quest for learning respected.
16. Know the fine line between encouragement and pushing.
17. Be a welcomed person at your child's school.
18. Provide an intellectual atmosphere—books, discussions, etc.
19. Parents of gifted children are people, too.
20. Don't expect your gifted child to be gifted all of the time.

STAFF DEVELOPMENT

Teachers and ancillary personnel often acknowledge that they feel unsure of themselves with parents of gifted children. This is not surprising, since few teachers have had more than one college course dealing with family involvement, and many have had no training whatsoever in this area. In addition, courses on family involvement do not usually focus on the gifted/talented child. Inservice training of staff is, therefore, basic to an effective family involvement program. In this section, basic assumptions about staff development will be reviewed, and alternative ways of promoting staff development will be considered.

Assumptions on Which to Build a Staff Development Program

Inservice training that will lead to the effective involvement of the family in the educational program of their gifted/talented child should be built on the following assumptions.

Reluctance of professional staff to involve parents is due in large part to inadequate skills. Inservice training must, therefore, provide the information and skills staff need to feel confident and to perform competently.

Inservice training must be flexible and individualized. Not all staff have the same professional needs, and there must be a match between individual needs and professional training. Staff members, therefore, should play a major role in assessing inservice needs and planning ways of meeting those needs.

Successful staff development requires strong and effective leadership. Leadership may be provided by a director or supervisor of the gifted, a principal, a director of a preschool program who wishes to improve offerings to gifted/talented children, or an ancillary staff member assigned to coordinate the parent involvement component of the program. A committee is not usually as effective as an individual in this leadership role.

The budget must reflect a commitment to professional growth. While it may not be necessary to have a large budget, no budget at all suggests little support by the administration for such training. Purchasing professional books, inviting an expert to conduct a workshop or make a presentation, or sending staff members to conferences on parent involvement all require financial resources.

Ongoing evaluation of inservice training is necessary to determine the worth of activities for professional growth and to make decisions regarding future plans. Both staff and family members should be involved in this evaluation. It is crucial that staff members be aware of their progress in acquiring the skills and knowledge to improve family involvement.

Last, but by no means least important, every professional is capable of continued growth. The ability to work effectively with parents of young gifted children is acquired only over time, through experience and ongoing training.

Alternative Ways of Promoting Staff Development

While group meetings are only one method of promoting professional growth, it is nevertheless important for all personnel working in the gifted/talented program for young children to meet on a regular basis. Steinberg and Ryan (1982) have offered the schedule in Figure 8-2, which has been used in the University of Illinois program for bright and gifted/talented children.

The initial meeting of the staff prior to the opening of the school is very important. There must be an understanding of and commitment to family

FIGURE 8-2
Schedule for Staff Development Relative to Family Involvement

MEETING	1	2	3	4	5
DATE	**August** At least a week before school opens.	**September** 1 to 2 weeks after school begins.	**October-November** After the family needs assessment has been analyzed.	**January** Midway through the school year.	**June** After parent end-of-year questionnaires have been analyzed.
TOPICS	Rationale. Staff needs assessment. Communicating with parents.	Needs of families with gifted children. Record-keeping techniques.	Decision-making and planning for group meetings.	Formative evaluation results. Revisions in program plans.	Evaluation results. Planning for the following year.

involvement. Goals for the family involvement program must be set. Although there is room for flexibility in how parents are to be involved by individual staff members, all are expected to follow certain guidelines. A needs assessment of parents is, for example, essential for everyone, as are a certain number of individual conferences during the year and a certain number of group meetings of parents. Record-keeping will also be relatively uniform.

Staff meetings are an efficient way of communicating information regarding procedures and requirements that affect all staff members. General topics for group discussion have been included in the five-meeting schedule because those topics seem to occur in most situations. Experience indicates that a minimum of five group meetings a year will be required to maintain the momentum of a family involvement program. When a program is going smoothly, the number and content of meetings will change.

In addition to staff meetings, there are many ways in which individual staff members may improve their skills in working with the families of young gifted children. Among them, of course, is reading the latest professional literature. Following the lead of a supervisor or principal who is knowledgeable about working with parents of gifted children is also helpful. Conferring with a teacher who has a successful parent involvement program and visiting successful family involvement programs are excellent ways to learn new strategies. Enrolling in a course on parent involvement and attending workshops during the summer provide interaction with other teachers of gifted children and new information.

SUMMARY

1. It is impossible for the school to take full responsibility for the education of the gifted child. Parents and other family members need to be involved to ensure the child's optimal development. The gifted child needs an ongoing manager of his or her educational program as well as a strong advocate, and parents are the most appropriate persons to assume that role.

2. The family has the most profound influence on the child's values, attitudes, and behavior. Family members know more than others do about a child's interests and needs and should be asked to share this information in developing an educational program. They can also reinforce and extend the educational program at home.

3. Professionals have the responsibility to provide family members with information that leads to a better understanding of their gifted child and to train them to interact more effectively with that child.

4. Research findings indicate that certain parental behaviors are closely related to positive growth in the child. Family members should be made aware of these findings and helped to evaluate their own behavior so that areas where change is needed can be identified. In some cases, school personnel can help parents locate community resources where they can obtain counseling or other services.

5. Knowing what research says about the effects of parental behavior on the child, professionals should conduct training sessions to help parents become more competent in rearing their gifted children. Through ongoing inservice training they can acquire the skills and knowledge that will make them more self-confident in working with the parents.

6. Studies dealing with parental concerns for gifted/talented children help professionals determine the information and services that parents need and want. It is advisable, however, to conduct a specific needs assessment with family members of young gifted/talented children, since each child and family are unique and their needs may not be identical with those disclosed in reported studies.

7. Professional personnel must cope with a number of problems when attempting to involve parents in the educational programs of their young gifted/talented children. The busy schedule of working mothers, reluctance of some parents to participate, and failure of fathers to become involved are typical problems. Professionals must be especially sensitive to the needs of parents and willing to try innovative ways of securing the participation of family members.

8. The success of a parent involvement program is contingent on the professional competencies of the staff. Inservice training is necessary to help professionals become effective in interacting with parents and other family members.

9. A coordinator of the parent involvement program is highly desirable, especially if the program is large. This person should be selected with

care, taking into consideration demonstrated skills with parents, knowledge about gifted children, and understanding of what makes a sound educational program for this segment of the preschool population.

10. Any effective parent involvement program must be individualized. No two parents of gifted children are alike; thus, their needs, abilities, and interests will differ. Professionals must recognize and respond to these differences.

11. Families should play a major role in determining their entry level in the gifted child's educational program. Options for involvement should be clearly delineated and varied, and family members should assist in making the match between what they want to do or feel capable of doing and the options for involvement open to them.

12. There are certain things parents need to know and do to ensure the optimal development of their gifted children. Parents need support, assistance, and feedback from knowledgeable professionals to improve their understanding of and interaction with their gifted child.

13. Parents of gifted children should be encouraged to initiate their own association for the gifted. They need opportunities to interact with and learn from each other and to develop skills that will enable them to become better advocates of their gifted/talented children.

An organized educational program for the gifted preschooler can only supplement the offering of the home, but home and school working together can foster the development of the child more efficiently and effectively than either working alone. Research and experience tell us that the first 5 years of the child's life are extremely important in developing the child's attitudes, values, and habits. The parents serve as the models for the child, and their child-rearing practices can either foster positive development or inhibit the development of the gifted child. Professionals, therefore, have the responsibility to provide parents with the knowledge and training to interact appropriately with their gifted child and to use available resources to promote their development. As the attitude of teachers toward parent involvement in educational programs for gifted children becomes more positive, so will the parent involvement program become more successful. The overall program for the young gifted child will be improved when parents actively work with the school. A closer relationship between home and school benefits teachers and parents, but most of all it benefits children.

REFERENCES

Bachtold, L. The creative personality and the ideal pupil revisited. *Journal of Creative Behavior,* 1974, *8* (1), 47–54.

Baldwin, A., Kalhorn, J., & Breese, F. Patterns of parent behavior. *Psychological Monographs,* 1945, *58* (3), Whole No. 268.

Bayley, N., & Schaefer, E. Correlations of maternal and child behavior with the development of mental abilities: Data from the Berkeley Growth Study. *Monographs* of the Society for Research in Child Development, 1964, *29* (6), Whole No. 97, 3–79.

Bing, E. Effects of child rearing practices on development of differential cognitive abilities. *Child Development*, 1963, *34,* 631–648.

Bloom, B. *Stability and change in human characteristics.* New York: Wiley, 1964.

Bloom, B., & Sosniak, L. Talent development vs. schooling. *Educational Leadership,* 1981, *39* (2), 86–94.

Bridges, S. *Problems of the gifted child: IQ 150.* New York: Crane & Russak, 1973.

Callahan, C., & Kauffman, J. Involving gifted children's parents: Federal law is silent, but its assumptions apply. *Exceptional Education Quarterly,* 1982, *3* (2), 50–63. (Monograph)

Cassidy, J. Parental involvement in gifted programs. *Journal for the Education of the Gifted,* 1981, *4* (3), 284–288.

Ciha, T., Harris, R., & Hoffman, C. Parents as identifiers of giftedness, ignored but accurate. *The Gifted Child Quarterly,* 1974, *18,* 191–195.

Clements, J., & Alexander, R. Parent training: Bringing it all back home. *Focus on Exceptional Children,* 1975, *7,* 1–12.

Colangelo, N., & Dettmann, D. Conceptual model of four types of parent-school interactions. *Journal for the Education of the Gifted,* 1982, *5* (2), 120–127.

Dave, R. *The identification and measurement of educational process variables that are related to educational achievement.* Unpublished doctoral dissertation, University of Chicago, 1963.

Debinski, R., & Mauser, A. Parents of the gifted: Perception of psychologists and teachers. *Journal for the Education of the Gifted,* 1978, *1* (2), 5–14.

Dettman, D., & Colangelo, N. A functional model for counseling parents of gifted students. *The Gifted Child Quarterly,* 1980, *24,* 158–161.

Dewing, K. Family influence on creativity: A review and discussion. *Journal of Special Education,* 1970, *4,* 399–404.

Drews, E., & Teahan, J. Parental attitudes and academic achievement. *Journal of Clinical Psychology,* 1957, *13,* 328–332.

Dwinell, P. *Parent education for gifted preschool.* Paper presented at the 55th Annual Council for Exceptional Children International Convention, Atlanta, Georgia, April, 1977. (ERIC Document Reproduction Service No. ED 139 169)

Ehrlich, V. *The Astor Program for gifted children: Pre-kindergarten through grade three.* New York: Columbia University, Teachers College, New York City Board of Education, Brooklyn NY, 1978. (ERIC Document Reproduction Service No. ED 166 889)

Fine, B. *Underachievers.* New York: E. P. Dutton, 1967.

Fisher, E. Being a good model for your gifted child. *Gifted Children Newsletter,* 1981, *2* (6), 1–2.

Flanagan, J. *The American high school student.* Pittsburgh: University of Pittsburgh, Project TALENT Office, 1964. (Cooperative Research Project No. 635)

Gallagher, J., & Crowder, T. The adjustment of gifted children in the regular classroom. *Exceptional Children,* 1957, *23,* 306–312; 317–319.

Ginsberg, G. "Homework" with the gifted and talented children. In *Parents speak on gifted and talented children.* Ventura CA: National/State Leadership Institute on the Gifted and Talented, 1976. (ERIC Document Reproduction Service No. ED 131 616)

Gordon, I. *Early child stimulation through parent education* (Final report to the Children's Bureau, U.S. Department of Health, Education and Welfare, PHS-R-306, PHS-R-306 01). Gainesville FL: Institute for Development of Human Resources, College of Education, University of Florida, June 30, 1969.

Gowan, J. Twenty-five suggestions for parents of able children. *The Gifted Child Quarterly,* 1964, *8,* 192–193.

Gowan, J., & Torrance, E. P. (Eds.), *Educating the ablest: A book of readings on the education of gifted children.* Itasca IL: Peacock, 1971.

Groth, N. Differences in parental environment for degree achievement for gifted men and women.*The Gifted Child Quarterly,*1971, *15,* 256–261.

Hackney, H. The gifted child, the family, and the school. *The Gifted Child Quarterly,* 1981, *25,* 51–54.

Hess, R., Block, M., Costello, J., Knowles, R., & Largny, D. Parental involvement in early education. In E. Grothberg (Ed.), *Day care resources for decisions* (Pamphlet 6106-1). Washington DC: Office of Economic Opportunity, 1971.

Hess, R., Shipman, V., Brophy, J., & Baer, R. *Cognitive environments of urban preschool Negro children* (Report to the Children's Bureau, Social Security Administration). Washington DC: U.S. Department of Health, Education and Welfare, 1968.

Hunt, J. McV. *Intelligence and experience.* New York: Ronald Press, 1961.

Israelson, J. Toward a realistic image of parents: A teacher's point of view. *Exceptional Parent,* 1980, *10* (5), 3–4.

Jacobs, J. Effectiveness of teacher and parent identification of gifted children as a function of school level. *Psychology in the Schools,* 1971, *8,* 140–142.

Karnes, M., McCoy, G., Zehrbach, R., Wollersheim, J., Clarizio, H., Costin, L., & Stanley, L. Factors associated with underachievement and overachievement of intellectually gifted children. *Exceptional Children,* 1961, *25,* 167–175.

Karnes, M., Studley, W., Wright, W., & Hodgins, A. An approach for working with mothers of disadvantaged preschool children. *Merrill-Palmer Quarterly,* 1968, *14,* 174–184.

Karnes, M., Teska, J., Hodgins, A., & Badger, E. Educational intervention at home by mothers of disadvantaged infants. *Child Development,* 1970, *41,* 925–935.

Karnes, M., & Zehrbach, R. Flexibility in getting parents involved in the school. *TEACHING Exceptional Children,* 1972, *5* (1), 6–19.

Kelly, E. *Parent-teacher interaction: A special educational perspective.* Seattle: Special Child Publications, 1974.

Khatena, J. *The creatively gifted child: Suggestions for parents and teachers.* New York: Vantage, 1978.

Kroth, R. The mirror model of parental involvement. *The Pointer,* 1980, *25,* 18–22.

La Crosse, E. *Parent involvement.* Monmouth OR: Western States Technical Assistance Resource, 1982. (WESTAR Series Paper #12)

Leonard, J. *Chapel Hill services to the gifted/handicapped: A project summary.* Durham NC: Seeman Printery, 1978.

Levenstein, P. *Verbal interaction project: Aiding cognition growth in disadvantaged preschoolers through the mother-child home program* (Final report of Child Welfare, Research and Demonstration Project R-300). Washington DC: Children's Bureau, Office of Child Development, U.S. Department of Health, Education and Welfare, 1971.

Malone, C. Education for parents of the gifted. *The Gifted Child Quarterly*, 1975, *19* (3),223–225.

Mathews, F. Effective communication with parents of the gifted and talented: Some suggestions for improvement. *Journal for the Education of the Gifted*, 1981, *4* (3), 207–211.

McQuilken, C. Parents of the gifted—Look homeward. *Gifted/Creative/Talented Children*, 1981, *17*, 28–29.

Meyers, E., Ball, H., & Crutchfield, M. Specific suggestions for the kindergarten teacher and the advanced child. *The Gifted Child Quarterly*, 1974, *18*, 25–30.

Milner, E. A study of the relationship between reading readiness in grade one school children and patterns of parent-child interactions. *Child Development*, 1951, *22*, 95–112.

Milner, J. Family involvement in British schools. *British Journal of Educational Psychology*, 1971, *14* (4), 84–97.

Moss, H., & Kagan, J. Maternal influences on early IQ scores. *Psychological Reports*, 1958, *4*, 655–661.

Naumann, N. Learn all you can at school conferences. *Gifted Children Newsletter*, 1981, *2* (10), 1–3.

Newman, D. It's time to get together on gifted programs. *Curriculum Review*, 1981, *20* (2), 114–117.

Niro, L. *Forming a local parent association for gifted and talented education*. Reston VA: The Council for Exceptional Children, 1978.

Nolte, J., & Dinklocker, D. Paraphernalia for parents. *Gifted/Creative/Talented Children*, 1981, *17*, 44.

O'Neill, K. Parent involvement: A key in the education of gifted children. *The Gifted Child Quarterly*, 1978, *22* (2), 235–242.

Passow, A. (Ed.), *The gifted and the talented: Their education and development* (78th yearbook of the National Society for the Study of Education). Chicago: University of Chicago Press, 1979.

Perkins, H. Classroom behavior and underachievement. *American Educational Research Journal*, 1965, *2*, 1–12.

Peterson, D. The heterogenously gifted family. *The Gifted Child Quarterly*, 1977, *21* (3), 396–398.

Pierce, J., & Bowman, P. Motivation patterns of high school students. In *Cooperative research monograph no. 2: The gifted student* (OE-35016). Washington DC: U.S. Office of Education, 1960.

Pringle, M. *Able misfits: A study of educational and behavioral difficulties of 103 very intelligent children*. London: Longmans Group, 1970.

Rau, L., Mlodnosky, L., & Anastasiow, N. *Child rearing antecedents of achievement behaviors in second grade boys* (Cooperative Research Project No. 1838). Palo Alto CA: Stanford University Press, 1964.

Robinson, H. *Current myths concerning gifted children* (Brief No. 5). Ventura CA: National/State Leadership Training Institute for Gifted and Talented, 1977.

Rosen, B., & D'Androde, S. Race, ethnicity, and the achievement syndrome. *American Sociological Review*, 1959, *24*, 47–60.

Schaefer, E. Family relationships. In J. Gallagher (Ed.), *The application of child development research to exceptional children*. Reston VA: The Council for Exceptional Children, 1975.

Shaw, M., & McCuen, J. The onset of academic underachievement in bright children. *Journal of Educational Research*, 1960, *51*, 103–108.

Sherman, W. The importance of parent/teacher cooperation in gifted education. *Roeper Review*, 1982, *5* (1), 42–45.

Staples, T., & Baer, D. An implicit technology of generalization. *Journal of Applied Behavior Analysis*, 1978, *11*, 590–620.

Steinberg, D., & Ryan, K. *Guide for family involvement: Families with gifted preschoolers*. (Mimeograph.) Urbana IL: Institute for Child Behavior and Development, 1982.

Terman, L., & Oden, M. The gifted group at mid-life: Thirty-five years' follow-up of the superior child. In L. Terman (Ed.), *Genetic studies of genius* (Vol. V). Palo Alto CA: Stanford University Press, 1959.

Thiel, R., & Thill, A. A structural analysis of family interaction patterns and the underachieving gifted child. *The Gifted Child Quarterly*, 1977, *21*, 167–275.

Walsh, A. *Self-concepts of bright boys with learning difficulties*. New York: Teachers College Press, Teachers College, Columbia University, 1956.

Weikart, D. *Ypsilanti Carnegie infant education project* (Progress report). Ypsilanti MI: Department of Research and Development, Ypsilanti Public Schools, September, 1969.

Whitmore, J. The etiology of underachievement in highly gifted young children. *Journal of the Education of the Gifted*, 1979, *3* (1), 38–51.

Wolf, R. *The identification and measurement of environmental process variables related to intelligence*. Unpublished doctoral dissertation, University of Chicago, 1964.

Yoshida, R., Fenton, K., Kaufman, M., & Maxwell, J. Parental involvement in the special education pupil planning process: The school perspective. *Exceptional Children*, 1978, *44*, 531–534.

CHAPTER 9

Evaluation

Allan M. Shwedel

How can you ensure that efforts to set up a preschool program for the gifted will meet with success? Alas, there is no royal road to a perfect program, but there are procedures and techniques that can increase the likelihood of making wise choices and minimize the consequences of unwise decisions. In this chapter we will describe a systematic approach to evaluation that can be applied to an entire program or to a single classroom for gifted preschoolers. Our goals are to foster in the reader a positive attitude toward evaluation and to provide the reader with strategies to develop, modify, and assess key components in the preschool programs for the gifted. Topics to be covered include brief overviews of four basic approaches to program evaluation, a description of the relationship between "questions" and "evaluation data," and a discussion of the evaluator's role *vis-à-vis* setting goals, developing a project timeline, monitoring program implementation, and assessing project effectiveness.

While there are many ways to view the evaluation process, the approach taken in this chapter is eclectic and geared to the needs of those responsible for developing or implementing new programs for gifted preschoolers. From the perspective of program developers, effective evaluation is in many ways analogous to the functioning of the human nervous system. Our bodies are composed of numerous subsystems—circulatory, digestive, muscular—which must operate properly and in synchrony in order for the entire system to function effectively. Similarly, a preschool program for the gifted is made up of numerous interrelated components—identification, staff training, parent involvement, programming. The nervous system's role is to collect and transmit information. The information flow goes in two directions, from the subsystems to the brain and from the brain (central decision maker) to the subsystems. Thus, the nervous system is operating at maximum efficiency. So, too, is evaluation used to monitor and to regulate the activities of the program components so that effective decisions can be made. Decision makers need to know both how a component is expected to function and how it is actually functioning. When a discrepancy between intended and actual functioning is observed, corrective action can be taken. An ideal evaluation program provides a continuous flow of information to and from those who make decisions about the program.

There is, however, an important difference between evaluation and the nervous system: we are born with a nervous system; it is built in, and in most cases it functions adequately. In contrast, evaluation procedures must be designed for each educational program, sometimes with resistance from those who could benefit from an effective evaluation component. Whenever possible, an evaluation component should be included in a new program from its inception.

The role of an evaluation component in the development of a preschool program for the gifted should be to:

1. Assist in the development of achievable goals and objectives.
2. Assist in the development of a time frame for the implementation of program components.
3. Monitor the implementation process and ongoing functioning of a program in order to provide feedback to designated individuals regarding the degree of success and the nature of problems in implementing a given program component.
4. Assess the effectiveness of each component in terms of program goals and unintended outcomes.

Later in the chapter these four evaluation activities are described within the context of preschool programs for the gifted. At this time no books focus on evaluation procedures for preschool gifted programs, but Appendix A lists references that cover various aspects of program evaluation. Of particular note are the work of Renzulli (1975) on the evaluation of programs for gifted students and that of Huberty and Swan (1977) on the evaluation of preschool programs for handicapped children. The following section contains summaries of prototypical approaches to program evaluation.

EVALUATION MODELS

Program evaluation has assumed an important role in educational planning and innovation over the past 15 to 20 years and, consequently, numerous models have been proposed to guide workers in this area. Worthen and Sanders (1973) presented a detailed comparison of some of the major evaluation models along with articles written by the developers of these models. For the purposes of this chapter, Popham (1975) has provided a useful classification schema for the major evaluation models: (a) goal-attainment models,

(b) judgmental models emphasizing intrinsic criteria, (c) judgmental models emphasizing extrinsic criteria, and (d) decision-facilitation models. Following is a brief overview of the four.

Goal-Attainment Models

This category includes models that assume that the worth of an educational (instructional) program can be assessed best by determining the degree to which the program goals, as specified by the program developers with input from the community, have been met by the program. The keys to this type of evaluation are first, the specification of measurable objectives derived from the program goals, and later, the use of appropriate instruments to measure performance. This model is exemplified in one of the earliest formal evaluation models (Tyler, 1942; see also Metfessel & Michael, 1967). In one form or another it still plays an important role in program evaluation.

Judgmental Models Emphasizing Intrinsic Criteria

Included in this category are models that specify that the evaluator must utilize criteria to assess program worth which are independent of the outcomes attributable to the use of that program. That is, the evaluation criteria are based on characteristics of the program itself rather than criteria such as student outcomes. Popham (1975) has given a good example of the distinction between intrinsic and extrinsic criteria:

> The distinction between intrinsic and extrinsic criteria is rather straightforward. Suppose you are considering a number of electric drills with a view of purchasing one of them. You could judge them on the basis of such factors as their design, style, weight, and color. (Who wants an ugly electric drill?) These criteria are *intrinsic* to the object to be judged. You could also judge them on the basis of how fast or neatly they drilled holes. (Who wants a glamorous drill that won't dent butter?) These criteria are *extrinsic* to the object to be judged. Extrinsic criteria are associated with the effects of the object. (p. 24)

According to Popham (1975), classic examples of evaluations that utilize intrinsic criteria are the periodic district-wide school accreditation assessments carried out by organizations such as the state department of education. The accreditation evaluations tend to focus on issues such as teacher-child ratios, class size, and certification of ancillary staff. Popham also noted that intrinsic criteria are synonymous with process criteria.

Judgmental Models Emphasizing Extrinsic Criteria

The primary concern addressed by the evaluation models in this category is the outcome or payoff resulting from the use of a curriculum, an innovative teaching style, and so forth (Scriven, 1967; Stake, 1967). These models resemble goal-attainment models, but, among other differences, these judgmental models are much more sophisticated in the identification and assessment of extrinsic criteria. For example, Scriven (1967) noted that evaluators should not simply measure how well a program has met its own goals but should, in addition, assess the value of the goals themselves. If program goals are of little concern to anyone, then the fact that they have been achieved is relatively unimportant. Scriven (1972) also suggested that evaluators identify and appraise unintended outcomes, which, in some cases, are the major outcomes of the program being evaluated.

Decision-Facilitation Models

Popham (1975) differentiated models in this category from models in the other three categories primarily on the basis of the role played by the evaluator. Decision-facilitation models describe the role of the evaluator as relatively nonjudgmental. The evaluator's task is to gather data needed by the decision makers while leaving most judgments to them. Another important feature of these models is that evaluation is envisioned as an ongoing activity to be carried out in conjunction with program development, program implementation, and overall program assessment. Some of the judgmental models utilizing extrinsic criteria also call for ongoing evaluation, but ongoing evaluation is not the primary focus of these judgmental models. Examples of the decision-facilitation models can be seen in the work of Stuffelbeam, Foley, Gephart, Guba, Hammond, Merriman, and Provus (1971) and Alkin (1969).

The evaluation procedures to be outlined in this chapter borrow· heavily from the decision-facilitation models since the evaluator has a unique set of skills that can be effectively tapped during the development and implementation phases of a project. By making use of the evaluator's data-gathering skills and systematic planning skills during the early phases of a new project, the probability of implementing an effective preschool program for gifted children is greatly enhanced. While the decision-facilitation models often downplay the decision-making role of the evaluator, in many cases it is advantageous to include the evaluator as one of the decision makers, since the evaluator has a relatively complete picture of the strengths and weaknesses of the project.

QUESTIONS AND EVALUATION DATA

The content of this chapter is geared to the collection of information needed by those who are concerned with the day-to-day operation of preschool programs. Nevertheless, a brief discussion of the relationship between questions and evaluation data provides a useful framework for most of the information-gathering activities to be performed by the evaluator.

Many different audiences will be curious about a new program for gifted preschoolers, and, in part, the evaluator's job is to provide answers to their questions. In many cases, different audiences need different data in order to make decisions. An answer becomes meaningful only when it is used by someone to make a decision, and data that are used to make a decision are called *information*. For example, both parents and administrators are prone to ask, "Does the new preschool program for the gifted work?" However, the information needs of these two audiences differ considerably since parents will be deciding whether or not they should enroll their child in the new program, while administrators will be deciding whether or not the program should be funded for another year.

The first step in information-gathering is to determine the questions that need to be answered. One way to accomplish this is to identify the target audience(s) and to ask members of the audience(s) what they want to know concerning the preschool program for the gifted. Of course, people may ask more questions than can be answered or they may decide at some later point that other questions should be answered. Nevertheless, polling the target audience gives the evaluator some idea of which questions must be addressed.

The next step is to develop a plan to obtain the data needed to answer the audience's questions. One way to approach this task is to conceive of answers as being made up of three components: data source(s), data type(s), and data collection procedures.[1] Some common sources of data are gifted preschoolers, parents, teachers, and newspaper articles. Some common types of data include attitudes, factual knowledge, classroom behavior, and monthly expenditures. Finally, common measurement procedures include naturalistic observation, questionnaires, rating scales, standardized tests, and projective instruments. An example of the relationship between questions and evaluation data is given in Figure 9-1. One advantage of this conceptual approach is that it broadens the range of information provided to decision makers. This approach can also aid the evaluator when choosing among information types, since the evaluator can compare the strengths and weaknesses of the various types of information.

EVALUATION ACTIVITIES

The role of the evaluator changes during the evolution of a program. The activities described here focus on the major efforts of the evaluator during the various phases of planning and implementing a new program for gifted preschoolers.

Setting Goals and Objectives

Needs Assessment

Before planned change occurs, an examination and critique of what currently exists are necessary. In one way or another decision makers, be they admin-

---

[1] This notion was suggested to the author by Dr. Andrew Hayes of the University of North Carolina at Wilmington.

istrators, parents, or teachers, come to a consensus regarding the strengths and weaknesses of the current situation when they make a decision to change a program. The aim of the evaluator, however, is to provide a systematic way to examine and assess the existing program. This activity is usually called *needs assessment*. To plan for change, decision makers need the following:

1. A description of the existing program including its goals and objectives, major components, population, and cost—or, if a program does not exist, a description of the range of services available to gifted preschoolers. Of particular concern in the needs assessment is to determine whether or not an existing program provides an appropriate match between the abilities of the gifted preschoolers and the curriculum.
2. An assessment of the success of the existing program in meeting its stated goals.
3. An assessment of the existing program from the perspective of relevant interest groups such as parents, preschool teachers, elementary school teachers, and school board members. A program may be meeting its stated goals, but the community may have had a different set of goals in mind when it supported the original program. For example, parents of gifted preschoolers may view preschool programs in terms of acceleration rather than enrichment. If the teachers are providing a good enrichment program but the children still enter kindergarten rather than directly entering first grade, conflict may arise. In this situation, project planners may decide that the preschool program should be modified. Alternatively, they may decide that parent attitudes should be modified.
4. An assessment of the resources available to carry out the new program. Resources include both financial and political support. Figure 9-2 lists selected information sources that can be tapped during the needs assessment process.

Establishing Goals and Objectives

When the needs assessment has been completed and a decision has been made to change the existing program, the next step is to establish a set of reasonable goals and objectives. The importance of this step should not be underestimated. In the long run it does no good to have goals and objectives that are impossible to achieve. Similarly, it is a waste of time, money, and human resources to establish trivial goals and objectives. The aim is to specify a set of meaningful yet achievable goals and objectives. Once again, systematic evaluation techniques can be used to compile a pool of goals and objectives from which decision makers can draw.

There is no obligation to change goals and objectives whenever program modifications are proposed, and in some cases existing goals and objectives may remain appropriate. However, the needs assessment process often uncovers goals that have been omitted from the current program or identifies

FIGURE 9-1
Information Source Matrix

Question	Audience	Data Sources	Data Types	Data Collection Procedures	Strengths	Weaknesses
Do gifted pre-schoolers acquire positive attitudes toward school as a result of their participation in this program?	Administrators	1. Children	1. Attitudes	(a) Administer a Likert scale attitude questionnaire. (b) Observe children and record their willingness to engage in academic activities within the classroom.	(a) Collection and analysis of data are relatively easy. (b) High degree of face validity.	(a) Need to ensure that items are appropriate for the youngest children. (b) 1. Time consuming. 2. Scoring criteria need to be established. 3. Observer reliabilities may be difficult to establish.
		2. Teachers	1. Opinions	(a) Administer an open-ended questionnaire.	(a) Unexpected but useful information may be obtained.	(a) 1. Scoring responses may be difficult. 2. Reliability and validity will need to be established.

		Method	Advantages	Limitations
		(b) Have teachers rate children on the basis of preestablished criteria related to attitudes toward school.	(b) 1. Moderate degree of face validity. 2. Collection and analysis of data are relatively easy.	(b) 1. Rating scales may be difficult to establish. 2. Reliability and validity will need to be established.
3. Parents	1. Opinions	(a) Administer an open-ended questionnaire.	(a) 1. Unexpected but useful information may be obtained.	(a) 1. Analysis may be difficult. 2. Reliability and validity will need to be established.
		(b) Have parents rate their own children on the basis of preestablished criteria related to attitudes toward school.	(b) 1. Moderate degree of face validity. 2. Collection and analysis of data are relatively easy.	(b) 1. Rating scales may be difficult to establish. 2. Reliability and validity will need to be established.

Note: The degree of detail to be included in this type of matrix can vary considerably. A less detailed matrix is shown in Figure 9-2.

FIGURE 9-2
Selected Information Sources for a Community-Wide Needs Assessment of a Preschool Program for the Gifted

Issues to Consider	Data Sources	Data Types	Data Collection Procedures
Description of existing programs or evidence of need for a new program	(a) Current staff (b) Former staff (c) Newspaper articles (d) Project reports (e) Preschool classrooms in daily operation	(a) Attitudes (b) Descriptive comments (c) Classroom behavior	(a) Questionnaires (b) Interviews (c) Observation
Effectiveness of existing program(s)	(a) Current staff (b) Former staff (c) Children enrolled in the program (d) Preschool classrooms in daily operation (e) Newspaper reports (f) Previous evaluation (g) Local interest groups (h) Parents of young gifted children	(a) Attitudes (b) Academic skills (c) Social skills	(a) Questionnaires (b) Interviews (c) Observation (d) Standardized paper and pencil tests (e) Rating scales
Availability of resources for new or altered program(s)	(a) Yearly budgets (b) Administrators (c) Community leaders	(a) Program expenditures (b) Projected budgets	(a) Cost analysis

goals and objectives that are no longer of concern to the community or to school personnel. For example, a goal may have been to identify all of the children in the community between the ages of 4 and 5 who scored above 140 on the Stanford-Binet. With the changing conceptions of giftedness, it may be more important to identify preschoolers who exhibit high levels of creativity and task commitment (Renzulli, 1978).

Goals and objectives should be established for each program component in addition to those established for child progress. An example of a component goal would be to assemble a staff of teachers and paraprofessionals who have the competencies to work with gifted preschoolers. Goals for child progress could be in the areas of interpersonal and artistic skills in addition to goals related to academic skills. The evaluator's attention to the goal-setting process can facilitate this crucial step in program development.

Many techniques have been developed to guide planners in the selection of appropriate goals. One useful procedure is to have a group of individuals write a set of potential goals and objectives and then give this set to relevant interest groups. Members of the interest groups can add additional goals and then rank the entire set of goals. These ranked lists can then be given to the decision makers so that they will know community perceptions of the relative importance of various goals. For a more complete discussion of this and related processes, see Popham (1975), Morris and Fitz-Gibbon (1978a), and Hostrop (1975).

The final decision as to which goals and objectives should be included in the program plan depends on many factors, some of which are not related to the evaluation process per se. For example, given two goals that are inter-related, such as improving self-concept and improving attitudes toward school, parents may rate the goal of improving attitudes toward school very high and the goal of improving self-concept very low. If the decision makers, however, feel that a positive self-concept is a prerequisite to positive attitudes toward school, then irrespective of the parents' ratings the goal of improving self-concept will probably be included as one of the program goals. Financial considerations also need to be taken into account in the selection of goals. If a proposed goal is to identify 100% of the gifted preschoolers but there is only enough money to screen 50% of the preschool population, then the identification goal will need to be modified before it is accepted as a viable project goal.

Developing an Implementation Plan

Generally, the selection of specific innovative procedures is out of the evaluator's realm of expertise. When program procedures that are relevant to the stated goals and objectives have been specified, an implementation plan needs to be developed. This plan specifies the primary responsibilities of staff members and indicates target dates for initiating and completing project activities. A timeline is a convenient way to represent information about target dates and staff responsibilities (see Figure 9-3).

FIGURE 9-3
Timeline of Project Accomplishments

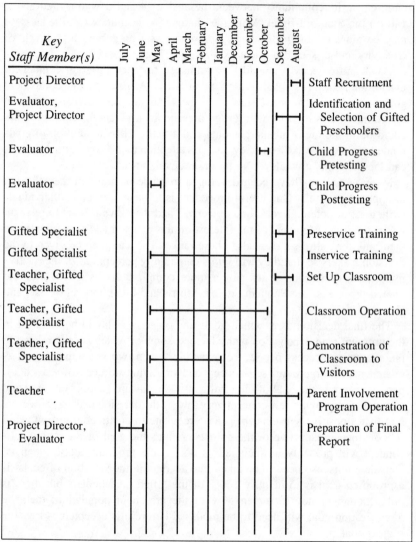

Key Staff Member(s)	July	June	May	April	March	February	January	December	November	October	September	August	
Project Director												⊢⊣	Staff Recruitment
Evaluator, Project Director											⊢—⊣		Identification and Selection of Gifted Preschoolers
Evaluator										⊢⊣			Child Progress Pretesting
Evaluator				⊢⊣									Child Progress Posttesting
Gifted Specialist											⊢—⊣		Preservice Training
Gifted Specialist				⊢————————⊣									Inservice Training
Teacher, Gifted Specialist											⊢—⊣		Set Up Classroom
Teacher, Gifted Specialist				⊢————————⊣									Classroom Operation
Teacher, Gifted Specialist				⊢————⊣									Demonstration of Classroom to Visitors
Teacher				⊢——————————⊣									Parent Involvement Program Operation
Project Director, Evaluator	⊢—⊣												Preparation of Final Report

A good timeline can be used to monitor the implementation of a new program or specific program modifications. If an event does not occur on schedule, the evaluator is alerted to the possibility that there may be problems with the implementation plan that need to be remedied in order for the program to function effectively. For example, suppose the timeline specified that screening of gifted preschoolers would be completed by October 1. If the screening is not finished by that date, the evaluator can begin to search for an explanation. The delay may have been caused by a factor unrelated to the program, such as a teacher strike that closed local preschools for 2 weeks. On the other hand, the delay may have been due to the fact that not enough testers were hired. If there is extra money, the problem can be remedied easily, but if no additional money is available, the staff may decide to modify the screening procedures by substituting a group intelligence test for the Stanford-Binet as an initial screening device. Then only those children who scored in the top 20% on the group test would receive follow-up testing with the Stanford-Binet.

In addition to its use as a monitoring device, the implementation plan can help the staff to allocate resources among project components. Resource needs vary over time among the different components of a project. The timeline indicates periods of high and low resource needs for each component and periods of high and low time demands on the staff. This information can be used to efficiently allocate limited financial and human resources among competing project components. Sometimes a cursory examination of a timeline is enough to indicate that the intended implementation strategy cannot be carried out effectively within the allotted time. In such cases, changes can be made to eliminate the problem before it occurs or to minimize its impact.

Monitoring the Implementation Process

Program monitoring is a crucial aspect of systematic evaluation (Morris & Fitz-Gibbon, 1978b). Information obtained via ongoing monitoring of each component can be used to assess how well the new program is being implemented and to document the actual operation of each component. Later this documentation of program operation can serve as an important source of information for the final assessment of the gifted preschool program.

There are many ways to monitor program implementation, and some are described here. One important consideration is that record-keeping can be both time-consuming and annoying, especially for the teacher who is busy trying to master new tasks. During this phase of the project the evaluator should make every effort to minimize and simplify the monitoring procedures. A useful guideline is to collect only the data that are obviously related to decision-making considerations. Figure 9-4 contains a portion of an implementation monitoring form that was developed for the PEECH Project, a model project for handicapped preschoolers (Karnes, 1978). One useful feature of this form is that it can be filled out either by the teacher or by a trained observer. This option gives the evaluator flexibility when balancing financial and staff concerns. The monitoring form also specifies the criteria that are used to rate the degree to which the component is being successfully implemented.

If the information collected via the monitoring process reveals that implementation is not occurring as intended, then the evaluator and relevant staff

FIGURE 9-4
Component Implementation Monitoring Form[1]

PEECH Model Component	Criteria for Observations	Present	Desired	OBS 1	OBS 2	OBS 3	OBS 4	OBS 5	OBS 6	OBS 7
12. Procedures that recognize that, in addition to the teacher's skills and the educational materials, the characteristics of other children in the classroom are important facilitators of the learning process. Systematically using some handicapped children's strengths as a model to demonstrate desirable cognitive, affective, or psychomotor behaviors may help facilitate each child's growth and development.	5. One-third or more of the children in the classroom are serving as appropriate models for other children in the areas of cognitive, affective, and psychomotor functioning.									
	4.									
	3. The behavior of one or more students in the classroom is systematically included as part of the instructional strategy for teaching other children.									
	2.									
	1. No systematic use of children as models.									
13. Procedures for planning an instructional program through lessons.	5. Individual lesson plans are written daily to achieve specific behavioral objectives and exist in four or more developmental areas of each child's greatest educational needs. Each plan specifies behavioral objectives, sequenced activities, and specific evaluation criteria.									
	4.									
	3. Daily individual lesson plans are written in two developmental areas (self-help, language, math, social, fine motor, gross motor) of each child's greatest educational needs. Each plan specifies behavioral objectives, sequenced activities, and specific evaluation.									
	2.									
	1. No lesson plans are written.									

[1] Adapted from the PEECH Model Components Observation Scale (Karnes, 1978).

will need to identify the cause of the problem and suggest ways to overcome the difficulty. In some cases the criterion level for that objective may need to be adjusted. For example, in a half-day preschool program it may be impossible to include 5 hours of child-directed exploratory activity per week in addition to other activities that are equally important for gifted preschoolers. Instead, 2 hours of child-directed activity may be feasible, and the 2 hours may be adequate for achieving the project's child progress objectives.

In other situations, however, the pre-established criterion level may not be flexible. If one of the project implementation objectives is to provide preschool teachers with skills for programming for gifted students on the basis of Meeker's adaptation of Guilford's Structure of the Intellect (SOI) model (Meeker, 1969), it will be necessary to ensure that the teachers have acquired the desired level of competency. To arbitrarily lower the competency level to meet this goal may mean that gifted preschoolers will not receive adequate programming in this area. In this case, the lowered implementation objective could be achieved, but the primary goal of enhancing the gifted preschooler's thinking abilities may be sacrificed.

Each component of the program needs to be monitored during the implementation process. Following are some suggestions for monitoring the basic components of a program for gifted preschoolers.

Child Identification

It is important to document that each step of the identification process is carried out in the correct sequence by properly trained personnel. Comments regarding difficulties in locating children, testing, or interpreting data should be elicited from the personnel who take part in the identification process. Their judgments regarding procedures and their suggestions for modifications should also be obtained. Finally, records should be kept regarding the number of children who were screened for entry into the program, the number who actually entered the program, and, if applicable, the number of children who were put on a waiting list due to insufficient facilities.

Staff Development

The implementation of the staff development component is crucial for the success of a preschool program for the gifted. Aspects of the training component that should be documented include such items as the number of inservice training sessions, topics covered at inservice sessions, attendance at inservice sessions, amount of additional coursework taken at local colleges, and amount of classroom observation done by individuals responsible for training teachers. Since staff training is an ongoing activity, effectiveness monitoring is an important aspect of successful implementation. In this case, monitoring the implementation of the staff training component is the same as monitoring its effectiveness. Methods for assessing the overall effectiveness of the training component are described later in the chapter, but it should be noted that the impact of the training component should also be monitored continuously. If training procedures are inadequate, teachers will have little to offer their students. If inservice workshops are the primary method for upgrading the skills teachers need to work with gifted preschoolers, then the effectiveness of each workshop should be measured by quizzes, teacher self-ratings, role-playing, or follow-up classroom observations.

Family Involvement

Monitoring the family involvement component is relatively easy once the resources are available. Process data should include information concerning the relevant issues: Do parent meetings occur at prescribed intervals? How many parents are participating? Are there any logistical problems, for instance, with meeting times, transportation, and so forth? Are parents actually participating, for instance, working at home with their children in their talent areas? Data sources should include both parents and teachers. If parents are being taught to teach their own children, then the effectiveness of these training procedures will also need to be monitored.

Programming

When people think of implementation, they usually think about the curriculum. Obviously, curriculum is the core component of a preschool program for gifted children, yet many projects fail to adequately implement their proposed curriculum. Until the curriculum has been successfully implemented, it is useless to try to assess the effectiveness of the project. Points to consider when monitoring the implementation of this component include the following:

1. Adequacy of materials for teachers and students (e.g., are there enough to go around?)
2. Adequacy of the training teachers receive in the use of the curriculum materials (e.g., do teachers know how to incorporate lessons based on the SOI model into their daily programming?)
3. Appropriateness of materials usage within classrooms (e.g., do teachers actually use the materials in the way intended by the materials designer, and are the materials or lessons being used with sufficient regularity?)

In most cases some classroom observation is needed to ensure that the gifted preschoolers are receiving the proper programming. In fact, ongoing classroom observation, with feedback to the teachers, should be a standard feature in any program for gifted preschoolers. In most cases this need not be done by the principal but by some other staff member or even the teachers themselves. Teacher X could observe teacher Y's class, teacher Y could observe teacher Z's class, and teacher Z could observe teacher X's class.

It takes both time and feedback to implement effective programming for gifted preschoolers. Without a system of ongoing monitoring, teachers are working at a real disadvantage. In addition, ongoing classroom monitoring may help to pinpoint why a correctly implemented procedure is not producing the intended outcome (Baker, 1974). With an effective classroom monitoring system, the evaluator or other observer is in an excellent position to help teachers find the best way to use innovative materials or teaching styles with a group of gifted preschoolers. Ongoing records of daily activities engaged in by children can also provide information about the degree to which children are being exposed to key elements of the curriculum. An example of a relatively simple record-keeping form to monitor the number of Structures of the Intellect activities engaged in by children enrolled in the University of Illinois Preschool Program for the Gifted is given in Figure 9-5.

Assessment of Component Effectiveness

Did the new program really produce results? Was it worth the effort? Should the program be continued? While many people associate evaluation with these value questions, it should be clear from the previous discussion that we view the evaluation process as a vital tool during the formative stages of a new program (Baker, 1974). Employing systematic evaluation procedures during the implementation phase is of prime importance since it makes little sense to assess the effectiveness of an inadequately implemented project. Of course, no functioning program is identical to the proposed program, but if it can be determined that there is a reasonable similarity between the two, then it is time to carry out the final major step in the evaluation process (Stake, 1967). (Actually, the evaluator's final step is to prepare a summary of the findings and a set of recommendations to be given to the relevant audience; see, for example, Morris and Fitz-Gibbon, 1978c; Renzulli, 1975; and Stake, 1969).

When assessing the effectiveness of a given component, there are two factors to be considered: outcomes and costs. The methods used to determine whether or not goals and objectives have been met vary considerably, so we will limit our discussion to some of the methods that are relevant to specific components of preschool programs for the gifted. It is beyond the scope of this chapter to describe the many research designs and statistical procedures available to evaluators, but a brief overview of the rationale for these designs and procedures may be helpful.

If someone claims that gifted preschoolers who participated in program X made significant gains in their ability to engage in divergent thinking, that individual is in fact implying three things: (a) that the measurement procedures produced reliable (i.e., consistent but not necessarily true) estimates of the amount of divergent thinking among these gifted preschoolers; (b) that the method(s) used to measure divergent thinking were in fact valid (i.e., true or accurate indicators of divergent thinking among the gifted preschoolers); and (c) that participation in the program was a causal factor in the development

FIGURE 9-5
University of Illinois Preschool Program for the Gifted
SOI ACTIVITY LOG

(Activity Number)				(Activity Title or Description)

Date	Child *(List Separately)*	Time Spent	Completed?	Comments

of divergent thinking among *these* gifted preschoolers. It is possible that any or all three of the implied claims could be false. Research designs and statistical analyses are the means whereby evaluators can provide meaningful evidence concerning the implied claims of reliability, validity, and causality (or association). Appendix B contains a list of useful references on research design and statistical analysis.

Identification. Goals and objectives for the identification component often focus on the rate of hits (correct selections), misses (incorrect rejections), and false positives (incorrect selections). A goal for this component could be (a) to increase the hit rate and lower the miss and false positive rates as compared to the rates for identification procedures previously used in a community; or (b) to include 50% of the gifted and talented preschoolers from a community in the program while excluding all children who are not actually gifted or talented. If the identification procedures are reliable and valid, it should be a relatively easy task to show the degree to which the identification procedures are reliable and valid.

The first step is to determine the reliability of the identification procedures—would the same youngsters be selected or rejected if the screening and selection were done again or done by someone else? A successfully implemented identification component is one that *consistently* includes certain children and excludes certain other children. The method used to determine the reliability or consistency of the identification procedure will vary depending on the type of procedure. For example, if behavioral checklists are used (Karnes, 1978; Renzulli, Smith, White, Callahan, & Hartman, 1976), reliability can be measured by having two people rate the same group of children. By comparing these ratings, the reliability of the rating instruments can be estimated. Reliability estimates should be obtained during the implementation phase of the project. If the reliabilities are very low, it may be necessary to modify the screening procedure. A low reliability index indicates a problem, but follow-up discussions with the observers or testers will be needed to isolate the source of the problem. For example, the variability between observers' ratings may have been due to something as simple as differences in the time of the day that the raters did their observing, rather than a weakness in the rating instrument itself.

The next step is to determine the validity of the identification procedures. Admittedly, this is a difficult task. Were the children selected for the program really gifted? One way to answer the validity question is to compare the identification procedures with another set of procedures known or at least assumed to be valid. Thus, the selections and rejections made on the basis of the checklist procedures and the selections and rejections made by an expert can be compared. If there is a high degree of agreement, then the *concurrent validity* of the identification procedures has been demonstrated (Kerlinger, 1973).

There are two other approaches to determining the validity of identification procedures that are more convincing than estimates of concurrent validity, but these alternatives are much more time-consuming and expensive. The first is based on the assumption that preschool children who are truly gifted should benefit from the program more than preschoolers who are not gifted. If it can be demonstrated that when enrolled in the same program children identified as gifted do better than children identified as not gifted, then the validity of the identification procedures has been established. To demonstrate this, both selected (gifted) and rejected (nongifted) children would have to be included in the program. Before this approach is used, the evaluator should be very confident that the program is geared specifically to gifted preschoolers. The identification procedures may be excellent, but if the curriculum is equally beneficial to both gifted and nongifted students, then it would be impossible to establish the validity of the identification procedures.

Another approach to determining the *predictive validity* of the identification procedure is based on the assumption that children who are gifted at the preschool level should, with adequate programming, also be gifted when they are in elementary school. If the correlation between preschool measures of giftedness and elementary school measures of giftedness for the same children is high, then it can be claimed that the preschool identification procedures are valid, that is, they are adequate for predicting the child's future level of functioning in areas of giftedness. While these last two methods for establishing validity are desirable, in most cases it is sufficient to demonstrate a high level of concurrent validity for identification procedures.

Staff Development. Goals and objectives for the staff development component often focus on attitude change or skill acquisition. If a new curriculum is being adopted, then a reasonable objective for staff training would be to expect that as a result of training teachers would be able to use the new materials with a high level of proficiency. An objective for staff training could also be to change attitudes of teachers and paraprofessionals toward working with parents of preschool gifted children.

To measure staff skills it is necessary to know which skills are to be acquired by the staff. Once the target skills have been specified, reliable and valid procedures must be developed to measure the level of staff skills at the end of—and, if possible, prior to—training. Data collection procedures include multiple choice examinations, self-report rating scales, ratings based on observation of simulated teaching activities, and ratings based on observation of classroom teaching practices. If the resources are available, the use of classroom observation procedures is strongly recommended. If the evaluator can actually observe teachers using or failing to use specific techniques in the classroom, the validity question all but vanishes. Furthermore, since classroom observation is a very effective tool to use during the implementation process, the same evaluation procedure can serve two very different purposes.

Attitude change is often measured by means of a self-report questionnaire. In general, self-report questionnaires share a common weakness: the relationship between responses on a questionnaire and real-world behavior is weak (Brannon, 1976). Often the intent of a questionnaire is obvious to the respondent, and consequently the responses tend to reflect the image that the respondent wants to convey to others. Furthermore, one typically fills out such a questionnaire in a quiet room—a setting quite unlike the classroom in which the actual teaching takes place. Teachers may respond to a question about a curriculum manual by indicating that they did not like the manual simply because they were comparing it to an ideal conception of a manual. The same teachers, however, may recommend the manual to other teachers simply because it is better than anything available; it is adequate but not perfect. One way to minimize the discrepancy between real-life behavior and a questionnaire is to frame items so that teachers have a concrete point of reference as the basis for their responses. The design of a good questionnaire is a time-consuming activity; nevertheless, measuring opinions both before and after training can be a useful way to assess changes in teacher attitudes as a result of inservice training.

Parent Involvement. In terms of long-range benefits to gifted preschoolers, the parent component is a key component of new programs. Goals for this component generally fall into three categories: attitude change, skill acquisition, and parent participation. Goals for attitude change could include the acquisition by parents of realistic expectations for their children and the development of favorable attitudes toward the child's academic program. Goals for skill acquisition tend to center on providing techniques for parents to use in fostering their children's talents. Goals for parent participation include increased contact between teachers and parents, increased parental participation in school activities, and increased parental involvement in activities at home that are geared to foster the child's talents. Of course, a needs assessment of parents helps to define the goals for parents and to pinpoint areas of possible program impact on parents. A sample of the parents' needs assessment is given in Figure 9-6.

In general, the techniques used to develop questionnaires and other instruments to measure attitude change among teachers can be applied to parents.

FIGURE 9-6
University of Illinois Preschool Program for the Gifted
Parents Needs Assessment

Please rank the following statements within each area according to your needs as parents of a young gifted child. (Begin with #1 to identify your area of greatest concern; rank the rest of the statements in order of diminishing importance, i.e., the highest number will indicate the least concern.)

I. Knowledge of Giftedness

_____ Increase your understanding of the characteristics of gifted children.

_____ Interest in appropriate interpretation of my child's developmental profile and test results.

_____ Increase your knowledge about early identification of giftedness in young children.

_____ Develop your understanding of special needs of gifted children.

_____ Increase your knowledge of cognitive, socio-emotional, and physical growth in young children.

II. Ways of Working With Your Child

_____ How to stimulate creativity at home.

_____ Ways to manage my child's behavior.

_____ How to develop task persistence.

_____ How to increase independence in my child.

_____ How to extend my child's self selected activities or projects.

_____ Ways to help my child develop a positive self-image.

Continued on next page

FIGURE 9-6 (Continued)

III. Peer and Sibling Dynamics

_____ Increase your general knowledge of sibling rivalry.

_____ Increase your understanding of the effects of a new baby or family member on other siblings.

_____ Increase your awareness of birth order in a family and its effects on children's social development.

_____ Increase your knowledge of developmental stages of peer relationships.

_____ Increase your knowledge of children's development of sex role identification.

_____ Increase your understanding of the effects of one sibling identified as gifted on other siblings in the family.

_____ Increase your knowledge of the development of "rules" for young children in peer and adult relationships.

Please * any written responses by you if they are more important to your needs than those identified in the ranking.

Identify three areas of concern you have as a gifted parent.

_____

_____

_____

Identify three goals you have for your child in this year's preschool program.

_____

_____

_____

What do you consider the most important characteristics parents of gifted children need to have or develop? (List at least three!)

_____   _____

_____   _____

_____   _____

How do you characterize your role as the parent of a gifted child in comparison to your role as the parent of a normal child?

_____

_____

_____

Please feel free to make any other comments regarding possible parent activities for the program.

_____

_____

_____

Similarly, procedures used to measure skill acquisition among teachers can also be transferred. The simplest procedure to assess parent involvement is to record the number of contacts between parents and teachers or to have parents keep track of the number of activities they participate in with their children (see for example Figure 9-7). While the parent component is important, the assessment of goal achievement poses no special problems to the evaluator.

Programming. The primary goal of preschool programs for gifted children is to serve their unique needs. In terms of evaluations, this is translated into the broad question: do children benefit from this program? More specifically, do gifted children gain more from participating in this particular program than they would from participating in some other program or no program at all? If gains *cannot* be observed, then there is really no way to justify the existence of a special and often expensive program for this relatively small group of children.

FIGURE 9-7
University of Illinois Preschool Program for the Gifted
Parent Contact Log

Name	Type Date/Time								

P
Phone
Contact

C
Conference

SC
Scheduled
Conference

M
Group
Meeting

O
Classroom
Observation

A
Participation
in
Classroom
Activities

Program goals may focus on changes in self-concept, task commitment, exploratory behavior, attitude toward school, and academic or talent performance. Typically, standardized, norm-referenced testing procedures are used to measure child progress. If norm-referenced tests are used, it is imperative that the instruments be relevant to the content of the program (Popham, 1975). Individual test items should be examined to determine whether or not they correspond to the content of the instructional activities that were carried out in the preschool classrooms. If the basic philosophy and approach to programming in the preschool program is to foster academic acceleration, then it may be appropriate to use the norm-referenced instruments used by the school district for kindergarteners and first-graders. However, if the philosophy and basic approach to programming is one of enrichment, appropriate norm-referenced tests may be impossible to find.

One solution to this problem is to create a criterion-referenced measurement instrument. According to Popham, "a criterion-referenced test is used to ascertain an in status with respect to a well-defined behavior domain" (1975, p. 130). Popham has suggested how an evaluator can develop a criterion-referenced test. Establishing a "well-defined behavior domain" is a difficult task, but if the project's goals and objectives are explicit regarding intended child outcomes, it is feasible to construct a meaningful criterion-referenced test. If the financial and technical resources necessary to create a new instrument are not available, it may still be possible to find a test that can be adapted to serve the project's needs. Appendix C lists sources for test reviews and test collections.

Of course, neither norm-referenced nor criterion-referenced assessment is restricted to paper-and-pencil instruments. Both naturalistic classroom observation and simulated activities can provide the evaluator with information regarding the preschooler's mastery of specific behaviors, skills, or attitudes. Program goals dealing with task commitment, exploratory behavior, and leadership can be assessed most effectively by observing gifted preschoolers in their regular classrooms. An example of a portion of the talent assessment checklist in the area of art developed for use with gifted/talented handicapped preschoolers is given in Figure 9-8 (Karnes, Steinberg, Brown, & Shwedel, 1982). Measurement issues in these areas, however, differ from measurement issues in areas related to skill or knowledge acquisition. We may not be concerned with estimating maximum levels of performance in task commitment, exploratory behavior, and leadership, but rather with determining typical levels of performance. In an area such as reading, it makes sense to say that a gifted preschooler has a reading vocabulary of 350 words, but it makes little sense to say that a gifted preschooler will persevere at a task for up to 1.2 hours. Thus, goal areas of particular relevance for preschool gifted programs do not fall neatly into either the criterion-referenced or the traditional norm-referenced category. Instead, the evaluator will need to develop systematic observation procedures which can be reliably used to record variables such as group composition, and frequency, duration, and location of behaviors

FIGURE 9-8

RAPYHT Project Talent Assessment Checklist: Artistic Talent (Visual Sensitivity Component)*

	Level I	Level II	Level III
A. Visual Sensitivity	1. Child notices visual characteristics of objects in the classroom, on the playground, on field trips (e.g., mentions that a toy is red like the shirt he's wearing, points out red berries on a bush, etc.).	5. Child mentions or describes visually perceptive changes that have taken place in the surroundings (e.g., is the first to notice berries on a bush in spring, notices that new books have been placed on the book rack).	9. Child mentions subtle visual changes in surroundings (e.g., calendar picture has been changed, angle of rug or a shelving unit is different, the paint brushes are smaller than ones usually used).
	2. Child examines or contemplates visual stimuli used in the classroom (e.g., book illustrations, bulletin boards, decorations, etc.) for longer periods of time than classmates.	6. Child makes simple descriptive or discriminative comments about visual materials used during reading or other subjects (e.g., "The colors in this book are different!").	10. Visual memory skill is evident from the detail appearing in child's art works.
	3. Child displays visual memory skill by replacing toys on a shelf, books on a rack, etc. much as they were previously arranged.	7. Child makes descriptive or discriminative comments about own and others' art works.	11. Child makes precise descriptive or discriminative comments about own and others' art works, or other visual stimuli (e.g., "The chimney should have bricks." "A squiggly line in that picture, a straight one in this!").
	4. Child prefers toys that require patterning or structuring, or spends time arranging and rearranging toys into patterns (e.g., alternating cups and saucers to make a tower in housekeeping, spending time setting and resetting the table).	8. Child selects or shows preference for books with similar illustration styles.	

*(Karnes, Steinberg, Brown, & Shwedel, 1982)

FIGURE 9-9
RAPYHT Cost Analysis Matrix 1978–1979[1]

RESOURCES	Talent Screening	Talent Assessment	Talent Staffing	Instructional Planning in Talent Areas	Implementing Instructional Planning	Evaluating Child Progress	Developing Family Involvement	Periodic Review by Planning Team
I. PERSONNEL								
Coordinator	N.A.	.4 hr/yr	.3 hr/yr	0	0	0	0	.1 hr/wk
Teacher	1.2 hr/yr	2.9 hr/yr	16.6 hr/yr	3.6 hr/wk	3.9 hr/wk	26.6 hr/yr	.37 hr/wk	.1 hr/wk
Ancillary staff	0	0	0	0	0	0	0	0
Child	N.A.	N.A.	N.A.	N.A.	2.8 hr/wk	5 hr/yr	N.A.	N.A.
Parent	N.A.	.3 hr/yr	N.A.	N.A.	N.A.	0	.5 hr/wk	0
Specialized resource personnel	0	0	0	0	0	35 hr/yr*	0	0
II. MATERIALS								
Checklists (consumable)	10.3/yr	N.A.	N.A.	N.A.	N.A.	N.A.	N.A.	N.A.
Manuals (resource)	4/yr	1/yr	N.A.	12/yr	N.A.	N.A.	8/yr	N.A.
III. SPECIALIZED MATERIALS FOR SPECIFIC TALENTS	0	0	0	$5.00/yr (1 site)	$18.00/yr (1 site)	0	0	0
IV. CONTRACTED SERVICES								

Consultants	0	0	$3.25/yr (1 site)	0	0	0	$4.25/yr (1 site)	0
Child Care	N.A.	N.A.	N.A.	N.A.	N.A.	0	0	0
V. EQUIPMENT								
Special equipment for talented areas	0	0	0	0	0	0	0	0
VI. SPACE								
Conference	0	0	0	0	0	0	0	0
Workshop	0	0	0	0	0	0	0	0
VII. TRANSPORTATION								
Special transportation for parent meetings	N.A.	0	$4.00/yr (1 site)	N.A.	N.A.	0	$4.50/yr (1 site)	0
Talent development experience	N.A.	N.A.	N.A.	N.A.	0	N.A.	N.A.	N.A.

N.A.—not applicable.
* = Illinois site only.
[1]From RAPYHT Project Performance Report 1978–79 (Bureau of Education for the Handicapped, HEW).

which are relevant to specific goal areas. For a detailed discussion of systematic observational procedures, see Sackett (1978). Day, Perkins, and Weinthaler (1979) have developed a naturalistic-observation system for preschool which is relatively easy to use and easily adaptable to the gifted preschool classroom.

Finally, certain goals and objectives can be assessed more easily and perhaps best by experts. The average teacher or evaluator is likely to have difficulty assessing achievement in talent areas such as dance, musical ability, and art. A perceptive expert who can make reliable judgments is an excellent "assessment instrument."

As this discussion indicates, the assessment of project outcomes is a complex, expensive, and time-consuming process. Yet this process is a necessary one. Without a systematic, relatively impartial examination of the results of a project's activities, decision makers are left with little but the comments of individuals who have vested interests, either positive or negative, in the project. The tools available to the evaluator, unwieldy as they are, provide crucial support for the continuation, termination, or modification of project components. It is well worth the effort to develop means to assess accurately the degree to which goals and objectives have been met.

Cost Analysis. Cost has been mentioned a number of times in this chapter. In addition to goal achievement, cost is an important variable in the final assessment of the viability of a preschool gifted program. Cost is also of prime concern to other administrators who may be interested in modeling their preschool gifted program on another program (Thompson, Rothrock, Strain, & Palmer, 1981). A brief statement of total expenditures does not provide decision makers or potential adopters with enough information about the actual costs of operating a program. Dr. Andrew Hayes of the University of North Carolina at Wilmington (Hayes, n.d.) has developed a cost analysis matrix that provides a breakdown of both financial and time costs by project component. The key feature of the matrix is that items are reported in standard units rather than in total amounts. The matrix is particularly useful for cost comparisons between a current program and earlier programs or programs in other locales. Even though prices increase due to inflation, it is relatively easy for anyone using this matrix to determine how much it will cost their school to implement the project even if the cost data were collected 2 or 3 years ago. Figure 9-9 contains an example of a cost analysis matrix designed by Dr. Hayes for a project serving gifted/talented handicapped preschoolers. A more detailed discussion of cost analysis issues can be found in Haller (1974).

SUMMARY

This chapter has provided an overview of the evaluation process as applied to new preschool programs for the gifted. Systematic evaluation procedures, when integrated into the development of a new project, can help to:

1. Set a target for the project to pursue (establish goals).
2. Keep the project on course during its journey (establish an implementation plan and monitor implementation).
3. Determine whether or not the project attained its goals (assess project outcomes).

Traditionally evaluation efforts have focused on item number 3. In many respects we feel that the best way to improve services to gifted preschoolers is to refocus much of our evaluation efforts on items 1 and 2. We hope that the reader is convinced of the importance and the feasibility of shifting from an exclusive emphasis on product assessment to a balanced approach that considers all phases of project development.

The following are guidelines to evaluate the effectiveness of your program as you go along:

1. Develop meaningful and achievable program goals.
2. Develop a timeline to guide the allocation of limited financial and human resources.
3. Monitor the implementation of the program components.
4. Assess the effectiveness of each component in terms of both the goals of the program and unintended outcomes.
5. Select and develop measuring devices for each phase of the project which will provide the necessary information economically and easily.
6. Maintain open lines of communication among the various groups of concerned individuals—teachers, administrators, parents, ancillary staff, and children.
7. Remember that evaluation activities are not an end but a means to an end—effective services to young children.

Getting there may be half the fun, but getting there effectively is the ultimate challenge and the best reward for everyone.

REFERENCES

Alkin, M. Evaluation theory development. *Evaluation Comment*, 1969, *2* (1), 2–7.

Baker, E. Formative evaluation of instruction. In J. Popham (Ed.), *Evaluation in education: Current applications*. Berkeley CA: McCutchen, 1974.

Brannon, R. Attitudes and the prediction of behavior. In B. Seidenberg & A. Snadowsky (Eds.), *Social psychology: An introduction*.New York: Free Press, 1976.

Day, D., Perkins, E., & Weinthaler, J. Naturalistic evaluation for program improvement. *Young Children*, 1979, *34*, 12–24.

Haller, E. Cost analysis for educational program evaluation. In J. Popham (Ed.), *Evaluation in education: Current applications*. Berkeley CA: McCutchen, 1974.

Hayes, A. *Cost analysis: A model for programs for the handicapped*. Unpublished manuscript. Available from School of Education, University of North Carolina, Wilmington, n.d.

Hostrop, R. *Managing education for results*. Palm Springs CA: ETC Publications, 1975.

Huberty, C., & Swan, W. Evaluation of programs. In J. Jordan, A. Hayden, M. Karnes, & M. Wood, *Early childhood education for exceptional children: A handbook of ideas and exemplary practices.* Reston VA: The Council for Exceptional Children, 1977.

Karnes, M.*Evaluation for PEECH replication, 1978-79.*Champaign IL: PEECH Project, Institute for Child Behavior and Development, University of Illinois, 1978. (U.S. Office of Education, Department of Health, Education and Welfare, Bureau of Education for the Handicapped, Grant No. G-00-77-00922.)

Karnes, M., & Associates. *Preschool talent checklists record booklet.* Champaign IL: RAPYHT Project, Institute for Child Behavior and Development, University of Illinois, 1978. (U.S. Office of Education Department of Health, Education and Welfare, Bureau of Education for the Handicapped, Grant No. OEG 00-75-00232.)

Karnes, M., Steinberg, D., Brown, J., & Shwedel, A. *RAPYHT Project talent components assessment checklist.* Champaign IL: RAPYHT Project, Institute for Child Development, University of Illinois, 1982.

Kerlinger, F. *Foundations of behavioral research* (2nd ed.).New York: Holt, Rinehart, & Winston, 1973.

Meeker, M. *The structure of intellect: Its interpretation and uses.* Columbus OH: Charles E. Merrill, 1969.

Metfessel, N., & Michael, W. A paradigm involving multiple criterion measures for the evaluation of the effectiveness of school programs. *Educational and Psychological Measurement,* 1967, *27,* 931–943.

Morris, L., & Fitz-Gibbon, C. *How to deal with goals and objectives.* Beverly Hills CA: Sage Publications, 1978. (a)

Morris, L., & Fitz-Gibbon, C. *How to measure program implementation.* Beverly Hills CA: Sage Publications, 1978. (b)

Morris, L., & Fitz-Gibbon, C. *How to present an evaluation report.* Beverly Hills CA: Sage Publications, 1978. (c)

Popham, J. *Educational evaluation.* Englewood Cliffs NJ: Prentice-Hall, 1975.

Renzulli, J. *A guidebook for evaluating programs for the gifted and talented.* Ventura CA: Office of the Ventura County Superintendent of Schools, 1975.

Renzulli, J. What makes giftedness: A re-examination of the definition. *Phi Delta Kappan,*1978, *60,* 180–184.

Renzulli, J., Smith, L., White, A., Callahan, C., & Hartman, R. *Scales for rating the behavioral characteristics of superior students.* Wethersfield CT: Creative Learning Press, 1976.

Sackett, G. (Ed.). *Observing behavior, Volume II: Data collections and analysis methods.* Baltimore: University Park Press, 1978.

Scriven, M. The methodology of evaluation. In R. Stake (Ed.), *Curriculum evaluation.* American Educational Research Association Monograph Series on Evaluation, No. 1. Chicago: Rand McNally, 1967.

Scriven, M. Pros and cons about goal-free evaluation. *Evaluation Comment,* 1972, *3* (4), 1–7.

Stake, R. The countenance of educational evaluation. *Teachers College Record,* 1967, *68,* 523–540.

Stake, R. Evaluation design, instrumentation, data collection, and analysis of data. In B. Worthen & J. Sanders (Eds.), *Educational evaluation: Theory and practice.* Belmont CA: Wadsworth, 1973. Originally published in J. Davis (Ed.), *Educational evaluation.* Columbus OH: Ohio State Department of Public Instruction, 1969.

Stufflebeam, D., Foley, W., Gephart, W., Guba, E., Hammond, R., Merriman, H., & Provus, M. *Educational evaluation and decision making.* Itasca IL: Peacock, 1971.

Thompson, M., Rothrock, J., Strain, R., & Palmer, R. Cost analysis for program evaluation. In R. Conner (Ed.), *Methodological advances in evaluation research.* Beverly Hills CA: Sage Publications, 1981.

Tyler, R. General statement on evaluation. *Journal of Educational Research,* 1942, *35,* 492–501.

Worthen, B., & Sanders, J. *Educational evaluation: Theory and practice.* Belmont CA: Wadsworth, 1973.

Appendix A

Selected References: Evaluation Methodology

Anderson, S., Ball, S., Murphy, R., et al. *Encyclopedia of educational evaluation.* San Francisco: Jossey-Bass, 1975.

Baker, E., & Saloutos, A. *Evaluating instructional programs.* Los Angeles: Center for the Study of Evaluation, 1974.

Cooley, W., & Lohnes, P. *Evaluation research in education: Theory, principles, and action.* New York: Irvington, 1976.

Evaluation bibliography (Tadscript #2). Chapel Hill NC: Technical Assistance Development System, 1973. (Available from ERIC Document Reproduction Service, No. ED 082 422.)

Evaluation studies: Review annual, I-IV. Beverly Hills CA: Sage Publications, 1976–1979.

Morris, L., Fitz-Gibbon, C., & Henderson, M. *Program evaluation kit.* Beverly Hills CA: Sage Publications, 1978.

Patton, M. *Qualitative evaluation methods.* Beverly Hills CA: Sage Publications, 1980.

Struening, E., & Guttentag, M. (Eds.). *Handbook of evaluation research, I & II.* Beverly Hills CA: Sage Publications, 1975.

Takanishi, R. *Evaluation of early childhood programs: Toward a developmental perspective.* Los Angeles: University of California at Los Angeles, 1978. (Available from ERIC Document Reproduction Service, No. ED 161 512.)

Appendix B

Selected References: Assessment Strategies

Campbell, D., & Stanley, J. *Experimental and quasi-experimental designs for research*. Chicago: Rand McNally, 1967.

Cook, T., & Campbell, D. *Quasi-experimentation: Design and analysis issues for field settings*. Chicago: Rand McNally, 1979.

Horst, D., Tallmadge, K., & Wood, C. *A practical guide to measuring project impact on student achievement*. Mountain View CA: RMC Research Corporation, 1975.

Harris, C. (Ed.). *Problems in measuring change*. Madison: University of Wisconsin Press, 1963.

Kratochwill, T. *Single subject research: Strategies for evaluating change*. San Francisco: Academic Press, 1978.

Morris, L., & Fitz-Gibbon, C. *How to measure achievement*. Beverly Hills CA: Sage Publications, 1978.

White, O. Practical program evaluation: Many problems and a few solutions. In May, M. (Ed.), *Evaluating handicapped children's early education programs*. Seattle: WESTAR, 1980.

Appendix C

Selected References: Assessment Instruments

Buros, O. *The eighth mental measurements yearbook*. Highland Park NJ: Gryphon Press, 1978.

Buros, O. (Ed.). *Tests in print, II*. Highland Park NJ: Gryphon Press, 1974.

Coller, A. *Self-concept measures; An annotated bibliography*. Princeton NJ: Head Start Test Collection, Educational Testing Service, 1971.

Goldman, B., & Saunders, J. *Directory of unpublished experimental mental measures, I*. New York: Behavioral Publications, 1974.

Haenn, J., Johnson, T., & Owoc, P. *Tests and measurements for early childhood education programs*. Chicago: National Program on Early Childhood Education, Central Midwestern Regional Educational Laboratory, 1972.

Hoepfner, R., Stern, C., & Mummedal, S. (Eds.). *CSE-CRC preschool/kindergarten test evaluations*. Los Angeles: Center for the Study of Evaluation and the Early Childhood Research Center, 1971.

Hoepfner, R. (Ed.). *CSE-RBS test evaluations: Tests of higher-order cognitive, affective, and interpersonal skills*. Los Angeles: Research for Better Schools, 1972.

Johnson, O. *Tests and measurements in child development: Handbook II*. San Francisco: Jossey-Bass, 1976.

Johnson, O., & Bommorito, J. *Tests and measurements in child development: A handbook*. San Francisco: Jossey-Bass, 1971.

Johnson, T., & Hess, R. *Tests in the arts*. St. Ann MO: Central Midwestern Regional Educational Laboratory, 1970.

Maranell, G. (Ed.). *Scaling: A sourcebook for behavioral scientists*. Chicago: Aldine, 1974.

Shaw, M., & Wright, J. *Scales for the measurement of attitudes*. New York: McGraw-Hill, 1971.

Simon, A., & Boyer, E. (Eds.). *Mirrors for behavior III: An anthology of observation instruments*. Wyncote PA: Communication Materials Center, 1974.

Test Collection Bulletin. Princeton NJ: Educational Testing Service.

Walker, D. *Socioemotional measures for preschool and kindergarten children*. San Francisco CA: Jossey-Bass, 1973.